ADVANCE PRAISE FOR Pierre Bourdieu
A CRITICAL INTRODUCTION TO MEDIA AND COMMUNICATION THEORY

"A compelling and comprehensive account that will surely be a touchstone for future conversations about Bourdieu and media studies."
—Rodney Benson, Associate Professor of Media Studies and Sociology, New York University

"If one imagined a Michelin Guide to theorists relevant to communication, Bourdieu would certainly merit 3 stars: worth a special trip. Yet, despite the powerful contributions Bourdieu's ideas and methods offer to communication and media scholars, it is all too familiar an experience to encounter his name invoked ritualistically, his terminology sprinkled like gold dust, and his concepts applied without appreciation for their subtlety and depth. This short but incisive book provides media scholars and students with a grounding in Bourdieu's work that removes any excuse for such intellectual laziness. Neither overstating his scope nor idealizing Bourdieu, this careful account offers a measured and therefore a valuable introduction and explication of key concepts that deserve to be part of any respectable communication scholar's intellectual toolbox."
—Larry Gross, University of Southern California

"This is a terrific book! I thought it was beyond any one scholar to unravel the many threads of Pierre Bourdieu's philosophically and empirically rich work and then put them together again in a synoptic account of what Bourdieu's many insights can contribute to media and communications research in the round. But David W. Park has pulled off this remarkable feat—with great elegance and considerable scholarship. The whole field should be grateful for him!"
—Nick Couldry, Professor of Media, Communications and Social Theory, LSE

GW00641060

Pierre Bourdieu

A CRITICAL INTRODUCTION TO MEDIA AND COMMUNICATION THEORY

David W. Park
Series Editor

Vol. 2

The Critical Introduction to Media and Communication Theory series
is part of the Peter Lang Media and Communication list.
Every volume is peer reviewed and meets
the highest quality standards for content and production.

PETER LANG
New York • Washington, D.C./Baltimore • Bern
Frankfurt • Berlin • Brussels • Vienna • Oxford

DAVID W. PARK

Pierre Bourdieu

A CRITICAL INTRODUCTION TO MEDIA AND COMMUNICATION THEORY

PETER LANG
New York • Washington, D.C./Baltimore • Bern
Frankfurt • Berlin • Brussels • Vienna • Oxford

Library of Congress Cataloging-in-Publication Data
Park, David W.
Pierre Bourdieu: a critical introduction to media and communication theory / David W. Park.
pages cm. — (A critical introduction to media and communication theory; vol. 2)
1. Bourdieu, Pierre, 1930–2002. 2. Mass media—Social aspects.
3. Mass media and culture. 4. Communication. I. Title.
HM479.B68P37   302.23—dc23   2014005965
ISBN 978-1-4331-0859-4 (hardcover)
ISBN 978-1-4331-0858-7 (paperback)
ISBN 978-1-4539-1339-0 (e-book)
ISSN 1947-6264

Bibliographic information published by **Die Deutsche Nationalbibliothek.**
Die Deutsche Nationalbibliothek lists this publication in the "Deutsche
Nationalbibliografie"; detailed bibliographic data is available
on the Internet at http://dnb.d-nb.de/.

© 2014 Peter Lang Publishing, Inc., New York
29 Broadway, 18th floor, New York, NY 10006
www.peterlang.com

Contents

Preface   vii
Acknowledgments   xi

Chapter One: Pierre Bourdieu's Legacy and the Study of Communication   1
Chapter Two: The Field of Media Production   19
Chapter Three: The Media Audience: Fluency, Strategy, and *Le Sens Practique*   53
Chapter Four: Symbolic Power and Authority: The Power/
       Communication Nexus   79
Chapter Five: Reflexivity and the History of the Field of Communication   105
Chapter Six: Conclusion: Communication as Practical, Relational,
       Historical, and Reflexive   131

Notes   141
References   157
Index   167

Preface

The question of what compels a communication scholar such as myself to become interested in Pierre Bourdieu's ideas is the kind of question that would have interested Bourdieu. My preparation for Bourdieusian thought derived in no small part from my experiences in college radio. When I was a college radio dj, I was immersed in a subculture dedicated to a feverish exploration of all kinds of music. Rarely could one find a more intense demonstration of how taste in music operated as a code. To be known to enjoy certain music was to become encamped with others who were like you, and by extension, to become opposed to some other camps. It quickly dawned on all of us that there was a kind of game being played. 'Pure' musical enjoyment may have been what we were all after, but through this, we djs became insinuated into a process of becoming aware of all this new music, and of having to choose sides in a conflict between different musical factions (ork pop, grindcore, grunge, and no depression were amongst the positions available) that were varyingly overlapping and opposed to each other. At the same time, the music we enjoyed (or hated) was created, distributed, promoted, sold, and criticized by record labels, small circulation magazines, and free weekly newspapers. It became apparent that organizations and institutions played no small role in holding this whole mess of music together, and that these organizations and institutions were linked up with the same games we were playing. It became very clear that 'culture' was not just something that dropped down on people like rain.

College radio showed me that this whole set of activities we call culture—even the seemingly minor developments in culture—depended on the interlocking activities of actual people, each of them in their own way a patriot of their own musical cause. I also learned that 'texts'—the actual content of songs, for instance—were not to be mistaken for the sum total of what constitutes a culture. By the time I graduated from college, I had an inchoate appreciation of the importance of issues I would only later find represented in the Bourdieusian master terms: field, habitus, and capital.

Shortly after I started graduate school at the University of Pennsylvania's Annenberg School for Communication, I read Bourdieu's *Distinction* not because it was assigned to me in a class but because it was the book that started the bitterest disputes amongst my friends. I was a graduate student in the 1990s, when cultural studies was enjoying its heyday. Of course this heyday was rather muted at Annenberg, where cultural studies was (sometimes reasonably, sometimes less reasonably) dismissed as being insufficiently empirical, non-falsifiable, and/or 'a fad'. It occurred to me that to read *Distinction* as an entry in cultural studies per se would be to miss the point. In contradistinction to much that was associated with cultural studies in the 1990s, the book is solidly empirical, with its reliance upon (oft-critiqued) statistical analyses, field research, and content analysis. Beyond this, Bourdieu's ideas seemed to have relatively little to do with the 1990s concern for texts and their varying potential for oppositional reads. Here was a sociologically trained French academic whose work was quite explicitly connected both to the American social science tradition *and* critical theory. Bourdieu's writing may not have been elegant, but I found in his long paragraphs a kind of unpretentiousness, a frustration with the expectation that research ought to be either deterministic or belle lettrist. I was hooked.

It was Bourdieu's focus on the parts of culture that other social theorists seemed so rarely to discuss—the patterns of behavior that animated almost every conversation at the college radio station back in the day—that got me fired up about Bourdieu. Bourdieu's understanding of cultural consumption's strategic tendencies, the use of culture as capital, the anticipation of profits from certain kinds of consumption, and the focus on cultural difference—or distinction, if you will—made me feel like I had found a scholar who had cracked the code.

My first attempts to use Bourdieu's ideas in research projects led me to experience certain difficulties. When trying to explain the cultural authority of popular psychology in the 20th century, I found Bourdieu's ideas regarding symbolic power to be most useful. However, I wished that Bourdieu had put more work into analyzing the role played by the media. His ideas concerning symbolic power, for instance, deal at length with language use and social space, but only rarely address how different media forms operate. Of course, this problem derived more from my own attempts to jury-rig Bourdieu's ideas than with Bourdieu's ideas themselves.

My simultaneous fascination with Bourdieu's ideas and frustration with how these ideas had yet to be mapped onto the domains germane to communication scholarship have led me to believe that we in the field of communication ought to invite him to our party. Bourdieusian perspectives on media production, media audiences, symbolic power, and the sociology of science could help us develop understandings of some of the most important issues facing the field. His avoidance of some familiar intellectual pitfalls in communication scholarship (such as: positivism, idealism, and materialism) leads me to believe that increased attention to Bourdieu's ideas could at the very least lead us to find new questions. The fact that Bourdieu—one of the most widely cited scholars in history, and one who has had a great impact on the fields of sociology, anthropology, education, and philosophy—is only occasionally seen as a figure whose ideas should matter to the field of communication should lead us not to sandbag him out of the field, but to draw on what he has to offer. I am not the only one to feel this way. Rodney Benson, Nick Couldry, and David Hesmondhalgh (to name but three) have all made significant contributions in the grander project of bringing Bourdieu's ideas into the field of communication. This book-length exploration of how Bourdieu could be incorporated into communication scholarship represents an effort more fully to draw on the promise of Bourdieusian thought in communication.

Acknowledgments

Though this book is not long, the list of people to thank for their help is quite lengthy.

First I wish to thank Mary Savigar at Peter Lang Publishing. I met Mary when we were both new to Peter Lang, and we have now worked together on a large and still growing number of projects. I cannot count the number of occasions when I have benefited from her insight or from her patience. Bernadette Shade and Sophie Appel—also at Peter Lang—are no less forgiving of my foolishness, no less hard-working. I salute them all.

Portions of this manuscript have appeared elsewhere in print. Chapter 2 was developed out of my article for *Democratic Communique*, titled "Pierre Bourdieu's 'Habitus' and the Political Economy of the Media." Chapter 5, in a slightly altered version, was translated into German and included ("Pierre Bourdieu und die Geschichte des Feldes der Kommunikationswissenschaft: Auf dem Weg zu Einem Reflexiven, Verkörperten und Konfliktorientierten Verständnis des Feldes") in a volume titled *Pierre Bourdieu und die Kommunikationswissenschaft*, edited by Thomas Wiedemann, Michael Meyen, and Alexis Mirbach. I am grateful to the editors of these publications for their willingness to allow me to develop these ideas in the form you find here.

Three of my friends helped me write this book. I owe a special thanks to Mark Brewin, who offered his commentary on three chapters, and whose ideas helped me to refocus, refine, revise, and reconsider what I was doing. Jennifer Horner offered valuable critical input regarding the introductory chapter of this book. Jeff Pooley offered editorial assistance and much-needed critical input for two chapters. One of the great things about my job is that I get to talk to Mark, Jen, and Jeff. I don't want to imagine what it would be like to do this job without them.

Another hearty thanks is due to one anonymous reviewer, who offered sweeping, honest, careful, and ultimately correct input on the book proposal and on a completed manuscript. Rare is the manuscript reviewer who knows Bourdieu so well; equally rare is the manuscript reviewer who brings so much care to the unheralded cause of reviewing.

I owe a kind of blanket perma-thanks to Steve Jones. Working with Steve at *New Media & Society* has given me a special appreciation for how the scholarly world operates, how it should operate, and how I might be of some use in the daunting collective project of pushing things closer to how they should work.

My colleagues in the Department of Communication at Lake Forest College should be called out as well. Liz Benacka, Helene DeGross, Linda Horwitz, Randy Iden, Rachel Whidden, and Camille Yale have been co-conspirators in the effort to make one of the great Communication departments on the planet. I am fortunate to work with such outstanding colleagues.

Students at Lake Forest College have helped me along. In particular, Chris Barnes, Meghan Grosse, and Nick Rennis have assisted me in the ongoing effort of figuring out what the world of people is all about. They have also reminded me frequently why anyone would ever want to be a college professor.

My wife, Sarah, is the best. I thank her for everything. This is convenient, because I also owe her everything.

CHAPTER ONE

Pierre Bourdieu's Legacy and the Study of Communication

Few individuals have been cited in scholarly work as much as Pierre Bourdieu (1930–2002). Bourdieu's ideas have left a vigorous legacy in sociology and anthropology, and have received ongoing if more fitful attention in fields as far flung as English, Art, and Education. The situation in communication research has been rather different. Bourdieu's ideas were so all-encompassing as to frustrate those not willing to dive in, and his reputation as someone who is "good to think with"[1] leads communication researchers often to refer to Bourdieu's ideas at an arm's length, either as distant inspiration or as bibliography padding. To adopt Bourdieu's thought for communication research, it is important to regard his ideas as more than inspirational touchstones and explore their applicability to specific questions relating to media production; media audiences; authority and symbolic power; and the history of communication research itself.

This book arrives at a time when the use of Bourdieu's ideas continues to grow and to become more conceptually diverse. In 2007, Jeffrey J. Sallaz and Jane Zavisca conducted a content analysis of uses of Bourdieu in sociology, and they found increasing numbers of citations of Bourdieu's work, and "increasingly comprehensive citations,"[2] to the extent that there is reason to believe that "at least some of Bourdieu's core concepts have become so taken for granted within the sociological lexicon that they may serve as building blocks for larger arguments and therefore their elaboration is no longer needed in the context of a journal article."[3]

Omar Lizardo outlines three phases of uses of Bourdieu's ideas in the U.S. Lizardo asserts that "the first phase of Bourdieu's U.S. reception revolved around *Reproduction* and *Distinction* and the second phase was centered on the essays collected in *The Field of Cultural Production*." The next phase "is beginning to take shape by revisiting what is quite likely Bourdieu's most difficult work: the revision of *Outline of a Theory of Practice* that became *The Logic of Practice*."[4] Clearly, Bourdieu's ideas are not being relegated to the dustbin of history. On the contrary, they are being used more, and being put to use in a wide variety of research contexts.

Beyond this, Bourdieu's ideas are being increasingly frequently applied to questions relating to media and communication. This has developed in large part because some prominent media and communication scholars have acted as ambassadors for Bourdieu's work, introducing his ideas to some of the most important research areas in communication. Rodney Benson and Erik Neveu have done the yeoman's work of applying Bourdieu's ideas to the study of journalism and beyond.[5] David Hesmondhalgh has developed some important points of contact between Bourdieu's theoretical corpus and the study of media production.[6] John B. Thompson has written numerous works concerning the application of Bourdieu's ideas to the consideration of media systems and to symbolic power.[7] And Nick Couldry has repeatedly (and successfully) shown how Bourdieu can offer us a better understanding of media practice.[8] The ground for this book has been well prepared.

If this book is to serve the field of communication as a bridge between our media and communication questions and Bourdieu's ideas, I would do well to at least acknowledge that Bourdieu was wary of the process by which his ideas could be misinterpreted and misapplied. He had a keen eye for how ideas from one continent could be deployed in very different ways on another. Bourdieu's interest in fidelity to context made him skeptical of many of those who hoped to apply his ideas without due diligence.

From the opposite point of view, there are those in the field of communication who could reasonably ask: 'Why do we need more ideas? And why would Bourdieu's ideas be more attractive than anyone else's?' Certainly the field does not suffer from a lack of competing theories. At times, the field is strikingly incoherent. Robert T. Craig argued in 1999 that "communication theory as an identifiable field of study does not yet exist," and that "[b]ooks and articles on communication theory seldom mention other works on communication theory except within narrow (inter)disciplinary specialties and schools of thought."[9] This situation has not changed since Craig wrote this, and things may have grown even less cohesive. Indeed, adding Bourdieu's ideas to the mix may actually intensify some of the incoherence, at least from the point of view of those who see one master discipline—say, social psychology or rhetoric—as the true lodestar for the field of communication.

Acknowledging these perfectly sensible objections to Bourdieu's potential relevance and benefit to the field of communication, I insist that Bourdieu's ideas help us to reconsider areas of research we find familiar in the field of communication. I have identified four areas where Bourdieu's ideas will lead us to reconceptualize—or reinvigorate—scholarship: media production, the media audience, authority and symbolic power, and the history of the field of communication. This book cannot single-handedly install Bourdieu as the one-stop shop for communication theory. Instead, the book engages Bourdieu's thought in order to ask different and better questions about the processes we are studying, while remaining faithful to Bourdieu's own goals in his scholarship.

To start, this introduction lays out some of Bourdieu's foundational concepts, and offers brief notes regarding their relevance to communication inquiry. Without a basic understanding of habitus, field, and capital—terms that recur throughout Bourdieu's considerable oeuvre—it would be difficult to proceed with any program for applying Bourdieu to questions of communication. These three terms underlie much of Bourdieu's work, usually operating in combination with each other. Each of these terms has been treated at length in the considerable secondary literature on Bourdieu.[10] Still, there is reason to inflect these terms with the accents of the communication scholar.

Habitus

Habitus is the best starting place for understanding Bourdieu's ideas, given his emphasis on embodiment and the importance of praxis to understanding culture and society. Adapted for various uses in some of his best-known and relatively obscure work, the concept of habitus has demonstrated a flexibility that threatens to undermine its conceptual utility. Bourdieu developed the concept in an effort to get beyond the structure/agency divide in the social sciences: the ongoing struggle between those who find the origins of the social world in individual agency and those who find it in social structures. To promise that an understanding of habitus could easily get the field of communication beyond the divide between these two tendencies would be foolish,[11] but the concept does offer us an opportunity to reflect on the interplay of structure and agency, itself no mean feat.

So what is habitus? Scholars of Bourdieu have treated habitus as an evolving concept, taking form in an iterative process that can be traced to his diverse research interests. Michael Grenfell helpfully traces the use of the term back to Bourdieu's early research concerning the lives of Béarn farmers, to his work in *Les Héritiers*, and in *La Reproduction*, where the concept of habitus "is used to express durable dispositions of individuals which guide social practice".[12] In *Outline of a Theory of Practice*, Bourdieu uses the concept to reject theories that "explicitly or implicitly treat practice as a mechanical reaction, directly determined by the antecedent conditions and entirely reducible to the mechanical functioning of pre-established assemblies," while also rejecting the idea that "we should bestow on some creative free will the free and willful power to constitute, on the instant, the meaning of the situation by projecting the ends aiming at its transformation."[13] Habitus was Bourdieu's attempt to develop a response to the structure-agency debate, a way to find the structure in the individual, and an individual in the structure.[14] Habitus is a way to envision societies and individuals as mutually constitutive. Instead of starting with individuals or with social structures in an effort to explain social processes, Bourdieu developed the idea of habitus as a way to consider individuals and structures in relationship to each other.

It is insufficient simply to go over what habitus is *not*. To get closer to a brass-tacks definition, Bourdieu explained that habitus is "the durably installed generative principle of regulated improvisations [which] produces practices."[15] Habitus is durable; it is embodied, and Bourdieu's emphasis on 'regulated improvisations' calls attention to how there is a pattern to even seemingly spontaneous actions. The simultaneously structural and individual levels of emphasis can be found in his assertion that these practices that habitus produces "tend to reproduce the regularities immanent in the objective conditions of the production of their generative principle."[16] This sounds circular because it involves a feedback loop at the heart of all social behavior: the patterns of perception, belief, attitude, and behavior all come from social structures, and these social structures are themselves held in place by the perceptions, beliefs, attitudes, and behavior. We see here how habitus was proposed as a concept closely linked to the perpetuation of regularities in social structures and in individuals.

The same emphasis on feedback loops is brought into greater clarity in Bourdieu's later description of habitus as "principles" that structure perception and behavior, and that emerge in a process of adaptation "to their outcomes without presupposing a conscious aiming at ends."[17] Individuals come to think, to feel, to act in certain ways that derive in large part from the structures that shape them, while at the same time these same modes of thought, feeling, and action generate the conditions necessary for the structures at work. To be more concise, habitus is "a socialized subjectivity,"[18] an embodied sense of the world that relates intricately, and intimately, to social structure.

Habitus represents an attempt to draw attention to the relational component of everything social, without unmooring behavior from context. David Swartz argues that the concept of habitus gives us "a programmatic research agenda for addressing the agency/structure issue," a research agenda that "derives from [Bourdieu's] theory that action is generated by the encounter between opportunities or constraints presented by situations and the durable dispositions that reflect the socialization of past experiences, traditions, and habits that individuals bring to situations."[19] If communication has a problem with the agency/structure issue—and I contend that it does—Bourdieu's thought provides an excellent point of entry for getting beyond this issue. Communication research already touches on numerous domains where the encounter Swartz describes—between opportunities/constraints and dispositions—can be found. In this sense, habitus has great promise for the field.

There are few limits to the applicability of this idea to communication. Interpersonal communication, for instance, can be considered in terms of the dispositions that have developed within individuals, and how interpersonal contexts relate differently to different dispositions. The job interview, the first date, and the doctor's appointment are all examples of interactions involving a collision of the socially-acquired dispositions of the interactants, themselves derived in large part from the roles played each interactant, and the history of interactions each has had in the past. Bourdieu himself often used examples of how individuals from different social classes come to interact with each other to illustrate the interpenetration of structure and agency.

Habitus is just as relevant to other domains of communication study. The production of messages in mass communication involves individuals working from durable dispositions to navigate work that brings with it its own set of opportunities and constraints. Imagine the journalist approaching a deadline, navigating, amongst other things: the interest in the 'good story,' the anticipation of an editor's red pencil, the need not to be seen as cow-towing to an editor, the recruitment of trustworthy sources, the anticipation of feedback from those involved in the story, and much more. All of this can be conceptualized as the kind of durable dispositions that social actors develop. This is to say that how media work comes to be understood by producers is an issue of habitus, and an issue of tremendous importance to understanding how we wind up with the media content that we have as well as broader issues relating to the sustenance of overarching media structures.

The reception of messages can also be helpfully construed in terms of habitus, as the moments of consumption, perception, and interpretation can all be conceptualized in terms that get us away from merely focusing on the presence or absence of agency, and instead lead us toward the nuanced manner in which structures work their way into all of these processes of media reception. Here, we find the durable dispositions at work found in: the varied sensibilities that inform what are often considered to be the 'rational' choices of media audience members, the sense of what the options are, the varied valuations given to different media content, and the audience member's self-identification vis à vis 'the media' writ large.

Before continuing, it is worthwhile to consider how the structure/agency divide has played out in communication inquiry. It is not difficult to find approaches in communication that emphasize one side of the structure/agency divide. Research emphasizing the structural side of communication could be found in much of the field's roots in the social sciences, extending most obviously to the political economy and production of culture approaches to the media. These explanations of media processes tend toward objectivist explanations of communication, using evidence about structures like media ownership and market forces to explain the rule-like mechanisms that shape how people behave. The agency side of the issue is taken up by those who explain communication processes in terms of what individuals are trying to do, as can be found in the uses and gratifications approach, much of what we call cultural studies (in communication), and audience research. These explanations focus on the subjectivist concern for individual intention/consciousness, and build from there. The media effects approach can arguably be found on both sides of the structure/agency divide. Some media effects approaches consider audience behavior only in terms of how some arrangement of independent and/or intervening variables could be considered as causes for behavior. Such research falls on the structural side of the divide, while also emphasizing what Bourdieu described as objectivist approaches to the social. Other media effects research—including so-called limited effects approaches—tends more obviously toward agency.

Habitus offers to the communication scholar a way to get beyond the now well-worn conflict between subjectivist and objectivist approaches to communication, between those attempting to understand human communication in terms of what goes on 'inside' people's heads (subjective modes of understanding) and those who attempt to do the same thing through reference to 'external' forces (objective forces at work in our lives). In 1995, Lawrence Grossberg posed the correct question vis à vis the conflict between political economy and cultural studies. His titular question—"Is Anybody Else Bored with This Debate?"[20]—referred to the frustration that comes from developing a self-reinforcing system whereby objectivist (political economy) and subjectivist (cultural studies) approaches collude to misunderstand each other in the field of communication, thus pushing inquiry to one side or the other on the divide between agency/structure. Bourdieu's idea of habitus offers us in communication an opportunity to bridge the agency/structure divide, to understand communication in terms of the intertwining of agency and structure, the elements of practice that bind agency and structure together. For this reason, the incorporation of Bourdieu's habitus into theoretical models of communication should not be anticipated as a win for any side in the theoretical/methodological squabbles carried out in the field, but instead should be a way to get past these squabbles.[21] Some may protest that habitus carries within it a bias for the structural, that the identification of habitus—as opposed to culture—as an essential explanatory factor tilts the Bourdieusian pinball table in the direction of structure. These concerns are not without merit, and yet habitus can still at least help us to begin the work of digging out of these intellectual foxholes and working toward mutual engagement on common problems.

The Field

If habitus is a way to help get social inquiry away from some familiar debates, it is only the first of some of the basic terms Bourdieu used. Bourdieu developed the term 'habitus' relatively early in his career. A more recent term, though one that has no less relevance for communication research, is 'field'. Bourdieu's notion of 'field' leads us to think relationally, to understand practice as something that plays out in relation to a range of other possibilities. The idea of the field provided Bourdieu with a term he required to put the workings of habitus into context. Field became, for Bourdieu, a way to consider the interlocking possibilities that make themselves available (or unavailable) to actors in the social world.

Given that Bourdieu's interest in the sociology of sport, it is fitting that one of his explanations of the term 'field' began with a comparison with games. Bourdieu noted that, in the context of games and sport, the field (the pitch or board on which it is played, the rules, the outcome at stake, etc.) is clearly seen for what it is, an arbitrary social construct, an artefact whose arbitrariness and artificiality are underlined by everything that defines its autonomy—explicit and specific rules, strictly delimited and extra-ordinary time and space.[22]

This differs from

> social fields, which are the products of a long, slow process of autonomization, and
> are therefore, so to speak, games 'in themselves' and not 'for themselves,' one does not
> embark on the game by a conscious act, one is born into the game, with the game; and
> the relation of investment, *illusio*,...is made more total and unconditional by the fact
> that it is unaware of what it is.[23]

We find ourselves operating in the context of social fields much of the time. Because of this autonomization of the process of involvement in the field, we come to take the field's operations for granted. We do not notice the kinds of games we play, the degree to which our perceptions are shaped through the fields in which we locate ourselves. We invest ourselves in numerous kinds of field-like scenarios: in our work life, in our cultural consumption, in our identification with groups. In our scholarship we find ourselves identifying with and against certain schools of thought, internalizing the structure of the fields in which we operate, taking as a given the stakes of academic work in the channels and backwaters in academia, understanding certain ideas and positions as strategically superior to others. When we consume culture, the game may be less obviously strategic, but we find parallel features to other field-like orientations. Even the more populist-leaning culturists amongst us recognize the distinctions at work between: going to an art gallery and watching a *Law & Order* marathon on television; attending a baseball game and an equestrian event; playing *World of Warcraft* and reading the new George R. R. Martin book. The sense of differences at play in these distinctions (some much finer than others) is something that we develop through immersion. Bourdieu showed us that these distinctions between positions in fields are constructed, and yet far from coincidental. The *illusio* functions so well because, though we are aware of the distinctions between these positions, we come to take them as given. The workings of the field become autonomized. This autonomization at work is particularly relevant to the field of communication, where so much of the work involves an attempt to make explicit processes that are routinized, evanescent, and embodied.[24]

The relevance of the idea of the field to communication can be made much more powerful. Bourdieu developed the idea of the field largely to account for patterns he observed in the production of culture, and this gives the idea a particular utility for communication scholars. Randal Johnson asserts that Bourdieu's idea of the field represents "an attempt to apply what Bourdieu, borrowing from Cassirer calls a relational mode of thought to cultural production."[25] Johnson continues: "In any given field, agents occupying the diverse available positions (or in some cases creating new positions) engage in competition for control of the interests or resources which are specific to the field in question."[26] In other words, fields have their own internal hierarchies, and these are related to other fields, each operating by its own specific logic. Think of the available positions, for instance, in such fields of interaction as: science fiction publishing, video game fandom, and political blogging and commentary.

A characteristically more prolix definition of a field comes from Bourdieu and Löic Wacquant, who called it "a network, or configuration, of objective relations between positions."[27] In order to distinguish between these positions, we are to look first to "the determinations they impose upon their occupants, agents or institutions."[28] This links the idea of the field to habitus, to the kinds of behaviors that allow social structure to make our activities (thoughts, behaviors, feelings) possible. Significantly, by tracing the field to both individual agents and institutions, Bourdieu and Wacquant are here emphasizing that the field structures both individuals and collectives. We distinguish between positions in a field in terms of their "situation (*situs*) in the structure of the distribution of species of power (or capital) whose possession commands access to the specific profits that are at stake in the field."[29] It is the idea of capital (see below) that makes fields mediators of power. Some positions in the field have advantages over others; not all positions are made equally. Finally, positions in fields can be distinguished in terms of "their objective relation to other positions (domination, subordination, homology, etc.)."[30] To think in terms of the field is to think relationally, to think in terms of the oppositions at play between any meeting between any two or more social positions, and to consider the advantages and disadvantages that come to those agents and institutions that are associated with different amounts or types of capital.

With the idea of the field in place, emphasis becomes focused on the contexts where much social behavior occurs, and on the coordinated relationships that these behaviors involve. Fields have objective being, in the sense that they do exist outside of the minds of the subjects who operate within them, but they also have links to the subjective, in the sense that these fields come to shape the formation of perceptions, strategies of behavior, and attitudes.

Field theory emphasizes the process by which subjects become oriented phenomenologically, without losing touch with the social aspect of individual practice. This sense of phenomenological detail is itself linked to institutions. John B. Thompson emphasizes the link between individuals' positions and institutions in his discussion of Bourdieu's notion of "fields of interaction," where "[i]ndividuals are situated at different positions within these fields, depending on the different kinds and quantities of resources available to them."[31] Institutions stabilize these positions, lending them a more definite shape, determining "rules," and arranging more durable "resources and relations"[32] in ways that coordinate individual activities. This gives some sense of how the idea of the field is to lend a sense of interactivity to any perspective on institutions and organizations. It is the positions in the field that are occupied by individuals (and the institutions/organizations through which the individual act) that set the stage for their practice. Picking up on this relational dimension of fields, Bourdieu and Wacquant told us that "[t]o think in terms of field is to *think relationally*,"[33] meaning that the field is intended to guide us toward how individuals' actions are carried out in relation to a range of other behaviors by differently placed individuals.

To perform an analysis that uses the idea of the field carefully "involves three necessary and internally connected moments."[34] In the first step, "one must analyze the position of the field" currently under consideration "vis-à-vis the field of power."[35] These positions (usually signified through the use of positive [+] and negative [-] symbols in Bourdieu's familiar charts) indicate dominance within the operation of a field, and the fields themselves could be within or outside the field of power itself. The workings of the field consist of familiar Levi-Straussian opposed pairs, with different fields—and different positions in those fields—operating in dominant and dominated positions. If the field under consideration is the literary world, as it often was for Bourdieu, this would be placed properly in the dominated position in the dominant field (the field of power). Other fields, such as the field of politics or the field of capitalist production would be placed elsewhere.

The second step requires the researcher to "map out the objective structure of the relations between the positions occupied by the agents or institutions who compete for the legitimate form of specific authority of which this field [is] the site."[36] This step finds the researcher plotting out how different factions within a field operate in competition with, in collusion with, and in terms of each other.

The third and final step requires the researcher to "analyze the habitus of agents,"[37] so that the agents' internalized dispositions are put into conversation with the stakes of the field. This final part hooks the overarching concerns of the macro-level sense of interfield concerns to individual agents, connecting the macro to the micro, and vice versa.

One might notice that there is very little actual content here. To propose that there are fields that orient social activity is to say very little about any particular field. Bourdieu insisted that this was an important component of the strength of the idea of the field, the fact that it "does not provide ready-made answers to all possible queries, in the manner of the grand concepts of 'theoreticist theory' which claims to explain everything and in the right order."[38] The "major virtue" of the idea of the field is that "it promotes a mode of construction that has to be re-thought anew every time."[39] In this sense, the idea of the field, paired always with a concern for habitus, is not a solution to any problem originally proposed in theoretical language. In a concerted effort not to force the researcher's hand, Bourdieu took a kind of constructivist half-step, insisting on the primacy of emic experience, while also avoiding the idea that agents are entirely in charge of constructing the world around them. The avoidance of substituting the language of the researcher for the practice of others led Bourdieu to develop a method that may seem too simple and yet too complex at the same time.

The idea of the field does many important things for Bourdieu, and it could have important meaning for communication research. Bourdieu developed the idea of the field as a way to get beyond subjectivism and objectivism in the social sciences. When carried over to the study of the media, this can be taken as a rebuff to positivist-leaning media effects approaches, and also to the oft-idealist approaches to culture that can be associated with cultural studies. With field theory, the effects of such structural elements as "class background, milieu or context… are *mediated* through the structure of fields."[40] This makes fields simultaneously material and symbolic. Bourdieu was no idealist; he still insisted that meaning does not emerge without connections to "social conditions of struggle that shape cultural production."[41] Much as Bourdieu attempted to get beyond the structure/agency divide in the social sciences, the idea of the field represented a concerted attempt to help us get beyond the materialist/idealist divide. It is worth pointing out that, in communication research, the general paucity of attention to Bourdieu may come in part from a tendency for the materialist, positivist, and idealist/culturist schools of thought to reproduce themselves, leading either to ignorance of Bourdieu's field-level analysis, or to an attempt to hitch it to pre-existing objectivist or subjectivist approaches to communication.

The relevance of the idea of the field is varied for the study of the media. It is difficult to understate the potential importance of this term for the study of media production. Benson and Neveu note that "the 'field' opens up a new unit of analysis for media research: the entire universe of journalists and media organizations acting and reacting in relation to one another."[42] A wealth of illustrative examples of such behavior springs mind: different newspapers jostling with each other in the battle over coverage of an event, competing movie studios positioning themselves to get the best box office receipts or the most Academy Awards, SNS platforms each trying to offer the most all-encompassing, user-friendly, and profit-friendly home for one's social network on the web. The possibilities are seemingly endless.

However, before we get carried away, it is important to point out that the idea of the field also has some limitations. Bourdieu made it very clear that not all social behavior occurs in a field as he intended for the term to be used. "As I use the term," he explained, "a field is a separate social universe having its own laws of functioning independent of those of politics and the economy."[43] Not everything is a field. It is only systems that have some set of laws of functioning, and some degree of autonomy from politics and the economy, that are to be treated as fields. Still, there is much that operates in communication in a manner similar to that of the field as proposed by Bourdieu, and there is great promise for the application of this term to the study of mediated communication, much of which does occur in 'fields.'

Capital

After habitus and field, the final of the three most important concepts for Bourdieu was capital. Capital is a perfectly recognizable term in and of itself. We recognize it as a basic term for understanding economies. However, as with 'field,' Bourdieu's use of the term requires a careful explanation. In keeping with familiar uses of the term, Bourdieu emphasized accumulation and exchange in his use of 'capital.' He cast economics as simply a special case for the exchange of capital. All kinds of modalities of accumulation and exchange are at work in a social system, and Bourdieu wished to call our attention to these processes.

One of Bourdieu's best definitions of capital (as he used the term) specified capital as "accumulated labor…which, when appropriated on a private, i.e., exclusive, basis by agents or groups of agents, enables them to appropriate social energy in the form of reified or living labor."[44] Capital "takes time to accumulate," and, "as a potential capacity to produce profits and to reproduce itself in identical or expanded form, contains a tendency to persist in its being, is a force inscribed in the objectivity of things so that everything is not equally possible or impossible."[45]

The emphasis on temporality ties any discussion of capital to history, and capital's non-random, unequal distribution means that capital becomes implicated in social reproduction. It is the accumulation and deployment of capital that keeps things much as they are, while also at times guiding subjects toward change. In a discussion that ties the idea of capital to his field theory, Bourdieu explained "kinds of capital" by comparing them to "trumps in a game of cards," in the sense that types of capital "are powers which define the chances of profit in a given field."[46] Working from this, we get the idea that capital can take on many forms, and that it is related to (figurative or literal) profit within the confines of a given field. As with habitus and field, with capital we have yet another component in Bourdieu's attempt to bind structure and agency to each other. The card game example highlights how capital is not something that simply happens; it is given power through agents' choices. But these choices are themselves shaped in large measure by what have been determined—as if it were natural—to be the trump cards in a game.

The concept of capital becomes a way to take a term most closely associated with economics and to broaden the term's meaning so that it can be understood that capital's place in economics is a special case. Bourdieu envisioned a "general science of the economy of practices" which, he insisted, "must endeavor to grasp capital and profit in all their forms and to establish the laws whereby the different types of capital (or power, which amounts to the same thing) change into one another."[47] If one type of power—like economic capital—were transferred into any other type of capital, that would be a reason to ignore the subservient types of capital. After all, if it all comes down to one trump card, why look anywhere else? Crucially, for Bourdieu, different fields came with different trump cards, and acquiring these trumps with others was in many cases rarely so easy.

Bourdieu's most influential use of the term 'capital' comes from his discussion of cultural capital, a term that is particularly relevant to the study of communication. Bourdieu's best definition of cultural capital posits cultural capital as existing "in three forms." First, it exists "in the *embodied* state, i.e., in the form of long-lasting dispositions of the mind and body." Second, it is found "in the *objectified* state, in the form of cultural goods (pictures, books, dictionaries, instruments, machines, etc.)." And finally, cultural capital is found "in the *institutionalized* state, a form of objectification which must be set apart because, as…in the case of educational qualifications, it confers entirely original properties on the cultural capital which it is presumed to guarantee."[48]

The idea of cultural capital comes from Bourdieu's attempts to understand discrepancies in the education system in a way that would get him past looking at such discrepancies as the result of differences in natural ability or in financial means. Bourdieu's pursuit of research involving cultural capital often concerned itself with differences in appreciation of art, but the relevance of cultural capital to the field of communication can be extended far beyond this. His discussion of cultural capital often emphasized the 'trump card'-like role of this capital as it came to fuel the reproduction of social privilege, as when elevated taste in cultural commodities becomes part of a game through which social privilege seems to derive from natural differences.

Social capital is another form of capital that occupies a major place in Bourdieu's work. He defined social capital as "the aggregate of the actual or potential resources which are linked to…membership in a group[,…] which provides each of its members with the backing of the collectively-owned capital."[49] Social capital is thus a kind of credit that goes to those who are connected to certain people. At the heart of this is a concern for group membership and social networks. Social capital, deployed semi-consciously by agents, can yield "material profits, such as all the types of services accruing from useful relationships," as well as "symbolic profits, such as those derived from association with a rare, prestigious group."[50] This is amongst the more obvious instances in which Bourdieu addressed the conversion of one form of capital to another. It is not difficult to envision how a social network can do material things for us. For Bourdieu's approach to capital, it is important to keep in mind how conversion from one form of capital to another plays a role in social life.

The maintenance of social networks is not unfamiliar to communication scholars, and Bourdieu's language in describing social capital should be of obvious importance to those who study communication. The work of maintaining social networks is not pursued from a calculating mindset. Instead, "the network of relationships is the product of investment strategies" aimed "at transforming contingent relations, such as those of neighborhood, the workplace, or even kinship, into relationships that are at once necessary and elective, implying durable obligations subjectively felt (feelings of gratitude, respect, friendship, etc.) or institutionally guaranteed (rights)."[51] These 'investment strategies' are not plotted on a spreadsheet. They feel right; they feel spontaneous. But they still bear the structural features of capital acquisition.

The significance of social capital for communication and media scholars is easy to refer to, but perhaps more difficult to instantiate. Any communication research that points to social networks, group membership, and rites of consecration can be linked to social capital. For Bourdieu, it was important that social capital not be considered in isolation from strategy or from other forms of capital.

Yet another kind of capital—symbolic capital—plays an important role in some of Bourdieu's later work. Though it did not occupy the place in Bourdieu's scholarship that cultural capital did, the idea of symbolic capital puts Bourdieu in contact with some important ideas in communication. Bourdieu's interest in symbolic capital stemmed from his concerns relating to the power of language. Distancing himself from what he deems "the illusion of linguistic communism,"[52] wherein all speakers/agents have the same access to the language, Bourdieu argued that agents vary in terms of their mastery of specific linguistic codes, and in terms of their power to compel attention and/or agreement. In essence, Bourdieu insisted (to those who concerned themselves with the primacy of the language or the text) that social processes, themselves tending to reproduce the social formation, shaped language use and authority. This sense of Bourdieu's rejection of what could be thought of as a purely linguistic approach can be found in his assertion that the "linguistic relation of power is never defined solely by the relation between the linguistic competences present. And the weight of different agents depends on their symbolic capital, i.e. on the recognition, institutionalized or not, that they receive from a group."[53] Bourdieu's emphasis is appealingly audience-oriented for media scholarship. The conditions that allow symbolic power to be wielded via symbolic capital require an audience that grants authority to the communicator. Significantly, these ideas concerning language can be applied to much more, as language itself would not seem to be the only thing capable of bearing the guarantee of delegation at work in symbolic power. Media scholars might be quick to point out that simply having access to certain media (e.g., being interviewed on televised network news in the US) is itself a display of symbolic capital.

It should not be forgotten that economic capital plays an important role in Bourdieu's work. In suggesting different types of non-economic capital, Bourdieu's main squabble was with economists who consider almost everything in terms of rational-choice models, and with Marxists who reduced all conflict to economic/class considerations. The potential for conversion between different types of capital (including economic capital) establishes a certain fluidity in this system, while the fact that such conversion requires effort and time means that not everything can be reduced to economics (or to any other capital). This did not make Bourdieu an anti-Marxist so much as someone who hoped to think "with Marx, against Marx,"[54] to apply some of Marx's ideas to others, in the hope of developing a creative, and, for that matter, accurate perspective on social behavior.

Bourdieu defined economic capital as the kind of capital that "is immediately and directly convertible into money and may be institutionalized in the form of property rights."[55] This may seem like an almost peremptorily short definition of such an important concept, but Bourdieu's interest in economic capital was not so dismissive. He paid significant attention to economic capital in his analyses of the conversions of capital. These conversions were not simple and direct, but involved what might be called transaction costs, or mediating factors. As he put it, the "different types of capital can be derived from *economic capital*, but only at the cost of a more or less great effort of transformation, which is needed to produce the type of power effective in the field in question."[56] In other words, possession of a large amount of economic capital cannot be instantly (note the emphasis on time) be transformed into social, cultural, or symbolic capital.

In perhaps regrettably indirect language, Bourdieu identified economic capital as mattering rather more than other types of capital. He proclaimed that

> economic capital is at the root of all the other types of capital and that these transformed, disguised forms of economic capital…produce their most specific effects only to the extent that they conceal (not least from their possessors) the fact that economic capital is at their root, in other words—but only in the last analysis—at the root of their effects.[57]

Economic capital is thus made to be fundamental in certain ways to other forms of capital, and yet it is the time and effort it takes to convert economic capital into other kinds of capital that prevents economic capital from always, and in all contexts, carrying the day.

This description of Bourdieu's theory of capital is of particular relevance to communication scholars, for it identifies what has been an ongoing, oft-misrecognized conflict in the field, and declares both sides of the conflict to be incomplete. Those who attempt to explain power in the media solely through reference to economic power or market share are in danger of succumbing to the weaknesses of economism here, by ignoring the other types of processes at work in the media, including almost all processes related to meaning. Those who attempt to explain media and communication solely through reference to the play of texts—and here I argue that numerous rhetoric and cultural studies scholars do this—risk forgetting the role played by power.

On Theoreticism

There is a serious danger of my allowing Bourdieu to stand as a pure theoretician. Frustratingly, the lingering sense that Bourdieu was simply a theoretically inclined guru is bolstered (particularly in the US) by Bourdieu's French-ness. Given that many of his writings took the form of screeds against pure theoreticism, and that he was so devoted to careful empirical work, it is important for me to point out that this book should be taken as an introduction to Bourdieu for those pursuing research in communication.

Bourdieu's dislike for pure theorizing was widely noted, and becomes quickly apparent in most of his work. Loïc Wacquant notes that Bourdieu stood "poised against…theoretical work done for its own sake, or the institution of theory as a separate, self-enclosed, and self-referential realm of discourse—what Kenneth Burke labels 'logology,' that is, 'words about words.'"[58] I have attempted to write this book (a book that consists largely of 'words about words') in a manner that demonstrates how Bourdieu's ideas can be linked to actual research. It is for this reason that this book finds me so frequently turning to issues in research. If this book is to achieve its goals, it will link up directly to research programs related to communication and the media. A book concerning Bourdieusian theory as something to be treated separately from the world of research (or from praxis) would be a failure in Bourdieusian terms.

My attempt to develop connections between Bourdieu's ideas and communication research finds me engaging a few related strategies. The most obvious and recurring strategy I employ is to describe Bourdieu's ideas and to explain their relevance to communication. Though Bourdieu never identified himself as a communication scholar per se, there is much to find in his work that relates to the questions we pose in communication. A thorough treatment of Bourdieu's considerable oeuvre is necessary and obvious in a book like this. A second strategy finds me, where applicable, showing how communication scholars have already used Bourdieu's ideas in their scholarship. Though I think that Bourdieu is underused in the field of communication, there is no reason to overstate my own case by claiming that he has never been applied, and a careful treatment of communication scholarship that has already used Bourdieu's ideas is an obvious necessity in this book. A third strategy, and one that carries with it a certain danger, involves lining up Bourdieu's ideas with communication scholars whose work does not explicitly cite Bourdieu. Here, the goal is to demonstrate how Bourdieu's concerns are not so different from our own, and that substantial overlap can be found between what he laid out and some of what communication scholars have done. There are numerous potential problems in this approach, where I am at risk of misrepresenting communication scholars, misrepresenting Bourdieu, or misrepresenting the potential connection between them. Still, this approach—a kind of inter-weaving of Bourdieu with extant communication research—strikes me as necessary if I am to demonstrate that Bourdieu's ideas can be successfully transposed for what will, perforce, be research goals that come from the field of communication.

As much as I attempt to weave Bourdieu's ideas into the tapestry of communication research, the real work will involve the kinds of research that Bourdieu himself modeled for the rest of us, including careful field research, large-scale surveys, content analysis, textual analysis, reflexive modes of taking on the role of the social scientist, and more. Bourdieu's work was empirical in a way that the "abstracted empiricism"[59] that characterizes much social science (and, in particular, much work in communication) is not. He amassed great piles of data, and developed theory around what he noticed. His approach was thus that of a social scientist, albeit a social scientist whose concern for reflexivity called his own authority into question. It would be wrong of me to claim that this book represents anything more than an introduction to the potential for applying his work to communication. This is not the first word on Bourdieu's relevance to communication, nor should it be the last.

Points of Contact: Bourdieu and the Media

The next four chapters will find me taking Bourdieu's ideas and moving them much closer to the study of communication and the media. In chapter 2, I show how Bourdieu's ideas of habitus and field can be posed in a manner that sheds new light on familiar concerns in the realm of media production. In chapter 3, I emphasize Bourdieu's long-lasting concern for codes and intelligibility at work in culture, showing how Bourdieu's ideas get us in touch with a particular approach to ritual in the media. In chapter 4, I expand on Bourdieu's sweeping perspective on authority, and sketch a media-centered approach to authority that preserves Bourdieu's concern for symbolic power. Finally, in chapter 5, I build on Bourdieu's own brand of sociology of science to show how the history of the field of communication can benefit from careful consideration of Bourdieu's habitus/field model.

CHAPTER TWO

The Field of Media Production

A cursory review of Bourdieu's writing indicates a clear concern with the production of culture. Two of his books—*The Rules of Art* and *The Field of Cultural Production*—address little *besides* the question of how culture comes to be produced. His identification with sociology inclines him toward institutions, and in particular with institutions that relate to cultural goods. Those who have applied Bourdieu's ideas to questions in communication scholarship often do so in the context of media production, as do Daniel Hallin and Paolo Mancini in their *Comparing Media Systems*.[1]

And yet there are reasons to doubt the applicability of Bourdieu's ideas to the domains of cultural production that have been of central concern to the field of communication. David Hesmondhalgh, who has considered the potential of Bourdieu's ideas for the study of media production, notes that Bourdieu's ideas have been received "with some ambivalence in Anglo-American media studies,"[2] and Hesmondhalgh himself is not without his own ambivalence. One limitation Hesmondhalgh finds in the potential for Bourdieu's application to media production is the fact that Bourdieu "focuses overwhelmingly on two types of field or sub-field of cultural production that are primarily expressive-aesthetic: literature and art," though Bourdieu "also published more briefly and polemically on journalism."[3] Thus an apparent limit to the applicability of Bourdieu's ideas is the fact that "the structure of the field of mass or large-scale production," which interests media researchers so much, "is an issue that Bourdieu scarcely addresses, at some cost to his theory."[4] Hesmondhalgh puts a fine point on his disappointment, concluding that

> [i]t is simply astonishing how little Bourdieu has to say about large-scale, 'heteronomous' commercial cultural production, given not only its enormous social and cultural importance in the contemporary world, but also its significance in determining conditions in the sub-field in which he is clearly much more interested, restricted production.[5]

This lack of attention is even more confusing and frustrating in light of the fact that Bourdieu's "work on cultural consumption is remarkably comprehensive."[6] Hesmondhalgh concludes that "Bourdieu misses the importance of the rise of the cultural industries for understanding the changing social relations of cultural producers."[7] On top of this, the same problem is apparent in works like *The Rules of Art*, where "Bourdieu has nothing to say about the combination of cultural production by multinational entertainment corporations across all cultural industries."[8]

Hesmondhalgh reminds us of Nicholas Garnham's point that the massive changes in the corporatization of media production in the late 20th century mean that "[t]he dominant fraction [of the dominant class] cannot safely leave the cultural field to be shaped by the interstatus group competition between subsets of the dominated fraction, since the reproduction of their economic capital now depends directly upon both the costs of production and the size of the markets for symbolic goods."[9] "Moreover," Hesmondhalgh continues, "with the rise in advertising, 'cultural taste publics are increasingly also market segments not just for symbolic goods but for an associated range of material goods.'"[10] Amplifying Garnham's earlier misgivings about the importation of Bourdieu's ideas to communication, Hesmondhalgh warns us that the properties of fields, as Bourdieu used the term, simply do not map so easily onto the world of media production we study.

But all is not lost for those of us arguing for the use of Bourdieu's ideas in the study of media production. I will pursue several lines of argument in this chapter, each making a case for the fruitful application of Bourdieu's ideas to questions of media production. First, I will argue that the concept of habitus provides the study of media production with a level of analysis that directly addresses questions about why we have the media systems, outlets, and messages that we do, and not something else. After this, I will make a case for applying the idea of the field to studies of media production. This may involve using Bourdieu's ideas against his other ideas—thinking 'with Bourdieu against Bourdieu'—but the utility of field-level analyses will be that they allow us to think relationally about media systems. My third argument in this chapter will suggest how we can adapt Bourdieu's interest in how autonomy and its opposite, heteronomy, can be related to inquiry about media production. In many media production contexts, it is something very much like Bourdieu's distinction between autonomy and heteronomy that interests us. Trying to figure out who is 'in control' and what cultural products come out of situations of relative autonomy and heteronomy can animate discussions of much besides the 'expressive-aesthetic' work that occupied Bourdieu's own attention.

Habitus and Political Economy

One point of connection that can be established between Bourdieu's ideas and media production pertains to the concept of habitus. When applied to questions of media production, the notion of habitus points to significant lacunae in much extant research concerning media production. The study of media systems and institutions outside of critical political economy often tends toward the descriptive, with only a diffuse sense of power or domination at work. The focus in the critical political economy study of the media defines itself largely in terms of a concern with power, frequently emphasizing the structures and institutions that are thought to dominate the system of mediated communication. I argue that habitus will give the political economy of communication a better sense of how structural arrangements come to matter, while also giving to the broader study of media systems and institutions a way of thinking through power and domination.

My emphasis here will be on how the study of media production can be shifted so that praxis—as it is connected to power structures—is brought more clearly into play. After all, the point for the study of media production should not just be the names of the corporations that have consolidated, or a catalog of their joint ventures and synergistic designs. If political economists and others who study media production are to understand processes of domination, the place to look would be at the practices made possible (and those made less possible) by these structural arrangements, as embodied by the producers themselves. Habitus could be the proper starting place for a reinvigorated political economy of communication. Its focus on the everyday, taken-for-granted aspects of life—on the micro-level—is what we should be casting onto the screen of structural arrangements.

The reason we study media institutions is because their arrangements can be demonstrated to have influence on how we wind up with the culture that we have. But culture does not come directly from an institution. It comes from practices that have emerged from past experience, are simultaneously constrained and enabled by structural arrangements (including legal, technical, and market concerns), and owe their existence to the strategic orientation of those whose labor is directly tied up with making media content. One of the most well-traveled hypotheticals for this would be the situation of the U.S. newspaper reporter, whose practices come not so much from the stated goals of a journalism school or a statement of professional values as from the day-to-day interactions with superiors and subordinates, sources and colleagues. Through this, the reporter (or any other producer of media content) gets a feel for the game: a feel that is embodied (and thus irreducible to simple, stated, logical-seeming rules) and a game that is taken seriously, though perhaps rarely understood in terms of the larger structural forces at play.

Seen this way, habitus gives us a way to think about media production as something that owes its shape partly to structural arrangements (and thus to power), but also as something that plays out in the everyday world of doing things. And for the political economist of communication, habitus tells us where to look for things like domination, hegemony, and reproduction. Much as Marx and Engels derided the "German philosophy which descends from heaven to earth," suggesting instead that we should "ascend from earth to heaven,"[11] the concept of habitus gives us a way to get down to the materiality that both follows from and subtends the structural arrangements we study.

This does not mean that it is time for the study of media production to turn away from institutions. Indeed, habitus can be linked up quite directly to institutions. It is through habitus that institutions reproduce the practices required for the social reproduction necessary for social sustenance. As Beate Krais has it, "[i]t is by habitus that the meaning objectified in institutions is reactivated, that institutions are kept alive, but only by imposing the revisions and transformations that are counterpart and condition of the reactivation."[12] In this sense, it is through habitus that institutions reproduce themselves (or reproduce the dispositions that make themselves sustainable), and it is through habitus that individuals develop the means through which to accommodate themselves to institutional needs/functions.

This emphasis on the inter-relationship of institutions and habitus links up smoothly with how Vincent Mosco envisions the work of the political economy of communication. Mosco argues for a renewed political economy of communication that "approaches social life as a set of mutually constitutive processes, acting on one another in various stages of formation, and with a direction and impact that can be comprehended only in specific research."[13] In pursuit of this, he tells us that "it is…more useful to develop starting points that characterize processes rather than simply to identify relevant institutions."[14] For Mosco, the processes of commodification, structuration, and hegemony make the best foci for political economy. His discussion of commodification identifies praxis as the central concern, noting that, in its past treatments of commodification, "political economy has tended to concentrate on media content and less so on media structures and the labor involved in media production."[15] It is under the rubric of structuration that Mosco identifies hegemony as an important part of the scholarship on political economy, describing hegemony as "a lived network of mutually constituting meanings and values, which, as they are experienced as practices, appear to be mutually confirming."[16]

Part of what Mosco is telling us is that a better political economy of communication will concern itself less with structures (institutions, organizations, policies) and media content, and more with the praxis connected to certain institutional arrangements. I am struck by the similarity between Mosco's ideas here and Bourdieu's description of his own scholarly project as "a general science of the economy of practices."[17] We see tremendous overlap in this vision of political economy and Bourdieu's ideas when we look at some of Bourdieu's starting points: the expansive sense of the term 'exchange,' the similarly expansive senses of 'capital' and of labor,[18] his pointed critique of rational choice theory,[19] and the "anticipation of profits" from symbolic exchange.[20]

In the hands of a critical political economist, habitus can be thought of as the medium through which commodity relations are internalized in daily practices. This applies not just to knowledge workers, but to everyone, to whole classes of people, where social relations and power are reified in daily actions structuring their choices and meanings as workers—who are tacitly bid to accept the terms of capital as doxa—and as consumers—who practice meanings and values in relations essential to the cycle of capital.[21]

Applying the concept of habitus to media production may seem relatively uncontroversial. In part, this is because some heavy lifting has already been done. Bernard Miège writes—in the context of the contemporary 'information revolution'—of "the importance that communication is presently gaining in the capitalist mode of production in the world economy in the context of globalization and liberalization."[22] One of the important points Miège makes is that the mode of production matters not only in terms of how large corporations and regulators relate to each other, but also in terms of how it shapes praxis, or, in the language of habitus, how it shapes the semi-conscious strategies at work in media labor. With more direct relevance to media production, Thomas Streeter has addressed how the field of possibilities was constructed culturally and embedded in praxis amongst the creators and managers of internet technologies in the 1990s.[23] Dallas Smythe's ideas are relevant here, too. Crucial to Smythe's sense of political economy of communication, after all, was a sense for how commodification operated in media markets to construct audiences as commodities.[24] Smythe focuses on power, while getting us beyond thinking only about regulations, corporations, and other large structures. What he was describing was how media producers come to understand and act toward audiences in specific ways, given the particular arrangements of corporate activity, and the over-arching demands of the capitalist marketplace, an issue ripe for consideration in terms of habitus.

Applications of habitus to media production can be found already in existence. Eric Darras has applied habitus to the situation of French journalists, where the "structural subordination of the journalistic field is made possible by journalistic self-censorship via the more or less confused absorption of the relative importance of political institutions (the constitution, the government, the Congress, the dominant parties, and especially in France, the National School for Administration…)."[25] As Darras puts it, the "most productive journalists are those who have best assimilated the theodicies that support representative government and the social system as a whole (the real power of politicians; the political participation of the 'people'; the 'separation of powers'; etc.)."[26] For Darras, habitus in journalism operates as a way to find the institution in the agent, revealing the power at work in the organization of praxis, the 'taken-for-granted.'

The application of the concept of habitus to questions of media production help us explain why the larger structural arrangements matter. In terms of habitus, structural arrangements (institutions, regulatory frameworks, corporations) do not so much matter in and of themselves, but matter a great deal in terms of how they arrange action, construct sets of possibles, tacitly introduce forms of self-censorship, and embody the rules of the game. From this vantage point, the capitalist mode of production matters in terms of its power to install doxa—taken-for-granted bits of knowledge—in the bodies of knowledge laborers. It is the job of the scholar to attempt to uncover these doxa, not as ideologies, but as lived habits that emerge from the social structure. As with Marx's cobbler, the effect of alienation comes from his relation to his labor, as it changes as a result of the development of modern capitalism; simply telling us who owns the shoe factory does not give us much of the story.

More than one daunting question haunts the effort to incorporate Bourdieu's habitus into a program for studying media production. One of the most important of these would be: what methods should be used to study habitus as it relates to production of culture? To study habitus as it relates to media production would be much better if habitus were, in the language of social science, a more readily operationalized concept.

Here it is worth considering what Bourdieu himself did. He is justifiably well known for employing numerous methods. He started off largely as a field researcher; his formulations of the term habitus come largely from his research on the Kabyle in Algeria.[27] In his work amongst the Kabyle, one finds exactly the kind of emphasis on nuance and praxis that field research should involve. It is worth pointing out that similar field-based research can retain a critical perspective. Critical ethnography, as described by Jim Thomas,[28] gives us a good sense of how a qualitative and field-based methodology can be linked with specific critical ends. The lessons of critical ethnography are apposite for the attempt to bridge habitus with political economy, an attempt already made quite successfully by Manjunath Pendakur, who helpfully outlined how ethnography could inform political economy in his analysis of media audiences in an Indian village.[29]

For political economy of the media the methodological significance of Bourdieu's work is its insistence on refusing to dissolve anything in a solution of ideological analyses, paying attention instead to the lived experience of power. From a Bourdieusian point of view, a focus on media institutions and structures simply would not be sufficient, since knowledge about political and corporate bodies and the formal rules they propagate does not tell us very much about precisely how domination is worked out. Furthermore, Bourdieu's ideas provide us with a way to get past the economic determinism in some strains of Marxian thought. Instead of responding to the problems of economic determinism through an embrace of populist assertions of agency, Bourdieu's broader sense of domination turns it into a more multivariate affair, where degrees of autonomy do exist in the confines of specific fields, and economics is not always the prime mover. Applied carefully to the consideration of media production, habitus gives us a way to join the nuance of fieldwork with the concern for power that we often associate with critical approaches. In this sense, a strength of habitus is its potential for joining the sociology of media production to critical goals.

Habitus lends a certain flexibility to the study of media production, and this flexibility is valuable as the field continues to be faced with the ongoing conceptual challenges presented by new media. The political economy of communication sometimes finds itself struggling to explain the importance of ownership and legal structures in a digital media context, where, if Henry Jenkins (for instance) is to be believed, the line between producers and consumers has become almost nonexistent, as a "collective intelligence" that is fostered in the current media environment begins to take hold, and new, more collaborative, means of creating culture emerge. From this point of view, domination seems to disappear, as 'produsers' reign. Though many scoff at Jenkins' conclusions, I believe they present a threat to the critical study of media production. In contradistinction to the arguments of political economists, Jenkins in essence argues that over-riding power structures no longer have any meaningful control. Others (non-political economists) who study media production are faced with the idea that new media have rearranged praxis, but that this has little to do with power. Both challenges demand a response.

The best response to Jenkins' ideas, I think, would be to apply his own methods (e.g., ethnography) to different parts of the media production/consumption process. Clearly, we still need to understand ownership and institutional control in the current 'new' media regime. What would Bourdieu do? Amongst other things, he would probably point out that the types of practice that Jenkins hails as a positive development of convergence culture are not evenly distributed, and that 'convergence' itself represents a potential tool for domination, as a potential form of misrecognition of a non-democratically arranged set of relationships. The seemingly populist tendencies Jenkins finds at work in activists' uses of Photoshop, for instance, could be more fully contextualized as the workings not just of people, but of specific parts of the population, themselves with particular cultural capital, and that many are left out of the process by which these activists "adopted technologies and techniques pioneered by fan communities and used them to mobilize voters."[30] There may be a kind of subversion of once-dominant political ideals and practices at work here, but a Bourdieusian analysis would also demand an appreciation of what kinds of inequality are (perhaps paradoxically) reproduced in these kinds of converged activism.

More broadly, current shifts in media production give us a rare chance to understand praxis, because they provoke actors in the media industry to do new things. A moment of cultural-technological change may give us the opportunity to unravel some of what has been going on—and some of what is coming—in the world of praxis. I suggest that many of Bourdieu's favorite themes in his research (misrecognition, *le sens practique*, adjustments in fields of play) become more accessible to the researcher when they are in flux. For instance, the popular music industry is currently experiencing difficult times. Old models for generating profit no longer work very well, new media have not been efficiently monetized, and the existing laws for intellectual property still highlight contradictions in the field more than the industry would prefer. For the agents involved—including audience members and consumers—this represents a time when well-worn subject positions become describable simply because they do not work as seamlessly as they once did. For those who study media production, it would be a mistake to only pay attention to institutions or, alternatively, to assume that power has melted away, at one of the moments—a time of technical/behavioral transformation—when praxis in the day-to-day has become fleetingly available. In other words, habitus helps us assess, in Roger Silverstone's words, "what is new about new media."[31]

The Field and Media Production

Habitus always operates in relation to fields of position-takings. Here, the "task [for the researcher] is that of constructing the space of positions and the space of the position-takings in which they are expressed."[32] Habitus becomes the means by which the field becomes internalized and embodied, with individuals occupying their own roles within the field, each reflecting differently off of other agents, hence the importance of relational thinking. Each position takes its form based in large part on its place in the field in which it is located (and the kinds of interaction/competition/collusion that take place within that field), and also on that specific field's place in relation to other fields of power.

As with much of Bourdieu's thought, one advantage—flexibility—is thwarted in part by the level of abstraction such flexibility often provides. So imagine that we are not talking about all of culture, but are instead discussing only the publication of a certain book. This book is produced because there is a homology between the book's content and the publisher's interests. The interests of author and publisher are coordinated in large part because they all operate according to the logic of the field in which they find themselves: the world of book publishing. And the arrangement of the entire field of book publishing is itself formed through that field's relationship to the field of power, as populated by political and capitalist-commercial interests.

Power is directly implicated in this model, as it is "by obeying the logic of the objective competition between mutually exclusive positions within the field" that "various categories of producers tend to supply products adjusted to the expectations of the various positions in the field of power, but without any conscious striving for such adjustment."[33] Operators within the field of cultural production do not develop strategies that are explicit reflections of their own interests; their competition with each other is subtly shaped by the contours of the field at hand. By simply working according to what presents itself as an obvious, even inevitable, course of action, agents work according to their position in the field, and this shapes culture. This is what Bourdieu refers to most when he declares that 'everything is relational.' It is out of relations between and within fields that culture is produced. Let us turn to the issue of interfield relations as they relate to media production, and then to the role played by intrafield relations.

Interfield Relations

The idea of the field has numerous points of relevance to the study of media production. The highest-level point of relevance involves so-called interfield relationships. Unfortunately, Bourdieu is frequently quite foggy in his description of how fields interact. Nick Couldry notes that "[h]ow fields *interrelate* has always been a difficult question for a research program whose first concern is always with the internal workings of particular fields."[34] David Swartz says much the same thing, noting that Bourdieu's work "thus far has acknowledged but not stressed the importance of *interfield* contradictions."[35] In much of Bourdieu's work, the attention to interrelationships between fields can be found in his efforts to orient discussions of the fields of cultural production (e.g., the literary and artistic fields) to the field of power, where they occupy a "dominated position."[36] In his later work, he would expand on this, with particular relevance to media studies, as when, in *On Television*, he expresses grave concerns regarding the relative autonomy of journalists and intellectuals within the field of power, in essence arguing that the necessary autonomy of journalists and intellectuals had been undermined by the encroaching fields of politics and/or the market.[37]

Thankfully, many scholars have stepped up and elaborated upon Bourdieu's ideas concerning interfield relationships. Rodney Benson has put considerable effort into mapping variations in the position of a field inside the broader field of power. Benson's ventures into this exploration of interfield relations concern journalism, as when examining the interfield relations between journalism, the market, and the state. He is particularly concerned with autonomy in journalism, and this issue compels him to ask "[u]nder what conditions do the semi-autonomous logics of national fields prove more or less powerful in resisting external pressures toward homogenization?"[38] Elsewhere, and more broadly, Benson pushes us toward interfield considerations by examining how "field position helps determine a field's relative vulnerability to external pressures for change." "[C]omparative research," Benson tells us, will allow us "to explore the question of how different types of fields vary in their tendencies toward cultural inertia."[39] In a similar way—but in a very different domain—Marion Fourcade applies Bourdieu's ideas relating to interfield relations to track how the field of Economics has related variably to the field of power in the United States, Britain, and France.[40]

A carefully attuned model for applying interfield concerns to the field of media production can be found in Daniel Hallin's work. Hallin explicitly spells out how interfield considerations can be connected to the study of journalism, contrasting Bourdieu's field theory with differentiation theory, which itself comes to us from Talcott Parsons via Jeffrey Alexander, who has applied differentiation theory to modern news media.[41] Differentiation theory tells us, in the context of journalism, that we should analyze how institutions become distinct from one another as they develop historically. The theory places great emphasis on patterns such as professionalism, wherein a specific institution becomes increasingly distinct (differentiated) from others. In the case of Western journalism, for instance, the "development of commercial media markets in the nineteenth century…permitted the differentiation of the media from political structures, and their reconstitution as independent structures increasingly central to the process by which public opinion was formed."[42] Hallin finds differentiation theory attractive "in part because it is such a rare attempt to do a comparative and historical analysis of the development of media institutions in relation to processes of social change at the system level."[43] He adds, however, that Bourdieu's field theory is "a useful alternative perspective against which to contrast Alexander's structural-functionalism."[44]

Field theory incorporates differentiation theory's concern for the degree to which different institutions establish degrees of distinctness and independence from each other, but does not buy into the assumption that institutions tend to become more distinct from each other over time. Hallin notes that Bourdieu and others who have applied field theory to the French media have pointed out that "the media have in recent years become increasingly de-differentiated in relation to the economic system."[45] Turning to US journalism history, Hallin reviews how journalistic autonomy in the US was for a time associated with commercial interests, as commercially run newspapers established themselves as relatively autonomous from political control. The "[p]rofessional autonomy" of journalists has "involved differentiation of the journalistic field from the economic as well as from the political fields."[46] Hallin builds to the idea that

> the distinctive 'media logic' that has developed during the twentieth century is in fact a complex hybrid influenced by both commercial and strictly 'professional' or 'intellectual' influences; these two are in many ways in tension with one another; and the balance is shifting toward the commercial.[47]

Hallin's focus here is on journalism, where the need to tease out the degrees and forms of autonomy and heteronomy seems relatively obvious. If, as Bourdieu argued in much of *On Television*, journalism finds itself moving toward a 'de-differentiation' from politics or commercial interests, that would matter tremendously, because there are good reasons we want journalists not to be making choices only for commercial or political reasons. Though there are reasons to be skeptical of the value of autonomy to journalism,[48] Hallin outlines a way to use Bourdieu's theory to assay the interfield connections and pressures between the media, the political field, and the field of commercial interests. He concludes that "one of the most central issues that needs to be developed from the perspective of field theory" is "the nature of the relation between the political and economic fields, and the intersection of journalism with these fields."[49]

Much as Hallin describes, we can work with field theory to orient ourselves to the interfield relationships that reside at the foundations of all kinds of media concerns. In the context of journalism, field theory gives us a way to treat the relationships between political, economic, and journalism fields as historically constituted factors that underlie much of the logic at work in media production. Many will recognize this as largely consistent with the critical political economy tradition, but it allows for greater emphasis on the structural origins of autonomy than political economy often does.

The same model can be applied to media production outside of journalism—to entertainment media. It may seem odd to regard 'autonomy' as much of a concern to media production that is not journalism, but such an attitude would be unfortunately tied to U.S.-based assumptions that non-journalistic culture can be safely assumed to be a commercially dominated affair. When considered in terms of field theory, the production of motion pictures, television, music, and more can be put on essentially the same interfield matrix as Hallin does with journalism. Imagine how the state, commercial interests, and media producers relate to each other. In the U.S., of course, media conglomerates control much of the content, and the question of interfield relations leads quickly to an initial sense that it is the economic field that holds sway. This does not mean that there is nothing interesting for field theory to tell us here. For instance, if the U.S. Federal Communications Commission functions as a 'captive' regulatory agency, that is a different way to say that the political field is dominated by the economic field in US media production, with resultant effects on how media structures are regulated, which itself affects all kinds of issues in media content. Beyond this, there is much to be said (and I will say more below) about the question of how autonomous media producers can be in a field configuration as is found in the U.S. Field theory can be used to point out how the configurations of interfield relationships found in different national contexts can vary. Hallin and Mancini's work is an example of an attempt to get to this level of analysis, where degrees of creative autonomy can be established if the commercial, political, and media fields are arranged in specific ways.

Bourdieu explicitly pointed out that not all social contexts operate in a field-like manner, and Hesmondhalgh has noted that this gives us limits for applying field theory to large-scale production. But understanding these interfield relation-ships can be a fruitful way to understand how high-level power dynamics can affect media production. And this seems to be even more helpful for understanding media production in a global context, where relationships between media corpora-tions/organizations, nations, and media workers make it clear that these kinds of interfield concerns matter.

If, as Hallin suggests may be the case, "an increasingly commercialized media are growing more central to social life," and that "they may be an important agent of this broader process of de-differentiation,"[50] there is much reason to focus on this concern for interfield relations. If it is the relative autonomy of journalists, or of media producers more broadly, that protects us from the dominance of the economic field, one can get a sense of Bourdieu's tremendous regard (to a fault, even) for autonomy. Beyond this, it is important to remember that the media are not like other institutions. In the context of this discussion, it bears pointing out, as Hallin explains, that "commercial media may in many cases be transmitters of the influence of the market into other areas of social life—and hence an agent of de-differentiation."[51] Seen this way, the interfield relations of the media take on far more relevance than Bourdieu himself would have had it, though his tools can prove invaluable for conceptualizing, analyzing, and responding to this de-differentiating influence of the market.

Intrafield Relations

The operations inside fields of production were where Bourdieu focused most of his attention, and on the face of things, that would seem to be unalloyed good news for the application of field theory to media production, keeping in mind Hesmondhalgh's reservations about a wholesale application of field theory to media production, since large-scale media production (as Bourdieu himself was careful to point out) rarely follows the rules of a field as Bourdieu laid them out. Despite this, there is much that field theory can give to the study of media production.

The study of the media has a built-in affinity for Bourdieu's consideration of the working of fields, because for Bourdieu the field itself acts as a medium, a factor operating in between the more direct concerns of class or corporation. Agents don't do what is 'natural' for them; the impulses are filtered, mediated, through fields. Working with the field approach gives Bourdieu's analyses a comparative lens. David Swartz describes how this was consistent with Bourdieu's desire "to emphasize the conflictual character of social life whereas the idea of institution suggests consensus," and also allows the field to remain "a concept that can cover worlds where practices are only weakly institutionalized and boundaries are not well established."[52] The structuralist logic at the heart of this emphasizes the mutual constitution of parts of any field. Swartz notes that "[f]ields are to be viewed as systems in which each particular element (institution, organization, group, or individual) derives its distinctive properties from its relationship to all other elements."[53]

The fact that Bourdieu assembled field theory as a rejoinder to opposed tendencies in micro- and macro-level approaches is something that makes it relevant to the study of the media. Rodney Benson tells us that Bourdieu's use in the study of the media is due largely to Bourdieu's "focus on the mezzo-level of the 'field,'" which allows us to bridge "the traditionally separated macro-'societal' level models of the news media, such as political economy, hegemony, cultural and technological theories, and micro-'organizational' approaches."[54] Benson notes that field theory "clearly distinguishes itself from 'vulgar Marxist' political economy approaches that seek to explain the news media's behavior by sole reference to its capitalist ownership and control."[55] At the same time, field theory differs from "organizational studies" in that "it takes care to relate particular media organizations to both their immediate institutional and broader societal environments."[56] Benson adds: "Field theory shares with the hegemony approach of Stuart Hall, Todd Gitlin, and Daniel C. Hallin a concern with how macro-structures of media power are linked to organizational routines and journalistic practices."[57] When put to work for the study of media production, Bourdieu's field theory gives us an approach that blends an anthropological concern for comparison while still maintaining an emphasis on power within and between fields.

Within individual fields, the focus for a Bourdieusian study of media production would be on how agents who operate in field-like structures find their actions shaped by the position-takings that the field allows, given the rules of capital within the field, and the possession of capital that they have. Many of Bourdieu's insights regarding the production of culture stem from this interest in how action derives in large part from agents' positions within a field. Frequently, this involves a focus on strategies that relate to how well-established different agents are. Swartz notes that Bourdieu identifies

> three different types of field strategies: *conservation, succession,* and *subversion.* Conservation strategies tend to be pursued by those who hold dominant positions and enjoy seniority in the field. Strategies of succession are attempts to gain access to dominant positions in a field and are generally pursued by the new entrants. Finally, strategies of subversion are pursued by those who expect to gain little from the dominant groups. These strategies take the form of a more or less radical rupture with the dominant group by challenging its legitimacy to define the standards of the field.[58]

Swartz describes the conservation and subversion strategies as related, in that "the two opposing strategies are dialectically related; one generates the other."[59]

Far from operating exclusively in the world of autonomous fields of high art, there is good reason to consider the interlocking strategies of different operators in the world of media production. Television production, for instance, has faced the introduction of new operators, each pursuing the kind of subversive strategies Bourdieu outlines, themselves matched against more established agents less impelled toward experimentation. When new networks are introduced, they often develop new kinds of programming. The introduction of the Fox Television Network in the U.S. in the 1980s, for instance, was an occasion that involved the attempt to develop new kinds of programming. Web-based television programming has been even more obviously subversive, experimenting with new formats and types of content. As Bourdieu indicated, the seeming subversion of new arrivals is matched with a conservation strategy from the old guard, and both strategies are developed in explicit contradistinction to each other. The strategy of succession represents an attempt to line oneself up to be next in line to be dominant, a low-capital attempt to become the new dominant position in time.

The question for Bourdieu is similar to the question that has faced generations of scholars who study media production: why look to the producers? If, in the media, it is a game of supply and demand, why not look to what the audience wants if we are to understand what we get? Bourdieu's answer is the same as that which comes from those who study media production: we look to media production because it is factors on the production side that represent the most proximal factors in explaining why we wind up with what we have. But Bourdieu's field analysis leads us away from the producers per se and instead focuses our attention on the fields in which the producers operate. As Swartz describes it, "[p]roducers struggle within the field of cultural production and their cultural products reflect more their respective positions of dominance or subordination in that struggle than they do the demands of consumers."[60] The field mediates the operations of any producer, both constricting the producers' ranges of choices while also enabling certain strategies. Bourdieu's emphasis on production also derived from his focus on homologies between cultural producers and their audiences. The assumption that there were homologies between producers and audiences—itself one of the reasons that seems to have kept Bourdieu focused on very tightly defined fields—led Bourdieu to understand reception largely in terms of these homologies. This itself can be called into question, particularly when we consider many of the mediated contexts for reception that we examine in media studies may involve less tightly connected pairings of producers and audience members.

Keeping in mind that Bourdieu himself seems to have had little interest in applying the field model to the field of mass production, one simple-yet-sweeping insight regarding the relevance of fields to media is that the fields of production in the media are largely defined by the media with which they are identified. Thus, there are fields of production associated with: television, cinema, radio, music, and all kinds of new media content. The 'field-ness' of these media producers' worlds— the degree to which the field mediates the producers' actions—varies, to be sure. But there is still utility in considering the kinds of competitions and alignments at work in the development of any media content.[61] To a great extent, these still involve within-medium comparisons. Someone producing a new television program will develop it to compete with other programs, to differentiate it but also make it similar to other programs in terms of: genre, intended audience, budget, and more. The strategies available to different producers vary in a non-random manner, with certain strategies more likely to be found from actors with different levels of capital and representing different parts of the lifespan of a media organization. Admittedly, this does not get us very far, and Bourdieu was always careful to insist that it was the researcher's job to follow the participants' definitions of the field (the emic sense of the field), rather than simply determining from the outside how a field is constituted. With this caveat granted, it is still perfectly apparent that many media operate as quasi-enclosed fields, with relations that follow from interactions that occur largely in terms of shared meaning related to specific media of communication.

Of course, even this is subject to change. Multi-media corporations have adjusted how actors in these fields envision themselves and those around them. Programming is created across divergent forms of media: television, movies, books, comic books, and even promotional items at fast food restaurants have been coordinated to become part of cross-media orientation. I suggest the consideration of individual media as fields of operation only as a provisionally useful idea. Cross-media programming is certainly showing us some limits to the presumption that individual media can be taken as ready-made fields. Bourdieu himself frequently took individual media as fields, following the emic understandings of fields at work in the operators he studied in *The Field of Cultural Production*. For Bourdieu, the field of painting and the field of literature were distinct because the operators who worked in the contexts of these fields understood them to be distinct. In later Bourdieu, we see an appreciation for how media do not always operate in their own terms, as in *On Television*, where he addresses the effects of television journalism on print journalism.[62] Bennett et al. have pioneered the consideration of multiple media at work in fields of audience practice[63]; there seems to be plentiful justification for remaining open to multiple media at work in fields of media production.

If we are to think of individual media as potential starting places for fields, we would want to consider programming within those media. Focusing on television in the 1990s, Bruce M. Owen and Steven S. Wildman observed that the "industry that supplies programs to the major broadcast networks is monopolistically competitive. Each program is different, and therefore the criterion of perfect substitutability among products required for perfect competition is not satisfied."[64] The uniqueness of each program, its differentiation from other programming, hints at some of the field-like operations of media production. Programs are designed to imitate other programs, but also to be differentiated from other programs. The programmers of media outlets rely on this play of similarity and difference in a manner not so very different from how, say, painters and literary figures in the late

19th century differentiated and aligned themselves against and with a host of others. This is admittedly not the working of 'the field' per se, but the kinds of insights drawn from field-based inquiry can certainly shed light on how, within and across types of programming (genres, media), there is Saussurean interplay between individual programming entries.

Attention to these kinds of similarities and differentiations offers a helpful, heuristic sense of fields operating through alignment and differentiation. We might also note how the alignments and differentiations are themselves derived from envisioned target audiences for programming. After all, it is the quest to 'capture' (in the language of advertising) audiences that provides the material heart for many programming decisions. The practice of symbolic violence and the establishment of a legitimate culture is carried out by actors who are not trying explicitly to do any such thing. They are simply trying to make more direct the relationships between specific programming, audiences, and producers.

Much of the value of Bourdieu's insights could be found in his insistence that we "look outside the 'field of discourse' for the principle which would cast light on each of the discourses within it."[65] To get beyond the merely heuristic use of Bourdieu, and to account for these inter-relationships outside of the programming itself, it is helpful to use Bourdieu's language of capital. The inter-relationships at work in fields of for-profit media programming develop as a result of the effort to link up: media products, media audiences, and media producers. It is not difficult to see how the workings of target-marketing, for instance, involve (relative to the past) precise definitions of who the audience will be, who the producers for this audience will be, and what programming will be developed to link them. Joseph Turow has argued that the increase in the number of media channels dovetails smoothly with target marketing, to the extent that media producers will be pushed increasingly to separate different market segments.[66] On the very surface of this, it seems likely that target marketing, because it brings what was formerly a mass-production ethic to smaller numbers, will create some more properly field-like considerations for production. But beyond this, what we find is a that the logic of target marketing also offers a proliferation of types of cultural capital, each one tied to a strip of the population. And, as Turow has been careful to point out, not all target markets are created equal. Some are given much more legitimacy than others, a symbolic order held together by a programming logic once thought to be most remarkable for dissolving differences.

Digital media have often been assumed to have changed how these kinds of distinctions get made. The new era of media convergence—itself frequently linked to the workings of digital media—has brought with it the promise of new kinds of media production as well as new ways to envision the fields at work in the media.

Media convergence need not be understood as a purely novel phenomenon. Janet Stager and Sabine Hake observe that it is "likely" that "print, movies, radio, television, and new media should never have been thought of as separate histories."[67] In keeping with this, there is reason to be suspicious of the effort to treat any medium (especially a mass medium) as truly separate. That said, new media do seem to upend the mutually reinforcing assumptions of media researchers and media producers regarding the separateness of media. We find ourselves in a moment of obvious transition, as producers struggle to develop new ways to approach converged media, while often still repairing to traditional definitions of fields. A fundamental Bourdieusian research issue to come out of this will be to attempt to get a grip on how media producers envision the fields in which they interact with other producers.

Autonomy and Heteronomy

Bourdieu's ideas concerning autonomy have particular relevance to the study of media production. Any time we use phrases like "creative control," "independent media," or even "freedom of speech," we are implicitly relying on some imagined importance of media producer autonomy, be it autonomy from the government, from capitalist interests, or from snooping parents. Bourdieu defined the field of large-scale production as functioning largely in a heteronomous manner (i.e., one in which actions are taken under the direction of others). This ought not be the last word on this. Hesmondhalgh points out that "[l]arge-scale production might be more differentiated than Bourdieu's work suggests, and the relations of heteronomy and autonomy might sometimes be more fluid and complex than he implies."[68]

Bourdieu defined autonomy in terms of the field. He envisioned fields operating with certain degrees of autonomy from the field of power, and he devoted much more attention to the degrees of autonomy available for agents *within* fields, especially those agents who found themselves in fields of restricted production (e.g., visual artists, literary figures). The autonomy in such a field "can be measured by [the field's] power to define its own criteria for the production and evaluation of its products."[69] These "cultural producers form a closed field of competition for cultural legitimacy" and "internal demarcations" come to "appear irreducible to any external factors of economic, political or social differentiation."[70] Within the autonomous subfield of the field of painting, for instance, the styles that are chosen appear to derive from, and are experienced as having derived from, internal considerations, not solely from a desire to sell. In the context of autonomous production, the act of producing culture is motivated by internal concerns for legitimacy, not by imposed concerns for selling culture.

Much of the emphasis in Bourdieu's description of autonomous production concerns differences that can be observed between internal (within-field) and external (outside-field) orientations. When a field of cultural production is characterized by a greater autonomy, the "principle of external hierarchization…is subordinated to the principle of internal hierarchization,"[71] meaning that it is the criteria developed by the producers/artists themselves that shape the work and the criteria to which the work is subjected. The more autonomous the field of cultural production,

> the more the break tends to be noticeable between the two poles of the field, that is, between the *subfield of restricted production*, where producers have only other producers for clients (who are also their direct competitors), and the *subfield of large-scale production*, which finds itself *symbolically* excluded and discredited.[72]

The subfield of restricted production thus operates "in the game of *loser takes all*, on an inversion of the fundamental principles of the field of power and of the economic field."[73] On the relatively autonomous side of the field of cultural production, symbolic value is assigned to those works that resist the blandishments of money and power. It is the "presumed adherence to the disinterested values" that identifies autonomy, though "lack of success is not in itself a sign and guarantee of election."[74]

One might be tempted to consider the ideal of autonomy instantly applicable to all kinds of media products that seem more concerned with legitimacy than with profit. Before the term can be applied to broad swaths of media production, however, it is good to keep in mind the emphasis Bourdieu placed on how autonomy often implies an opposition to 'bourgeois' art/culture. For instance, "in the purely literary domain of style," Bourdieu found a "rejection of the 'bourgeois' and of the 'people,'" as well as a "rejection of 'bourgeois art' and 'social art'" in the "purely literary domain of style."[75] As "artists affirm their autonomy and produce works which contain and impose their own norms of evaluation" they begin to "[push] the 'bourgeois' to the point where they are incapable of appropriating these works for themselves."[76] The reason I bring this up is to emphasize a potential difficulty in applying Bourdieu's idea of autonomy. Simply because a subfield of the field of cultural production involves some degree of seeming autonomy does not mean that the full meaning of autonomy—as Bourdieu uses the term—applies. Carrying the term over to the study of mass media production brings with it a near certain danger of broadening the term beyond its original purposes.[77]

The fundamental move at work in Bourdieu's work on autonomy and the field of production is his determined effort to establish the social structures at work in autonomy. One finds in this move an underlying motive on Bourdieu's behalf to undo the presumption that autonomy derives from individual talent or determination. It is an understanding of autonomy that he develops to demystify art, as a critique of the romantic vision of the artist. Instead of just trying to 'explain' art through reference to autonomy, Bourdieu was trying to show what autonomy and disinterest could do, provided that there were structures in place to prevent this autonomy from being undermined by political and economic forces (the field of power). Bourdieu's use of the term 'autonomy' was not intended to refer to any kind of ontological or radical freedom. Autonomy refers to fields, not to individuals. And autonomy represents a condition in constant peril. To a great extent, Bourdieu used the term 'autonomy' to establish how some arenas of behavior could set themselves up to act as a potentially powerful buffer against temporal powers such as the state or the market. Those looking for a purely materialist or idealist source for autonomy would be frustrated with Bourdieu's constant emphasis on *both* the material and cultural components of autonomy. And Bourdieu's emphasis quite clearly leads us to look for autonomy in fields, not in individual agency.

Bourdieu's later writings on journalism and on science made it very clear that he invested great hope in disinterest and autonomy. In *On Television*—his veritable ode to autonomy—he asserted that the "more a cultural producer is autonomous, rich in specific capital from a given field and exclusively integrated into the restricted market in which the only audience is competitors, the greater the inclination to resist." At the same time, "the more producers aim for the mass market (like some essayists, writer-journalists, and popular novelists), the more likely they are to collaborate with the powers that be…and to yield to their demands or their orders."[78] Fields that are autonomous from the political and economic powers are necessary for the sustenance of critical thought.

The development of a certain amount of autonomy was, for Bourdieu, the thing that made possible the modern field of art, with its emphasis on art for art's sake, as "evolution of different fields of cultural production towards a greater autonomy is accompanied…by a sort of reflexive and critical turning back by producers upon their own production, which leads them to distinguish its own principle and its specific assumptions."[79] We see autonomy in a "field of restricted production" evidenced by "its power to define its own criteria for the production and evaluation of its products."[80]

The inward-looking tendency in more autonomous fields is linked to disinterest. Bourdieu repeatedly described autonomous fields as kinds of upside-down worlds (from the point of view of the dominant class, or from the point of view of the market): "the literary order…presents itself as an inverted economic world: those who enter have an interest in disinterestedness."[81] History is centrally important in the story of autonomy, as the "degree of autonomy of the field (and thereby, the state of relations of force established there) varies considerably accord-ing to periods and national traditions." This degree of autonomy is itself "related to the degree of symbolic capital which has been accumulated over the course of time by the action of successive generations."[82]

Bourdieu opposed autonomy to heteronomy, wherein the goals and rules of production, and the collective ethos, are in a sense imported from outside the field. Heteronomy "occurs in effect through demand, which may take the form of the personalized commission formulated by a 'patron,' a sponsor or client, or the anonymous expectation and sanction of a market."[83] In the field of art, "threats to autonomy result from the increasingly greater interpenetration between the world of art and the world of money,"[84] as happens with sponsorship and under-writing of artistic production. More broadly, and more obviously relevant to the study of the media, Bourdieu pointed out that "[p]roducers attached to the major cultural bureaucracies (newspapers, radio, television) are increasingly forced to accept and adopt norms and constraints linked to the requirements of the market and, especially, to pressure exerted more or less strongly and directly by advertisers."[85] Heteronomy is thus established any time one field's logic becomes dependent on the logic of a different field. This kind of 'seepage' of the logic of fields tells us much about how Bourdieu understood political and market power, both of which are at all times likely to over-run the oft-fragile borders of the autonomous fields of production.

One finds in this vision of the benefits of autonomy a theme familiar from the work of Walter Lippmann and Jürgen Habermas. Though it is easy to make too much of Walter Lippmann's call for "interposing some form of expertness between the private citizen and the vast environment in which he is entangled,"[86] he en-visioned this as desirable because of the potential value of autonomous inquiry to informing the public. As Sue Curry Jansen explains, it is the fact that these experts "are interested in the work itself," and "not merely the profit that can be made from it"[87]—the precise 'interest in disinterest' that Bourdieu highlights in auton-omous fields—that led Lippmann to value experts. In the language of Bourdieu, what Lippmann was trying to do was to envision how an autonomous sphere of public information could be developed, to allow for an untangling of the problem of complexity of information in a world where almost all knowledge-holders had a strong stake in the game.

A parallel concern can be detected at work in much of what Jürgen Habermas describes at work in the emergence of a bourgeois public sphere. Habermas traces how "[e]lements of occupational status group organizations…developed into the sphere of 'civil society' that as the genuine domain of private autonomy stood opposed to the state."[88] It is the slow process whereby pockets of autonomy from the state emerged that Habermas emphasizes in his effort to demonstrate how a public sphere has existed in the past. For his part, Bourdieu envisioned an "*Internationale of intellectuals*" which would be "committed to defending the autonomy of the universes of cultural production."[89]

Beyond this concern for the constitution of the public, Bourdieu's ideas about autonomy can help to enliven inquiry into some of the fine meshes of cultural production. In pursuit of the applicability of Bourdieu's notion of autonomy, Hesmondhalgh notes that "there is now a huge amount of cultural production taking place on the boundaries between sub-fields of mass and restricted production; or, perhaps better still, that restricted production has become introduced *into* the field of mass production."[90] Perhaps some components of this phenomenon are not so recent. In 1971, Herbert Menzel suggested that "quasi-mass communication" would be a useful term for describing scenarios which "offer varying combinations of accessibility, search-language compatibility, responsiveness, fidelity in 'upward' communication, [and] capacity to link together with others of similar interest."[91] Menzel was considering "such phenomena as speakers who take part in election campaigns,…missionaries preaching in foreign societies, store-front information centers,…[and] selective dissemination services,"[92] but the point can be carried through to the idea that there is—and has been for some time—a great deal of cultural production that occurs on the margins between mass and restricted production. This is more consistent with Bourdieu's ideas than Hesmondhalgh describes these ideas, as Bourdieu's emphasis on relationality points us in the direction of a continuum between more- and less-restricted domains of cultural production. Also, Bourdieu makes something more than passing mention of "omnibus" media in *Distinction*, and this discussion explicitly mentions this kind of flexibility in the levels of restriction of production at work in fields of media production.[93]

The role played by autonomy in these realms between mass and restricted production is not difficult to notice. Certainly those who create zines, chapbooks, and pirate radio have given us important examples of relatively autonomous arenas of activity, and these all seem to exist somewhere between mass and restricted production. In this sense, the model provides numerous insights into how independent media production defines itself. Like many of the autonomous arenas of production that Bourdieu analyzes, independent media outlets often define themselves in opposition to ostensibly 'mainstream' media. The process of producing content for independent media outlets often involves the kind of anticipation of an audience of peers that Bourdieu highlights as a marker of autonomous production.

Examples of communication research that at least bump up against these Bourdieusian concerns are not hard to find. Chris Atton has done a good job of identifying how those who publish zines often play the role of "reader-writers,"[94] meaning that writers for one zine are often the audience for another, a situation quite reminiscent of the situation of the painters and literary figures Bourdieu described as having anticipated each others' responses as they pursued their art. Stephen Duncombe has also chronicled zines, and his ideas regarding how zines "[hold] a scene together"[95] resonates strongly with the group-constitutive power that Bourdieu finds in more autonomous portions of the art world. Rodney Benson describes in helpful detail how weekly alternative papers in the U.S. like San Francisco's *SF Weekly* and Seattle's *The Stranger* define themselves largely in opposition to other journalism, and even to other alternative newspapers. Citing Bourdieu's field theory, Benson describes this as an example of how "social fields" are "marked by the struggle for distinction."[96] The confluence of familiar issues from Bourdieu's field theory—the struggle for distinction, the concern for autonomy, the blurred roles of creator and audience member—support the contention that the study of independent and alternative media have much to gain from use of Bourdieu's ideas. These ideas, of course, are not sacrosanct, and they stand to be refined considerably by a careful application to specific media contexts.

Beyond this concern for alternative and independent media is the question of how digital media may have reshuffled cultural production. Mathieu O'Neil asserts that "online tribes" represent "the central value on the Internet, *autonomy*."[97] Though O'Neil is not using Bourdieu's definition of autonomy here, the argument is familiar: digital media lend themselves to the creation and sustenance of shared bonds of collaboration and consensus-building that represent important new threats to the temporal powers. A somewhat less sweeping account is offered by Yochai Benkler and Helen Nissenbaum, who suggest that digital media lead to "commons-based peer production."[98] Such arguments suggest that the quasi-mass character of much online communication lends itself, at the very least, to sustained Bourdieusian analysis of how digital media in particular relate to autonomy.

For example, take the field of comedy. In the U.S., comedy was often dominated by cultural production roles that were tied to the field of mass production. Standup comedians hoped for their big break on *The Tonight Show* with Johnny Carson, and comedy writers vied for positions writing for situation comedies on network television. Today, digital media have made it possible for comedy writers and performers to create and distribute content at relatively low expense, as has been the case with the recent U.S. program *Children's Hospital* (which started with web episodes, and was picked up by a cable network). At the same time, podcasts like Marc Maron's *WTF* and Jesse Thorn's *Bullseye*, which involve in-depth interviews by comedians with comedians, provide an outlet for what could be thought of as an 'inside' or autonomous aesthetic perspective on comedy. Similar small- to medium-scale circulation phenomena are not unusual, and the question of whether these represent meaningful autonomous developments is worth asking. There is little reason to doubt that digital media are associated with some kinds of adjustments in the world of autonomous cultural production, and there is much to be hoped for in applications of Bourdieu's ideas relating to autonomous fields of production to such phenomena as blogs, wikis, podcasting, peer-to-peer distribution, and more.

This exercise in autonomy as it relates to digital media highlights the fact that Bourdieu often treated media as relatively stable objects operating in the context of dynamic social forces. In contrast to this, we might instead begin to write media history into Bourdieu's ideas, extending these ideas to contend with the interplay between all the forces Bourdieu considers (field, habitus, capital) as they relate to the technology at work.

One good starting place for this project could be found in Marshall McLuhan's characteristically sweeping statement that "[e]ach new technology creates an environment that is itself regarded as corrupt and degrading. Yet the new one turns its predecessor into an art form."[99] What do we call old media? Frequently, we call them art. This would certainly be the case for the field of painting in the late 19th century, which was a kind of response to the development of photography. The same situation also describes the literary field that Flaubert occupied, wherein the relatively autonomous section of the literary field was responding in part to a growing trade in printed work (from popular novels to newspapers).

My point here is not so much that McLuhan was correct as it is that his mythic characterization of the historical long tail of media has something to it. To address this feature of media history better than McLuhan does would involve consideration of the social aspects whereby the relatively old medium becomes 'an art form.' There is reason to suspect that this part of the life story of media (the old age? middle age? decrepitude?) is often downplayed in our media histories. Ben Peters points out a blind spot in much media history. Citing numerous examples from some of the best-known examples of media history, Peters observes that "[m]any media histories address a period when a particular medium was new for the first time, and thus are, in a strong sense, already histories of new media."[100] Charles Acland concurs, noting that an "inappropriate amount of energy has gone into the study of new media, new genres, new communities, and new bodies, that is, into the contemporary forms."[101] One result of this is that we often wind up thinking relatively little about the later periods of media, and this pushes us away from some important arenas where media production operates in ways that are quite similar to the operations of fields. Another result of this tenacious focus on the new is a tendency to endorse tacitly the idea that media somehow replace each other, as if print was replaced by the telegraph, which was itself replaced by the telephone, and so on. For all its faults, McLuhan's idea that outmoded media became art was a rather successful reminder that we should not think that media simply disappear at the moment their novelty recedes.

If we accept the proposition that Bourdieu's applications of field theory to the literary field and to the field of art often involve something like residual media, we find a way into understanding how relative autonomy for producers can be established when what may have been a field of large-scale production becomes something quite different. New possibilities for autonomy—and new arenas of field-like behavior in media contexts—become available when media undergo certain historical shifts. The motion picture industry, threatened by the ubiquity of the newer medium of television, tacked toward creative autonomy in the 1970s, and continued developments in media technology have continued to allow an autonomous ('independent') cinema to sustain itself. Facing increasing competition from the internet, radio finds itself casting about for models of production, occasionally allowing more producer autonomy. Facing smaller and more targeted audiences, television production seems to have begun to internalize a more autonomous aesthetic.

It would be easy to go too far with this. I am not implying that there is a rule whereby all media have a 'late' or 'residual' phase that makes them embrace autonomy. I do think it is worth putting McLuhan's basic insight onto ground level and observing that the field of large-scale production is not all that we should be studying, and that there are a surprising number of contexts where field theory is quite directly applicable to what we study. In his edited volume *Residual Media*, Charles Acland applies to the situation of outmoded media Bourdieu's idea from *Distinction* that "nothing is more distinctive, more distinguished, than the capacity to confer aesthetic status on objects that are banal or even 'common'."[102] In this sense, 'residual' media lend themselves quite well to the concerns of field theory.

If we accept this idea that older media become art because they often lend themselves to field-like operations, what is it about older, outmoded media that makes this possible? Here, I think it would be wise to focus on structural and material concerns, which would be more consistent with a Bourdieusian approach, and would also act as a tonic for the more mythologizing tendencies of McLuhan. First, residual media often lend themselves to field-like operation because they frequently have relatively low barriers to entry. For instance, photocopying a zine, burning one's own music cds, posting music online, or setting up a podcast are all activities that can be potentially pursued by large numbers of people. These activities do not require the involvement of the massive amounts of capital available only to large media corporations. Second, residual media tend not to be so much the focus of political or industry regulation as the dominant media. Often taken as irrelevant to the political field, residual media can benefit from lurking underground, so to speak. A good example of this can be found in the alternative comic books sold at head shops in the late 1960s. These comics no doubt violated the spirit and the letter of the Comic Book Code (then fully in effect), but their distribution system bypassed this entirely, making the alternative comics in a sense too small to provoke much bother from the authorities. Third, residual media carry with them a certain exclusivity. Their departure from (even rejection of) ubiquity gives them a power to confer something about their producers and appreciators. They have caché in a way that is difficult to find in the field of large-scale production. Taken together, these factors predispose specific media for the field of restricted production that is described at such length by Bourdieu.

With older, residual, outmoded media on the one hand, and newer media on the other, both of them considered in terms of their fit with Bourdieu's field theory, we can adjust our perception of media studies in order to better appreciate the relevance of field theory to media. We may wish for Bourdieu to have done a better job of developing a system of thought that could more easily be applied to large-scale production, but there is also much that field theory, as proposed, can do for our understanding. From this point of view, it seems that treating large-scale production as the sine qua non of media studies ends up narrowing our focus too much.

Capital: Production and Prestige

The relevance of capital to media production may seem obvious at first, especially to media scholars in the U.S., where the fact that media production is a big business is hardly news. As we have seen, Bourdieu's use of the term 'capital' was intended to broaden the idea of capital beyond the economic consideration of capital as monetary value in an economy. That said, he does discuss economic capital, which he considers to be "at the root of all the other types of capital." He asserts that other types of capital are "transformed, disguised forms of economic capital" that "produce their most specific effects only to the extent that they conceal (not least from their possessors) the fact that economic capital is at their root."[103] Any discussion of the relevance of Bourdieu's notion of capital to media production must take note of this basic issue. Before other types of capital can be discussed, this must be established.

It would add little to this discussion to review the full panoply of academic labor that has considered the importance of economic capital to the world of media production. The application is obvious, and Bourdieu's ideas do little to refine the strict consideration of economic capital as the capital that "is immediately and directly convertible into money and may be institutionalized in the form of property rights."[104] Bourdieu helps us more by giving us the sweeping idea of cultural capital, and the transformation of economic capital into cultural capital.

I will take the second of these two issues first. The transformation of economic capital into cultural capital, according to Bourdieu, is 'laborious.' If it were not so laborious, fields would not work in the way that Bourdieu claimed they do. First, the relative autonomy of fields (of painting, of literature, of science) would be eroded, as economic capital would simply install itself as the one true king. Alongside this, there would be little room for the misrecognition and symbolic violence that Bourdieu so frequently described. Those who lack cultural capital would not accept the legitimacy of a class whose only claim to power derives from the possession of economic capital. Cultural capital—and the symbolic violence that comes from its deployment—depends on there being a kind of buffer between it and economic capital.

By asserting that the workings of relatively autonomous fields and cultural capital can be applied to the field of mass production, I am calling attention to the convenient lack of attention in Bourdieu's model to how logics of cultural capital play out in non-autonomous fields of production. Bourdieu gives us strong reason not to think that cultural capital matters much in the field of mass production. I think otherwise. Hesmondhalgh notes that "Bourdieu misses the importance of the rise of the cultural industries for understanding the changing social relations of cultural producers."[105] In particular, Bourdieu failed to account for the "ability of large-scale production to disseminate consecrated culture—assuming that we expand the term 'consecrated' to include new institutions of consecration, such as industry awards, the responses of other producers…, and the views of television critics of 'quality' newspapers."[106] Here I think Hesmondhalgh has it just right.

One of the things that falls into this expansive category of what Bourdieu misses is the persistent concern for legitimacy—for cultural capital—in the field of mass production of media. To find such concerns in the world of mass produced media goods is not difficult. Not long after motion pictures were developed as popular entertainment, Hollywood producers began to establish the legitimacy of the medium, usually through deployment of cultural capital. A classic technique involved using screenplays derived from works of legitimate culture, such as adaptations of Shakespeare plays, and established literature.

The production of television programming could be thought of simply in terms of large audiences sold for much money to the consumer goods industry, but we find in recent decades a focus on legitimacy that stems quite obviously from the strategy of targeting relatively well-to-do audiences.[107] The development of premium cable networks in the U.S. (such as HBO and Showtime) has spawned a renewed concern for lending to television production a legitimacy that had once been thought unreachable. Recent critical successes like the AMC Network's *Breaking Bad* or HBO's *The Wire* should provoke us to consider the degree to which the rules of cultural capital can be applied to cultural production that Bourdieu largely neglected. These recent examples of 'legitimacy' television are linked to (at least mythic) senses of charismatic writer-producers (David Simon, Vince Gilligan) whose freedom to create what they envision is a frequent refrain in journalistic coverage of their shows. This concern for legitimacy in television seems to have been accelerated at least in part by the reduction of audience size for shows, itself a tendency growing alongside the fragmentation of audiences so familiar to recent media history. At the same time, the concern for legitimacy also represents an important index of cultural distinction.

Consecration—the bestowing of legitimacy to a cultural object or to people associated with a cultural object—is the central issue here. Bourdieu described "three competing principles of legitimacy" in culture.[108] He identifies each as follows:

> First, there is the specific principle of legitimacy, i.e., the recognition granted by the set of producers who produce for other producers, their competitors, i.e. by the autonomous 'art for art's sake', meaning art for artists.[109]

Bourdieu presumed here that producers who produce for other producers were entirely separate from the 'popular,' though there may be reason (with digital and independent media, as above) to challenge this assumption, and extend this beyond the realm of art.

The second principle of legitimacy

> [corresponds] to 'bourgeois' taste and to the consecration bestowed by the dominant fractions of the dominant class and by private tribunals, such as salons, or public, state-guaranteed ones, such as academies, which sanction the inseparably ethical and aesthetic (and therefore political) taste of the dominant.[110]

Here we have something of straightforward relevance to the emergence of the kind of enhanced legitimacy that we have seen in recent middle-brow television programming. This programming is created in a manner that differs from classic mass produced entertainment (where Bourdieu would say that capital alone holds sway), and its consecration, as Bourdieu notes, is underwritten by innumerable testimonies from critics (themselves supported by bourgeois media outlets) and academics. With the rise of the target audiences—many of them elite bourgeois audiences—as a component in the mass communication process, I argue that we have seen a marked growth in this kind of legitimacy.

The last principle of legitimacy, "which its advocates call 'popular'" involves "the consecration bestowed by the choice of ordinary consumers, the 'mass audience.'"[111] This may not be the most meaningful sense of legitimacy, but it can be noticed in the distinction that is made between commonly recognized pop culture figures and those whose success is less widespread. It is the kind of legitimacy that obtains in U.S. television programs like *American Idol* and motion pictures like *Spider Man*. Bourdieu saw this legitimacy as mattering because, for the mass audience as he understood it, this kind of legitimacy was what was required for this culture to seem proper and fitting. Anything else would strike many in the mass audience as 'weird' or 'pretentious,' or 'not for me.'

The fuller extension of these ideas demands that we pay attention to these systems of consecration. Regarding the field of restricted production, Bourdieu instructed us that the full understanding of consecration depends on an analysis of

> institutions which conserve the capital of symbolic goods, such as museums; and, on the other hand, of institutions (such as the educational system) which ensure the reproduction of agents imbued with the categories of action, expression, conception, imagination, perception, specific to the 'cultivated disposition.'[112]

Much as it does with products of restricted production, where theoretically widely available consecrated works are still enjoyed almost entirely by specific sectors of society, in the context of media production, this understanding of consecration calls attention to the processes whereby audience members are, in a sense, 'made' for the works that are marketed to them. One extension of Bourdieu that is particularly worth pointing out is the fact that the media producers themselves seem to have the power to create the categories of perception required for certain kinds of reception of their products. I will return to that issue in the next chapter.

Given that autonomous 'art for art's sake' seems rarely to be the province of the media producers, there does still seem to be much in the way of consecration that applies quite directly to the mass media. Do producers in the field of mass media produce for other producers? An easy point to be made here would be that journalists often write their stories largely for other journalists (in their own organizations and beyond), as numerous journalism scholars have pointed out.[113] A similar pattern, perhaps indicative of a level of autonomy in popular music, seems to have evolved in a wide range of music production, as relatively subaltern musicians create music to a great extent in response to their peers. The consecration at work in these production contexts is certainly not what Bourdieu originally envisioned, so even this first form of legitimacy that Bourdieu describes may be surprisingly applicable to media production.

More obvious examples of the field of mass production being a site of consecration can be found in something like the 'private tribunals' that Bourdieu mentions. Here it seems apposite to consider the more recent workings of awards for entertainment excellence. Obviously, these are not fully disinterested tribunals. However, it is very clear here that awards for entertainment excellence (such as the Academy, Emmy, Grammy, and other awards) do represent an attempt to consecrate some culture in a manner that endows it with at least a sense of being set aside from popular entertainment. Film critic Jonathan Rosenbaum has argued that the creation of lists of 'great' movies (as with the creation of the American Film Institute's list of the top 100 movies) is really "about the increasing lack of any viable distinction between corporate greed and what used to be called public works."[114] Rosenbaum is concerned that the film industry's version of consecration represents an all-too-interested promotional effort more than a disinterested consideration of the movies. The broader point to be taken from award shows is that consecration does exist in the field of mass production, and that award shows are only the tip of the iceberg. Bourdieu's relative neglect of the field of mass production would leave us to think that anything operating outside of an autonomous field of production may lack for legitimation rituals. Not so. As he himself makes clear in his tripartite vision of legitimacy, art for art's sake is but one of three types of legitimation at work in culture. Certainly the concern for legitimacy in bourgeois and popular art are major concerns for those who study media production. As Hesmondhalgh puts it, there are certainly arenas in media production "where prestige and popularity are not necessarily so much in contradiction as in Bourdieu's schema."[115]

A separate point to be made regarding consecration concerns the possibility of the fragmentation of consecration processes that may attend the fragmentation of audiences. The idea of the fragmentation of mass communication audiences is certainly not new. The classic expression of the idea of audience fragmentation in a new media environment comes from W. Russell Neuman, who in 1991 entertained the idea that the "ultimate result of electronic integration into a single integrated system, paradoxically, will be intellectual pluralism and personalized control over communications."[116] If we assume that this fragmentation is happening, we can begin to appreciate cultural capital as a somewhat less centralized set of practices than Bourdieu had it. In the context of media production, a segmentation logic has accelerated, as many producers find ways to aim precisely at demographically precise audiences, defined according to the terms advertisers find most useful for their own needs.[117] Elihu Katz has lamented the loss of television's position as a "shared public space," as it becomes "a medium of segmentation."[118] Certainly television is not the only medium engaged in this logic of segmentation.

The segmentation logic of contemporary media points to the possibility that the forms of cultural capital at work in the media may be multiplying and becoming decentralized. To apply Bourdieu's ideas about consecration to cultural capital, it would seem that all three types of consecration may be fragmenting. Certainly this seems likely to be the case with the consecration at work in the 'popular.' With new, fragmented definitions of popularity, the legitimacy associated with popularity has probably shifted. Katy Perry and *American Idol* in the U.S. simply do not have the broad audiences of the most popular programming from, say, the mid-20th century. And there is much left to be said about what this means in terms of popular cultural legitimacy.

The most middle-brow version of legitimacy—the one that is associated with 'bourgeois' taste—has certainly fragmented in many media markets, leading perhaps to a proliferation of types of cultural capital amongst different demographic segments of the bourgeoisie (at least). If we understand the workings of capital to be a kind of centripetal force, similar in their way to the workings of the high modern mass media themselves, we can try to chart the degree to which cultural capital retains some power to coordinate societies or groups within societies. Bourdieu's take on cultural capital as it relates to dominance within a field could be extended to attempt to measure both the degree to which segmentation logic has adjusted the workings of cultural capital (if at all), as well as the dynamics of cultural capital within and between different cultural segments. The proliferation of market segments may portend the proliferation of types of cultural capital. It bears pointing out that this is not necessarily a bad thing.

A final issue worth considering in the relationship between capital and media production is suggested by Rodney Benson, in his observation that one of the most important issues for field theory is that of "which form of capital—economic, bureaucratic, etc.—exerts the *dominant* outside power within the field."[119] To put this in the context of US media seems like a classic no-brainer. Economic capital seems to be firmly in charge. As Benson points out, "[h]aving had a commercially-dominated radio-television system almost from the beginning in the United States, questions of the effects of commercialization have seemed rather beside the point, if not quite difficult to study."[120] But before this issue can be dismissed as irrelevant, it is worth considering how these kinds of interfield determinations at work in capital still play important roles in shaping culture. As an example to illustrate his point, Benson points to how the "rise of journalists and media intellectuals in France provides another case study to illuminate what is lost when journalists largely displace intellectuals in public debate."[121] Benson's example demonstrates two things that are relevant here: first, the potential for change to occur in media fields, and how this change relates to capital; second, the potential for Bourdieu's notion of capital to highlight international comparisons in media systems. Interfield relationships—and their variance across international media systems—certainly have much to do with the manifold processes of capital at work in media production.

Conclusion

What Bourdieu's combination of habitus, field, and capital has the potential to do for the study of media production is to provide a way to understand media production that: lends itself to empirical study, captures conflicting interests in the production process, steps aside of purely objective and subjective approaches, can be adapted to the specific forms of differentiation germane to the field under consideration, and incorporates a thorough concern for power and agency. Less consensus-oriented than much sociology of media production, more flexible in its understanding of power, Bourdieu's tools for understanding cultural production have much to recommend them.

The approach outlined here links up nicely with a new understanding of how change occurs in the media. Rodney Benson argues that field theory contributes something important to the study of the media because it "emphasizes the issue of media change."[122] Though Bourdieu is concerned about reproduction, the overall theoretical mechanism he outlines (in part because it remains vague on particulars) suggests much more about how change can occur in the media than hegemony studies (or organizational theories, or technological theories) do. Benson notes that "[i]n field theory, changes in the structure of fields are produced from two basic sources."[123] The emphasis Bourdieu put on distinctions made between positions in the field means that there is a "constant production of change as new actors attempt to enter and make their mark in the field,"[124] each bringing strategies internalized from their position and vector in the field. Additionally, "changes in closely related fields such as the university or politics, set in motion by their own internal dynamics, can have important cross-over effects on the journalistic field"[125] and, I suggest, on other media fields. Though his work is often criticized for being determinist, Bourdieu's ideas offer themselves as perhaps surprisingly open to the idea of change. The emphasis is often placed on reproduction, but unlike many Marxist/hegemonic approaches, the Bourdieusian approach develops a socially grounded understanding of how change does occur and has occurred.

The changes at work in fields often develop from interfield relations, from 'external' forces. Though Bourdieu shows us how shifts in fields can develop from intrafield relationships, he rather clearly indicates that it is the relationships between fields that tends to create major changes. In *The Rules of Art*, he points out that, "however great the autonomy of the field, the chances of success of strategies of conservation and subversion always depend in part on the reinforcement that one or another camp can find in external forces (for example, in new clienteles)."[126] At all times, it is forces external to these fields that shapes them, and can even threaten to adjust them beyond recognition. In even more pointed language regarding changes to fields, Bourdieu asserts that the "most decisive of…changes" in fields "are the political ruptures, such as revolutionary crises, which change the power relations at the heart of the field,…or the appearance of new categories of consumers who, having an affinity with the new producers, guarantee the success of their products."[127] These 'external shocks' occur not infrequently in media production, be they changes in trade agreements, media regulations, ownership structures, or more.

What Bourdieu offers to the study of media production is a kind of in-between-ness. The habitus/field/capital model's strengths and weaknesses are mostly connected to this, the 'mezzo' level that Benson describes at work in Bourdieu's ideas. When held alongside, say, hegemonic theory, Bourdieu's ideas seem rather lacking in content, like a map for conflicts that could play out anywhere. For this reason, the promise of Bourdieu's model has taken some time to hold the attention of media scholars. It is difficult to summarize, flexible enough to seem ambiguous, and does not align very well with most well-established methods of studying communication. Its relevance to communication is getting put to the test much more in recent years. Certainly the study of media production stands to gain from the in-between-ness, and there does seem to be the promise that Bourdieu's ideas are more relevant to media production than even he ever realized.

CHAPTER THREE

The Media Audience: Fluency, Strategy, and *Le Sens Practique*

If Bourdieu's ideas are to invigorate the study of media and communication, it would be important to apply his ideas to the situation of the audience. In this chapter, I put forward some potential points of contact between Bourdieu's scholarship and audience research. Though Bourdieu's ideas are no cure-all for whatever ailments one might find in audience research, they do help us to think anew about the familiar questions of domination, determination, structure, and agency as they relate to the situation of the audience. Bourdieu's understanding of the audience takes some effort to identify. Certainly his approach to the audience differs markedly from the kinds of understandings we associate with media effects approaches to the audience. It is safe to say that, like many audience researchers in the field, Bourdieu's rejection of purely objective accounts of social processes—accounts that do not take heed of an agent's own perceptions—puts him very much against much of the media effects perspective on the audience.[1]

This antipathy toward media effects assumptions, however, does not necessarily translate into a celebratory vision of audience behavior. Bourdieu's work is a poor fit for the kind of upbeat scholarship of popular culture audiences that James Curran has described as "reheated…old pluralist dishes."[2] Bourdieu himself averred that studies of popular culture suffered from an over-weaning desire to align the scholar with the audience, with the people. The assumption that research that presumes to take the point of view of 'the people' actually defends their interests cannot hold; it represents what Christian Vermehren calls "a false identification with lower social strata which derives not from social proximity, but from similarity of position in homologous and relatively separate power structures."[3] To focus almost entirely on the process of interpretation of media messages, or on texts themselves, would not live up to what Bourdieu hoped the social sciences could provide. Nick Couldry describes how "Bourdieu rejected a method of 'reading' the social world as if it were ready for interpretation and replaced it with an investigation into the preconditions of action."[4] This has perhaps come off as overly sociological to audience researchers hoping to focus on transgression, play, and agency.

In sum, Bourdieu does not fit comfortably into the categories of communication research, which is at least arguably one of the reasons he has been neglected (or misinterpreted) by those in the field of communication.[5] Yet there is good reason to believe that much more could be done to apply Bourdieu's ideas to the study of the audience. In pursuit of his thesis that there is substantial distance between Bourdieu's positions and that of the Frankfurt school, Erik Neveu demonstrates that Bourdieu was in fact very much interested in the role played by media audiences, and in the range of audience responses. Certainly Bourdieu took an active interest in some of the ideas and writings that inspired the formations of cultural studies in the UK. He helped to get Hoggart's seminal *Uses of Literacy* published in France, and "used his journal *Actes* to translate texts by E.P. Thompson, Raymond Williams, and Paul Willis."[6] Far from being a scholar who "gives intellectuals a monopoly over reflexivity and the ability to resist the media,"[7] Bourdieu dedicated tremendous effort over many decades to examining the wide range of audience response. In fact, it could be argued that one difference between Bourdieu and the cultural studies camp was that Bourdieu was even more interested in audience response than were many in cultural studies, opposing as he did actual empirical studies of cultural consumers to the "semiological orientation"[8] of much cultural studies work, which was tied up with the study of texts. Bourdieu regarded meaning as relational at all times, and repeatedly pursued research projects that focused on systematic descriptions of varied audience responses. Neveu concludes that Bourdieu's relevance to a sociology of media involves what he calls "a three-dimensional approach,"[9] wherein a focus on the "space of production—a field—a structured system of institutions, organizations, and social roles"[10] can be combined with a focus on "the materiality of images, in their grammar,"[11] and finally with an examination of "reception, of the social uses of various cultural goods."[12] Neveu emphasizes Bourdieu's concern for reception, and highlights three of Bourdieu's books (*Photography: A Middle-Brow Art*, *The Love of Art: European Art Museums and their Public*, and *Distinction: A Social Critique of the Judgement of Taste*) as exemplars of his attention to audience processes.

Carefully applied, Bourdieu's ideas promise to get the field of communication past some of its more stubborn structure-agency disputes. Taking a couple of steps back from his oeuvre, the hopeful observer can find much in Bourdieu's ideas that makes a good fit for audience research. His best-known book in the U.S., *Distinction*, could be thought of as audience research, with its use of a survey method to develop an understanding of the strategies at work in the consumption of culture. More broadly, the oft-invoked idea of habitus could propel all kinds of consideration of the experiences of the audience. Indeed, there is great potential for the idea of habitus to inform audience studies regarding the meaning of embodiment as it relates to reception, which is often in danger of being conceptualized in idealist/textual terms. The notion of 'strategy' also has much to offer the audience researcher interested in patterns of interpretation, given how Bourdieu used the concept as the emergent practice that comes out of the intersection of field and capital. Additionally, Bourdieu's background in anthropological approaches to social practice lends itself to a study of the ritual dimension of reception. This anthropological approach may be closer to the American cultural studies approach than might easily be expected from a scholar who insisted that his work was (in some ways) so characteristically French. However, the American cultural studies tradition in communication shares with Bourdieu's outlook a fractured ritual perspective on how meaning relates to society, and this element of a shared tradition could be meaningful to communication scholars interested in developing an approach to culture that goes beyond what we normally associate with cultural studies. The fact that Bourdieu's ideas are not more frequently included in audience studies research tells us more about the field of communication's insularity than it does about Bourdieu's relevance to consideration of the media audience.

Tacit Knowledge and the Audience

To apply Bourdieu's model of practice to audience processes should involve a careful understanding of his emphasis on how practice could not simply be boiled down into 'discourse' or 'ideology.' This was one of his most stubbornly held positions, one that connects the more anthropological Bourdieu of the 1970s with the more polemical Bourdieu of the 1990s. His point is that, even though language practices are a kind of practice, this does not mean that all (or even much) practice can be laid out in linguistic or representational terms.

Bourdieu calls our attention to the importance of practice, and with it, to the non-textual. As Aaron V. Cicourel tells us, what Bourdieu thought was needed was "to understand practices from within the activity of their accomplishment and their dialectic relationship to the access afforded by the objective structures."[13] Here I would like to emphasize this idea of looking at practices 'from within.' This approach promises to allow us to understand practice as something more than just an outcome, which is obviously what media effects theories do with practice. Less obviously, cultural studies and constructivist approaches threaten to do the same thing, to think of things that we do simply as the results of the meanings to which we subscribe. To try to understand practice 'from within' could be a way out of this, to go immediately to the thing that interests us—what do people do with the media?—and to appreciate how practice itself can shape understanding and take on social meaning.

Of course social structure matters here, too. Cicourel refers to the dialectic at work between practices and the 'access afforded by the objective structures,' meaning that not all practices are equally available to all people. This is what puts these practices in context, and puts power into the equation. Simply working from this barebones gloss of Bourdieu, there is an emphasis on practice that stands in direct contrast with many cultural studies approaches and everything related to media effects theories.

A keynote in Bourdieu's social theory is the avoidance of what he called an intellectualist approach, which treats communication "as a *logos* as opposed to *praxis*."[14] Bourdieu approvingly cites Marx's insistence that we not mistake "the things of logic for the logic of things."[15] Jacques Bouveresse helpfully reminds us that Wittgenstein would refer to this same error as "taking as a predicate something that is merely a mode of representation."[16] Bourdieu's habitus demands that scholars consider more than just texts and representations, that the practical knowledge at work in social life is really where the action is. For audience studies in communication, it could be argued that the same concern about treating messages purely as messages has already been installed as a justifiable (if difficult to live up to) norm for how to regard audience activity. After all, audience research since at least the 1980s has been defined largely in opposition to a media effects tradition that often showed almost no interest in audience activity, as well as an opposition to a textually oriented approach that focused largely on messages themselves (texts), often with the assumption that the categories worked out by scholars could be logically deduced to be at work in audiences. One of the stirring insights repeatedly offered in audience research has been the insistence that meaning is not just found on paper, but is actually practiced, done, lived. In this sense, there is substantial overlap between Bourdieu's approach and many of the current tendencies in audience research.

This still leaves much to be established in terms of how precisely we are to engage with these ideas. Bourdieu insisted that researchers "have to include" in their theories "the real principle behind strategies, namely the practical sense, or, if you prefer what sports players call a feel for the game."[17] This *sens practique* becomes tacit but no less powerful upon the achievement of mastery. It is a mastery that is "acquired by experience of the game, and one which works outside conscious control and discourse," much as "techniques of the body do."[18] This sense of mastery links up with Bourdieu's sense of doxa, which he defined as "the pre-verbal taking-for-granted of the world that flows from practical sense."[19] The muscle memory of the tennis player is, in this way, much the same as the conceptual knowledge of the chemist. It is worth noting the parallels between Bourdieu's method and the radical empiricism of William James and other pragmatists.[20] For our purposes here, however, the key is that without *le sens practique* as a backdrop, without a sense of the factors that make communication possible, without an emic sense of the precise nature of the situation, we will have relatively little to say about what audiences do, what their practices are.

In the previous chapter, I asserted that a Bourdieusian approach to media production leads away from the flat structuralism of concern for ownership and toward an appreciation of the generative habits of media workers. In much the same way, a Bourdieusian approach to media audiences leads away from the intellectualism that favors ideologies or texts as starting points, and leads toward an appreciation for what audiences do. This represents a move that is quite consistent with many trends in audience studies. Janice Radway's *Reading the Romance*, to choose an obvious example, is a major work of audience studies that concerned itself with much the same move away from the text that Bourdieu espoused.[21]

A way to sum this up would be to consider 'loaded language' and 'loaded questions.' We are accustomed to the idea that language can be assembled to shape someone's frame of mind, and furthermore, we understand that this loaded-ness does not require any intentional manipulation. The idea of social constructions of reality gets us this far. Bourdieu's vision of practice invites us to consider practices as every bit as loaded as language. More to the point, he invited us to think of language as a kind of practice. Every practice in which we engage invites us into a particular worldview, a worldview that has social—not natural—origins. To apply this to the situation of the audience involves asking how different audience practices are loaded, if you will. When we do things with the media, we do so because of how the field of media options is made available to us, and we engage our existing understandings (coded bodily as habitus) to do what 'comes naturally.'

It is difficult to think of anything more natural-seeming than media audience practices. A focus on the habitual tendencies of media audience practices can highlight some of what Bourdieu's ideas can do for this area of study. In a consideration of Bourdieu's idea of rule-like behavior, Charles Taylor argues that our sense of what we are as rule-following beings often overstates the level of explicit thought, choice, and elaboration that goes on when we act on the world, or when we follow rules. Taylor emphasizes that "much of our intelligent action in the world, sensitive as it usually is to our situation and goals, is carried on unformulated…[flowing] from an understanding which is largely inarticulate."[22] Taylor calls representations mere "islands in the sea of our unformulated practical grasp on the world."[23]

And indeed, there is great reason to think of much audience behavior as relying less on explicit goals than on unformulated practical tendencies, or habits. The study of the media audience can get past the intellectualism of much research in part by theorizing the audience in a manner that places less emphasis on meaning construction (or resistance, or negotiation), and more on habit. Bourdieu's focus on the homologies between producers and audience members leaves interpretation almost completely unproblematic. The linkage between the moment of production and the moment of reception is so pre-programmed—so pre-loaded—as to be rather less pliable to an individual's agency as many audience researchers have described it as being. The place of media habits may offer one way to access this vision of the media producer and the media audience acting in some kind of twinned coordination. The concept of media habits has had a recent resurgence among media researchers. Robert LaRose addresses media habits as "a form of automaticity in media consumption that develops as people repeat media consumption behavior in stable circumstances." Such habits occasionally get forgotten and rediscovered.[24] LaRose uses some obvious examples of habitual media consumption to orient his remarks, but his stronger case is that "[b]y overlooking the habit construct, or at best submerging it deeply, prevailing theories of media consumption behavior implicitly favor active selection processes to the exclusion of automatic and nonconscious ones," an insight quite consistent with Bourdieu's emphasis on the practical, and his insistence on avoiding the intellectualism that comes with a focus on explicit choices and strategies. On a cognitive level, these habits can be thought of as being "nonconscious and automatic responses to stimuli, acting alone or together with conscious intentions framed by expected outcomes to determine behavior."[25] Though LaRose's emphasis is on individual audience members, there is no reason to leave these insights tethered to this individualism. Considered in terms of the social origins of practice that Bourdieu outlined, we can start by reminding ourselves that media habits do not come out of nowhere. The job before us is to uncover the system of oppositions loaded into these habits. A Bourdieusian approach would demand an understanding of habits that takes into consideration the distribution of different kinds of habits in different parts of the social topology.

Communication Competence: Beauty Is a Rarefied Thing

One habitual component of media audience processes is the exercise of symbolic competence. Bourdieu dedicates much attention to the competence that is required for receiving messages and consuming culture. Bourdieu's *Distinction* is a sustained argument that seemingly transparent or 'natural' processes of reception such as the enjoyment of art and other symbolic work is anything but natural. This emphasis on the tacit and necessary component of the development of communication competence allows us to reconsider the meanings of such familiar terms as audience activity and decoding.

That audiences require competence is not a new idea for communication theory, though it often takes a backstage position. Larry Gross positions competence as a central issue in the study of communication. Building from the idea that "[c]ompetence in a symbolic mode involves the ability to perceive and/or manipulate symbols,"[26] Gross argues that "some minimum level of competence is the basic precondition for the creation or comprehension of symbolic meaning within" any such mode.[27] Within this, it is to be understood that there is a "tacitness"[28] at work in this skill; for the most part, the audience member receives messages and interprets them using frameworks that are not applied explicitly. In other words, receiving messages is a developed skill, but it is often misrecognized as being a formal operation. As Gross has it, "much if not most of the physical, perceptual, and cognitive elements of skillful performance are not amenable to being coded and comprehended verbally."[29] Like all practical performances, receiving messages is something more complicated, non-verbal, and multidimensional than a term like 'reading' (oft-used to describe what audiences do) leads us to believe.

Gross's emphasis on competence is important because it calls attention to how messages are produced—in almost all contexts, from interpersonal to mass communication—in anticipation of specific audience skills. By telling us that the "ability to intentionally structure meaning is dependent upon the ability to perceive and comprehend it,"[30] he calls attention to the distribution not of hegemonic forces per se, but to the distribution of skills for understanding. If "the existence of a subculture of competent appreciators is required for the occurrence of highly creative innovation,"[31] we should consider the power of the media to reinforce existing communities of appreciation, or perhaps, their power to inculcate new regimes of appreciation. The emphasis on audience competence places front-and-center what many studies of ideology and many explorations of content tend to set aside: the question of 'getting it,' of intelligibility.

Intelligibility seems initially to be rather weak tea for anyone hoping to understand power or domination as they relate to the media. The path to interesting analyses of audience processes does seem indirect, at best, but Bourdieu argued that "to speak of 'ideologies' is to locate in the realm of *representations*...what in fact belongs to the order of *belief*, that is, to the level of the most profound corporeal dispositions."[32] These 'corporeal dispositions' are where the Bourdieusian action happens, where patterns are established that set the stage for all kinds of behaviors. The habitus of the audience member should be considered in terms of these kinds of corporeal dispositions, and certainly competence in a symbolic code can be thought of as one of the most important corporeal dispositions at work.

Competence is socially produced, and distributed in non-random ways. Bourdieu emphasized in the outset of *Distinction* how "consumers of cultural goods, and their taste for them, are produced,"[33] indicating his concern for how receiving/consuming cultural goods as an audience member is something quite different from the relatively autonomous process associated with audience activity in much communication scholarship. As Bourdieu explained, a "work of art has meaning and interest only for someone who possesses the cultural competence, that is, the code, into which it is encoded."[34] More directly, he asserted that "[o]bjects are not rare, but the propensity to consume them is."[35] Leaving aside for the moment Bourdieu's analysis of the meaning of the unequal distribution of symbolic competences, it is important to note his concern for how audience members are produced, and how this production involves instilling code-relevant competence in individuals. For Bourdieu, the process of receiving a message is rather less 'free' than it often appears in much audience research in communication. Reception is always embedded in social structure, and thus bound to reproduce social structure. This explains much of Bourdieu's relatively downbeat sense of audience activity. Whatever dream of flying may be conjured up by others addressing ostensibly transgressive audience practices, Bourdieu insisted that our practices are always linked to social origins.

This is when Bourdieu's idea of cultural capital takes the stage. John B. Thompson defines cultural capital as "knowledge, skills and other cultural acquisitions, as exemplified by educational or technical qualifications,"[36] and it is safe to consider symbolic competence as cultural capital at its most communication-relevant.[37] One arena that seems quite ripe for Bourdieusian critique and research is that of media literacy. His focus on code mastery leads him to question how it is that individuals come to think of much mediated culture as 'not for them,' similar to those who do not feel qualified to have an opinion in a public opinion survey.[38] Like media literacy advocates, Bourdieu addressed how culture acts as a code. Unlike media literacy advocates, Bourdieu was careful to note that efforts to distribute art appreciation, for example, can unconsciously mask deeper stratifying effects, as when he describes "[t]he school" as "the institution which...transforms socially conditioned inequalities in matters of culture into inequalities of success."[39] Even those who espouse "critical media literacy"[40] tend not to account for the full sweep of Bourdieu's arguments regarding the differentiating impact of education. Media literacy, in Bourdieu's hands, would remain an important issue, albeit one lacking an easy-to-find ameliorative program of education.

Some of Bourdieu's critics doubt that taste in things can be mapped as thoroughly as Bourdieu would have us believe. Richard Peterson and Roger Kern use U.S. survey data to support their argument that "ominvorousness"—the consumption of a wide variety of cultural materials—"is replacing snobbishness among Americans of highbrow status."[41] Tony Bennett and his coauthors complicate this picture somewhat. Building on survey and other data from Britain, Bennett et al. find some omnivorousness in music taste, but also find that "there are key boundaries that are much more rarely crossed."[42] In *Culture, Class, Distinction*, Bennett et al. give us a rather fine-grained understanding of the different boundaries in different taste cultures operate. Their analysis extends Bourdieu's work in *Distinction* in ways that point the way to applications of Bourdieu to different media. They posit that reading (of print), for instance, operates on a different level from some other fluencies, perhaps operating as "a crucial avenue, or intermediation, for the accumulation of cultural capital" of many kinds.[43] In their consideration of cultural capital at work in television viewing, Bennett et al. find that television viewing differs not only in terms of the content that is preferred, but also in terms of the relationship audience members assume toward that content. They describe how the "pedagogic value of television contrasts with the values of escapism or entertainment," and how these values operate in the system of television viewing habits.[44] These kinds of insights provide a model for extending Bourdieu into mediated culture, and for appreciating how fluency in codes can operate simultaneously on numerous levels, including: the cultural code, the mode of expression, and the medium of communication.

Beyond media literacy per se, the Bourdieusian emphasis on symbolic competence guides our attention to numerous issues related to practice. In particular, it pushes us to consider the kinds of symbolic competence that are required in order to understand media content. This in turn provokes questions about the distribution of a specific competence within a specific context, and the 'capital' aspect of symbolic competence shines through if we pivot to ask about the 'feel for the game' that Bourdieu addressed. Here is where the most probing questions begin. For it is here that we can ask, of symbolic competence of a specific kind: what sense of the world is provided through this competence? What vision of the social topology emerges from this practice of symbolic competence? How do audience members' exercises of symbolic competence lead them—via habitual, practical affairs—to create cognized maps of the social world around them? If practice is 'loaded' as I assert above, how are audience practices loaded?

The Circuit of Culture

Bourdieu's emphasis on symbolic competence came with a sense of how media producers and audiences are synchronized. The process he outlined has many similarities with the model of communication associated with British cultural studies. This gives us an enriched sense of how the production and reception of media messages are linked to each other.

In particular, Bourdieu's ideas line up with those of Stuart Hall, who opened up the idea of media audience reception as "decoding," thus charting a course for media research that was not centrally concerned with media effects. As with Bourdieu's emphasis on the 'codedness' of messages, Hall asserts that "[b]efore [a] message can have an 'effect' (however defined), satisfy a 'need' or be put to a 'use,' it must first be appropriated as a meaningful discourse and be meaningfully decoded."[45] Taking issue with those who act as if "the referent of a televisual discourse were an objective fact but the interpretive level were an individualized and private matter," Hall says that "the opposite seems to be the case."[46] To clear this up, he explained that the

> televisual practice takes 'objective' (that is, systemic) responsibility precisely for the relations which disparate signs contract with one another in any discursive instance, and thus continually rearranges, delimits and prescribes into what 'awareness of one's total environment' these items are arranged.[47]

With this in place, Hall moves on to offer his famous discussion of the "dominant-hegemonic," "negotiated," and "oppositional" codes through which televisual messages can be construed.[48] Like Hall, Bourdieu focused on the symbolic competences of the audiences at work and considered the common cultural ground that was involved at moments of encoding and decoding. Unlike Hall, Bourdieu's concern for homologies and fields paints a somewhat less open arena for interpretation and agency.

But where do these symbolic competences come from? How do we come to internalize certain codes/practices? Asking these kinds of questions will get us beyond some of the familiar dilemmas that have faced the study of audiences for some time. Rodney Benson argues that the model of practice that Bourdieu and his colleagues provided is one that "challenges the dichotomy of 'passive' versus 'active' audiences, insisting on the pre-established harmony of circuits of production and reception."[49] Bourdieu clearly pointed out that production and reception take the forms that they do largely because of producers' proleptic assessment of audience response, and because of audience members' proleptic assessment of what is out there and how to consume and interpret messages. Producers and audience members both develop a 'feel for the game' that is particular to their relative location in social space, though also mutually coordinated. This is quite consistent with the "circuit of culture" model laid out by Paul du Gay and his co-authors in *Doing Cultural Studies*, where they put consumption, production, identity, representation, and regulation together into a model of inter-connected meaning-making.[50]

This argument for the interwoven practices of media production and reception is also suggested by Robert Entman, who, in his discussion of journalism, asserts that it is difficult for the public to demand better journalism if they have not been exposed to better journalism. Mastery of a given code is difficult to find amongst those who have limited exposure to the code. Entman finds a journalism market that is limited by the fact that the consumers do not know how to pursue options that the market itself has never made available to them.[51] Robert W. McChesney says much the same thing when he describes how "[p]eople are exposed to the media fare that the giants can profit from, they develop a taste for it, they consume it, and then the media giants claim they must make more of it to satisfy demand.... To paraphrase Say's Law, supply creates demand."[52] This process is directly concerned with the intelligibility of media content, and how the audience habitus comes to be shaped by the field of options the producers make available. Producers themselves feel simultaneously constrained and enabled by the same process.

Through a consideration of habitus, we could attempt to understand processes of production and reception as reciprocally structuring events (which is not to say that audiences and producers have equal power) whereby audience members come to develop a sense of the possible through repeated exposure to a specific field of options. From these options, individuals develop a sense not only of what is possible, but also of where they fit. This is the sense of the game that Bourdieu described so often, and it is what media programmers attempt to account for in their increasingly detailed research about media markets. On the audience side, supply creates its own demand as audience members themselves internalize the options made available to them. This is emergent practice, self-perpetuating, and probably not as stable as it seems to be, not as inevitable as we often presume.

To connect this back to code fluency, we can learn much about media consumption by considering Bourdieu's statement that, in the context of art museums, "only those who exclude themselves are ever excluded."[53] He elaborates that "[i]f it is indisputable that our society offers to all the *pure possibility* of taking advantage of the works on display in museums, it remains the case that only some have the *real possibility* of doing so."[54] The same is true of media culture more broadly. Though the media are just as much (if not more) open to public enjoyment, audience habits create structures of consumption, thus showing how the field of media choices comes to be shaped in particular ways, resulting in the same kind of unequal (if also quite structured) distribution of audience competences.

So what does this have to do with reception? Bourdieu's emphasis on competence (redolent of the sociology of education) emphasizes the role played by the routinization of cultural praxis. He calls to mind the situation of the outsider at the art museum, noting that "understanding of a conduct or a cultural work is always a case of *mediate decipherment*."[55] Bourdieu invested much in the "interiorization" at work in the mastery of any symbolic code. This interiorization often comes from the family.[56] Audience researchers may want to consider media as both the family and art museum in one: as purveyors of messages and as ubiquitous suppliers of the skills of interiorization that are at work in culture. In the context of avant-garde art, Bourdieu remarked that "the most innovative works tend, *with time*, to produce their own audience by imposing their own structures, through the effect of familiarization, as categories of perception legitimate for any possible work."[57] Though audiences for popular culture are often not adjusting their own expectations all that frequently, there is much work to be done to understand how audiences' categories of perception relate to the media environment in which they live.

Technical Competence, Practice, and New Media

What we often call 'new media' today prompt some questions that provide important parallels to this consideration of symbolic competence, and Bourdieu's model of practice provides an excellent tool with which we can gain a deeper appreciation for new media practices. Of course newness is not new. All currently 'old' media were once new, and the media we now consider as new will in time be taken for granted, as natural, or as given. Communication researchers often approach the spread of new media from the point of view of diffusion of innovations theory, and, with the internet and other new media, we have found no small amount of attention paid to the so-called 'digital divide' between information 'haves' and information 'have nots.'

The classic way to explain the digital divide is to call attention to the degree to which different segments of society have different levels of access to new media. Lisa Nakamura does an excellent job picking apart some of the assumptions common to some discussions of the digital divide, pointing out how these discussions often presume that the internet "is de facto 'enriching.'"[58] In place of this divide,

Nakamura suggests we consider the different ways that different groups use the internet. Working from cross-sectional survey data, Nakamura observes that the digital divide at work across different races in the U.S. is less of a difference between 'haves' and 'have nots' than it is a range of differences between different kinds of online practices. She concludes that it "may be helpful to envision various *categories* of online citizens rather than thinking in terms of gaps and divides."[59] She offers a comparison of internet use with the categories of passengers on airlines. These "'classes' of service cut across race in interesting ways," she notes.[60] Elsewhere, she asserts that "the Internet [works] to differentially screen users by race, ethnicity, and language use."[61] When considered in Bourdieu's terminology, what Nakamura offers is a sense of technical competences distributed differently across different races of internet users, giving each a different way of being online. Differential amounts and modes of cultural capital in the form of technical competence lead to different formations of practice associated with different groups (race being only the beginning) to reproduce social divisions. Though Bourdieu would presumably offer criticism regarding Nakamura's privileging of race over class, and of her use of categories of race that derive from artificially naturalized divisions suggested by survey research, the analysis she offers of competences being variably distributed across the social formation are quite consistent with his vision of the distribution of cultural capital.

Though the idea of a 'digital divide' got us started on this, these issues of technical fluency are not unique to the internet. The situation whereby those who master a new communication technology is familiar, and has been described at work in new media of a different time. Carolyn Marvin describes how "technological literacy" functioned "as social currency" in media that were introduced in the U.S. during the 19th century.[62] This operated in at least two different ways. First, technicians who were involved in creating early electrical communication media (such as the telegraph and telephone) "were wont to indulge a powerful impulse to identify aliens and enemies, those suspect in electrical culture and perhaps dangerous to it, in terms of their textual competence."[63] For these experts, technical competence functioned as cultural capital, sorting out the insiders from the outsiders, reinforcing a divide between experts and the lay public. Secondly, and more broadly, this technical 'ability' acted as a way for dominant classes to reinforce their own sense of themselves as refined, as naturally separate from other groups. Bourdieu asserted that "[t]aste classifies, and it classifies the classifier."[64] There is reason to believe that technical competence does much the same thing, creating a field where differences in practice (each of them world-constitutive) get sorted out socially.

It is not hard to find latter-day parallels to what Marvin describes. Technical expertise continues to operate as a kind of cultural capital. Obvious examples abound in recent history: the tech guru playing soothsayer in meetings with venture capitalists;

information technology professionals in myriad offices around the world who make much of their own ability to solve problems no one else can; wealthier youths taking as a given their own familiarity with the newest high-tech gadget. Once we orient ourselves to the importance of fluency in the codes we use—including html code and its successors—the activity of the audience can be better understood.

Relationality and the Field of the Audience

Bourdieu impressed on us the idea that "the real is the relational,"[65] and by this he emphasizes both the fluidity and stubborn fixity of practice. The set of practices that exist in the world are not randomly strewn about the social field, nor are they placed in a necessary relation with a set of social classes as static stand-ins or signifiers. Instead, at all times, we must consider "a set of social positions which is bound by a relation of homology to a set of activities (the practice of golf or piano) or of goods (a second home or an old master painting) that are themselves characterized relationally."[66] By 'characterized relationally,' Bourdieu meant something similar to the structuralist emphasis on difference as it relates to meaning. The things we do are never simply themselves. They are practices that come to seem natural or different to us because of their relation to other practices, and because of our own positions in social space. Golf, for instance, has a position in the field of leisure activities which has homologies with certain social positions. The position of golf can change along with the shifting positions in the social space; there is an ongoing dialectic between the relational positions of practices and social positions. This kind of correspondence between social space and practices represents Bourdieu's attempt to create a non-determinist picture of how practices become possible through their relation to social position, and also of how practices can change for the same reason. There is a materialism at work here, where culture is not given the position in the driver's seat. Instead, it is the relationality of social space that generates the system of practices.

This approach to cultural practice is most famously dealt with in *Distinction*, where Bourdieu addresses the issue of homologies at great length. Bourdieu stated in *Distinction* that

> [c]hoosing according to one's tastes is a matter of identifying goods that are objectively attuned to one's position and which 'go together' because they are situated in roughly equivalent positions in their respective spaces, be they films or plays, cartoons or novels, clothes or furniture; this choice is assisted by institutions—shops, theatres (left- or right-bank), critics, newspapers, magazines—which are themselves defined by their position in a field and which are chosen on the same principles.[67]

The social formation reproduces itself through the mechanism of the homology, as audience members come to find certain cultural products to be a good fit for themselves. This sense of something being a good fit comes from the homology that obtains when an agent's social position is felt to match the position of the cultural good in question. We come to develop a feel for the game that tells us that some messages are 'for us,' while others occur to us as being white noise, a distribution of meaningfulness reminiscent of Norbert Wiener's notion of "'To-whom-it-may-concern' messages,"[68] as he imagined them at work in any number of human and non-human contexts. Some messages (or practices, or cultural products) call out to us. Bourdieu constructed the idea of the homology to explain how some things do (and some do not) call out to us.

Bourdieu's use of the term 'homology,' however, at times yields more confusion than clarity. He was notably unclear about which homologies would produce meaningful identifications, and which would not. Still, the grander idea of homologies between media producers and audiences deserves careful explanation, in part because it promises to pull together the study of these two groups, potentially bridging one of the more unfortunate divides in media studies.

Bourdieu posited links between producers and audience members in his discussion of fashion. We see "change in fashion," he explains, in conflicts between the "established and the challengers," or, "in other words…between those who have the social properties associated with accomplished adulthood and those who have the social properties associated with the incompleteness of youth."[69] Though Bourdieu tied this to specific tendencies at work within the dominant class, there is some promise for broadening this so that it is brought to bear on how youth media audiences are developed, and how they come to find enjoyable some of the culture that has been created 'for' them. In the sphere of media production, new ideas in culture come from those who have nothing to lose and something to gain from dismissing the old ways. The same is largely true for younger media audiences, who also have little to lose from breaking from what has come before. In this sense, there is a homology—a shared logic of 'newness,' of the distinction bestowed upon the novel—at work in the creation of youth culture. In this sense, we can think of youth culture as one of the first niche cultures created by the media industry. A homology between the producers and audience members sets the whole thing into motion. This does not mean that capitalist forces are held at bay, but simply that the profit motive must contend with these issues of social space.

That these homologies often go unacknowledged by both producers and audience members is an important component of how they work. Everything seems to click into place, as everyone involved pursues more or less what seems to come naturally. This separation between producers' and audience members' intentions can be most dramatic. Bourdieu asserted that the field of cultural production follows a logic that arranges the products it creates "to be predisposed to function differentially, as means of distinction, first between the class fractions and then between the classes."[70] This all happens while the producers, as Bourdieu maintained in a discussion of theater producers, remain "totally involved and absorbed in their struggles with other producers, convinced that only specific artistic interests are at stake and that they are otherwise totally disinterested."[71] The homologies at work between the competing factions amongst producers and the less obviously competing audience members pull the entire system into a kind of coordination.

Bourdieu confined much of his discussion of these issues to the field of limited production (and its audiences). Applying these ideas to the field of large-scale production, where commercial interests often carry the day, is more difficult. Bourdieu contrasted the autonomous arena of production from production concerned with 'heteronomous' success. He cast this as the difference between production that "serves no other demand than the one it itself produces," and "a production which secures success and the corresponding profits by adjusting to a preexisting demand."[72] This latter kind of production implies that the homology between producers and audience members may be less precisely coordinated in cases of large-scale production. Large-scale production in many arenas requires a focus on the lowest common denominator that differs markedly from the more targeted logic in small-scale production. I am reminded of the advice given to the newly ensconced NBC President Brandon Tartikoff when he was chided for favoring television programming more likely to be critically acclaimed than to be popular: "Take your camera to the New York bus terminal, photograph the first 100 people arriving, and whenever you make a decision think of those faces and say, 'Now I like it, but will they like it?'"[73] I suspect that this gives us a hint about why Bourdieu did not extend his logic of homologies into much popular culture; he did not see the homologies as holding up in the same way in mass production. However, one might point out that some rough homologies would remain. The producers of a reality show intended for a broad audience, for instance, would likely have less cultural capital than their counterparts producing, say, a critically acclaimed drama for a subscription-based cable television network.[74]

Bourdieu did, however, write at some length about the reception of this culture that comes from large-scale production. In particular, he examines the popular aesthetic, which certainly can be applied with some success to the situation of the audiences for large-scale production media. As with other audience tendencies, and in a manner that links up with Saussure's ideas regarding opposition and negation, he described this aesthetic in terms of rejection. He contrasted the popular aesthetic with the 'pure' aesthetic found in audiences for autonomous production by describing the popular aesthetic as "the refusal of the refusal which is the starting point of the high aesthetic, i.e., the clear-cut separation of ordinary dispositions from the specifically aesthetic disposition."[75] Even if the architectonic system of homologies does not apply seamlessly here, there is still a logic of rejection at work in the consumption of mass produced popular culture. This logic is perhaps best described in his description of how different photographers operate, where he noted how, "feeling that a more demanding practice is impossible and prohibited, one *prohibits oneself* from developing a taste for it and avoids liking it."[76] The enjoyment of the products that come from the field of mass production is thus made out to be no less of an act of distinction, of asserting difference (without trying to do so), than is the case with high art. This tells us little about homologies, alas, but it does link up nicely with some important insights related to the how the social formation is reproduced through media consumption.

Distinction may be a growing—or at least more obvious—part of the consumption of popular culture. As I have already discussed in the context of media production, we may be witnessing the erosion of the classic 'mass audience.' Much as this leads to consideration of Bourdieu's applicability to the newer systems of production, there is also much to consider in terms of the audience side of the new non-mass audience. Rodney Benson has suggested that, "[a]s cable television leads to the proliferation of news channels and programs, television may begin to operate more as an agent of class differentiation, as it already has in the United States."[77] If the tendency of mass communication to operate as a kind of "[o]pen scatter"[78] often makes it difficult to find much in the way of social differentiation at work, the fact that many media we have associated with mass communication have become oriented much less around this kind of open scatter should be food for thought. The tendencies of social differentiation at work in media audience practice may be changing with adjustments in how media are programmed in an age of proliferating channels, the internet, and mobile media.

We find the logic of social differentiation—the very heart of what Bourdieu means by 'distinction'—quite frequently in our media programming today. Just as there are social positions that relate to an individual's annual income, level of education, ethnicity, sex, and age, so are there television networks pitched to these positions in the social field. As Joseph Turow puts it, "the new portraits of society that advertisers and media personnel invoke involve the blending of income, generation, marital status, and gender into a soup of geographical and psychological profiles they call 'lifestyles'."[79] This can be found outside the world of television, too. Magazines, satellite radio channels, manifold types of online content, and even AM Radio have now been long at work tapping into the logic of differentiated audiences. To apply Bourdieu's ideas to this as a research program concerning audience behavior would involve looking at this not solely as a market phenomenon, but instead asking the kinds of questions about practice that concerned Bourdieu. The shift to programming for target audiences no doubt involves an adjustment in the kinds of relationality at work in the media; there seems to be an elaborated sense in which simply watching one television show is to choose not to watch much else, to locate oneself much more precisely in the field of cultural positions. To turn this into a question about praxis, we may wish to ask what kinds of 'corporeal dispositions' can be linked to programming such as this? How does it come to seem natural to consume it? What kinds of codes does it involve, and what kinds of fluency must be used to decipher it?

Things get rather more pointed when we focus these kinds of questions on internet audience practices. Social differentiation was once made out to be something like a non-factor in internet-based communication, as when Howard Rheingold described Multi-User Dungeons as a virtual space "where magic is real and identity is fluid."[80] Many now agree that social differentiation may in fact play an accentuated role in online communication, where users have tremendous opportunities for public display. Blogs, social networking, and other forms of on-line communication represent a meaningful expansion in opportunities to display cultural consumption. danah boyd and Nicole Ellison cite Jenny Sundén's idea that online profiles provide a way to "type oneself into being."[81] They describe the Social Network Site as services based largely on the construction of "a public or semi-public profile within a bounded system."[82] Sonia Livingstone presents a detailed description of the ranges of aesthetics at work in youths' social media profiles, with a particular focus on "identity as display."[83] Even more suggestive of Bourdieu's ideas, Zizi Papacharissi has examined Twitter in terms of how it lends itself to performances of self, which she considers as "deliberately improvised performances of a digital orality."[84] In short, much online communicative behavior takes the form of a kind of public display of the self.

These ideas dovetail smoothly with Bourdieu's considerations of social differentiation. Using his logic, these kinds of performances of the self are always group-relevant, always pregnant with meanings relating to the classification of others and the classification of self, performed not intentionally but 'naturally.' The classic Bourdieusian concern for classification is best summed up in Bourdieu's difficult statement that the

[c]lassifying subjects who classify the properties and practices of others, or their own, are also classifiable objects which classify themselves (in the eyes of others) by appropriating practices and properties that are already classified (as vulgar or distinguished, high or low, heavy or light etc.—in other words, in the last analysis, as popular or bourgeois) according to their probable distribution between groups that are themselves classified.[85]

Social network sites and other forms of online communication—with their blending of producers, distributors, and audience members—show us two things. First, the fragmentation of audiences we find in the world of new media may indicate that we will find a fragmentation in the system of classifications at work, with the popular/bourgeois divide suggested here being replaced by other kinds of divides (political, lifestyle, geographical). Beyond this, audiences are not only being fragmented. Audiences are also, via the affordances of new media, being enlisted into more direct assertions of their distinctions. When someone posts to Facebook a link to a favorite song (or political idea, or restaurant, or television show, or blog post…), a whole system of discernment is re-summoned into existence. New media have not *created* this process, but they do seem to have adjusted a part of it so that Bourdieu's ideas regarding cultural consumption seem even more relevant than before.

Audience Practice as Ritual

Bourdieu's discussion of the media audience strikes many researchers as lacking in depth, due to Bourdieu's tendency to focus very much on the distribution of cultural products across different points in the social topology. In other words, Bourdieu focused very much on the act of consumption, and concentrated rather less on issues of interpretation. His focus on consumption is consistent with his insistence on talking about practices over and above interpretation, his oft-invoked impulse not to take an 'intellectualist' standpoint that mistakes the things of logic for the logic of things. The result leaves many audience researchers wanting more, which is understandable. An important connection between Bourdieu's focus on practice and the study of the media audience can be found in the idea of ritual as it relates to media audiences.

The idea of ritual media usage is not new. When contrasted with many studies of media audiences that focus on resistance or on fandom, the focus on media audiences and ritual can demonstrate that audiences are not particularly active. Alan M. Rubin's study of ritualized television is a kind of broadside against the idea of a meaningfully active audience, as when he points out that, in ritualized television use, "activity would involve the notion of utility, but apparently not a great degree of intentionality or selectivity."[86] He concludes that, while "instrumental television use means a more *involving* viewing experience[,],…ritualized television use is a more *important* viewing experience," and that "television viewing is clearly a time-filling activity for some viewers."[87] This kind of understanding of ritualized media use demonstrates the potential distance between those who espouse ritual understandings of media use and those who focus on active, contested audience interpretation processes.

Just because an audience is not seen as particularly active does not mean that there is not much going on. Much of the importance of Bourdieu's focus on symbolic codes, after all, is that there is a tremendous amount of communication 'going on' when we seem to be doing very little. When this is plugged into a ritual understanding of the media, we can start to develop a better sense of how audiences use media.

It is not difficult to link Bourdieu to ritual theory. Bourdieu was critical of some of the social theorists most associated with theories of ritual (and especially of Durkheim), criticizing both "structuralist semiology and Durkheim's concept of 'collective representations'" for carrying "an implicit theory of consensus."[88] However, much of what he laid out in his model of habitus/field/capital involves an attempt to elaborate upon anthropological approaches to society in an effort to make these approaches amenable to treatments of power and multi-polarity, elements that he found lacking in much Durkheimian scholarship. The idea that one unified symbol system was somehow the natural way of things struck Bourdieu as a way for scholars to ignore symbolic violence, the tacit process whereby the dominated in a society accept the categories of the dominant as natural. Bourdieu's relative emphasis on differentiation relies on an assumption that there are some basic cognitive structures at work, but eschews the idea that meaning works in the same way for all people. A careful reading of Bourdieu tells us that distinctions generated by social praxis "are predisposed to simultaneously generate *social* as well as logical classifications by making dichotomous social as well as logical groupings, by creating forms of social inclusion and exclusion as well as at the level of symbols."[89] This is the very core of what Bourdieu intends to describe at work in distinction, and "[j]ust as the double meaning of 'distinction' indicates, this fundamental logic identifies the precise character of symbolic power: the simultaneous act of making conceptual and social discriminations."[90] Broadly conceived, this approach to meaning, with its focus on practical ways of knowing and acting, connects quite well with much of what exists in the study of media ritual.

To transport Bourdieu's concepts regarding the operation of symbol systems and practical knowledge to the study of the media, I argue that we can think of his social theory as one that emphasizes how schemata for understanding the world are developed through practice—including communicative practice—without explicit thought. Much as Bourdieu's emphasis was placed on the tacit exercise of fluency within symbolic systems, and how these symbolic systems relate to power, the closest harmonies with Bourdieu's approach in the study of media ritual come from those who share Bourdieu's concern for worldviews. James W. Carey's famous ritual view of communication emphasizes "the maintenance of society in time" and "the representation of shared beliefs."[91] This leads Carey to consider the reading of a newspaper as "a situation in which nothing new is learned but in which a particular view of the world is portrayed and confirmed."[92] Significantly, Carey emphasizes that reading the newspaper (when considered from the ritual view) does not so much give us information about the world as much as it "invites our participation on the basis of our assuming, often vicariously, social roles within it."[93] The audience is here thought of not as being acted upon, but as taking part in a process, albeit a process that has usually been construed long before the audience arrived on the scene. And this is roughly appropriate for Bourdieu's understanding of the audience, where the emphasis is placed on the process of re-enacting the social, and on the repetitive performance of visions of the world. Of course, Bourdieu critiqued the Durkheimian ideal of a unified social symbolic 'center,' and the same critique carries over to how Bourdieu would differ from Carey. Bourdieu gave us a picture of a shared social space, but a shared social space that is fractured into separate spheres.

Some of the best points of contact for Bourdieu's ideas and the study of the media audience come from Nick Couldry's ideas concerning media rituals, a term that Couldry defines as "the whole range of situations where media themselves 'stand in,' or appear to 'stand in,' for something wider, something linked to the fundamental organizational level on which we are, or imagine ourselves to be, *connected* as members of a society."[94] More broadly, Couldry refers to the "ritual space of the media" as "the whole interlocking mass of practices that must be 'in place' for there to be ritual action oriented to the media."[95] Of tremendous importance to both rituals and the ritual space of the media is "the body that passes between them: the ritual body which has internalized the organizing significance of ritual's category differences."[96] And here is where Bourdieu's focus on practical reason becomes most relevant. Bourdieu claimed that it is a kind of bodily knowledge that emerges from experience of given fields of interaction. "Having acquired from this exposure a system of dispositions attuned to these regularities," the body

> is inclined and able to anticipate them practically in behaviours which engage a corporeal knowledge that provides a practical comprehension of the world quite different from the intentional act of conscious decoding that is normally designated by the idea of comprehension.[97]

On the level of embodied, practical dispositions, the audience member comes to internalize a fluency (itself inflected by class/status origins and trajectory) that is attuned to the form at work in the media. Couldry reasons that, in the analysis of media ritual, "our primary concern is not with the 'ideas' that might be 'expressed' through, say, a media text, but with the formal relations at work in a particular type of action."[98]

Instead of turning to media rituals per se, I suggest that we focus on the meaning of this broader sense of the ritual space of the media, in large part because it has so much relevance to the understanding of prosaic media practices, and to practical knowledge at work in audience behavior. One of the best things about this approach, if it is carried out carefully, is its avoidance of thinking about audience behavior only in terms of intellectualized processes such as 'reading' or 'interpreting' that fail to grasp the tremendous amount of practical knowledge put into play with all media behavior. Roger Silverstone described how the "language of television, in particular through its narrative structure, narrowly defines the range of expression and the limits of response."[99] It is this kind of everyday limning of the basic forms of expression and experience that Bourdieu's ideas promise to bring to audience studies. Couldry examines how rituals give us "frameworks of understanding," and that "the actions comprising rituals are structured around certain *categories and/or boundaries.*"[100] Bourdieu's concern for how habitus is structured around categories (and paired opposites within these categories) does a good job of showing us how to approach what Silverstone calls the "common-sense world and its judgements of the appropriate," illuminated and made coherent.[101]

Bourdieu emphasized the ritual observance of time in his earlier and more anthropological work, and much of what he said can be applied to how audiences relate to the media. Temporal categories and boundaries certainly play an important role in our media practices as audience members. Bourdieu described how

> [s]ocial disciplines take the form of temporal disciplines and the whole social order imposes itself at the deepest level of the bodily dispositions through a particular way of regulating the use of time, the temporal distribution of collective and individual activities and the appropriate rhythm with which to perform them.[102]

This is relevant to the study of audiences in at least two ways. First, there is a sense in which media usage lends itself to the kind of temporal disciplines Bourdieu described at work. Here I call attention to the temporal regularity of much media use: television is often watched in the evening, newspapers (online and paper) are often read in the morning, radio is often listened to during a commute to work. The point here is that media use has often taken the form of a kind of temporal practice that becomes an important part of our practical sense of the world. Bourdieu asserted that temporal "formulae, commonly used to reassert solidarity, contain an implicit definition of the fundamental virtue of conformity, the opposite of which is the desire to stand apart from others."[103] Through temporally arranged practices of media consumption, we become members of a community of temporal practice. In a broad sense, media usage becomes a way to attain a tacit sense of solidarity with others.[104]

Second, our practical sense of time is supplied to us out of the ceremonies that we create. The ceremonies become temporal guide-posts, moments when time stands still, which are used in reference to each other to offer a sense of shared temporal experience. This is the kind of thing that Daniel Dayan and Elihu Katz refer to when they tell us that media events "have the power to declare a holiday, thus to play a part in the *civil religion*."[105] These are special occasions when the "ceremonial roles assumed by viewers—mourner, citizen, juror, sports fan—differentiate holiday viewing from everyday viewing and transform the nature of involvement with the medium."[106] The audience members for media events, or media rituals if you prefer, take part in the re-framing of temporal experience. The social experience of temporality is coordinated through media events that give us something that is happening in real time, meant to be remembered and used for future reference. Social time is thus organized at moments of events/rituals/ceremonies, when we are given major signposts for time's passage, as well as in more mundane experiences of the media, when we are given the opportunity to play a part in ongoing rituals concerning the temporal element of practice.

This excursion into temporal practice shows us that there is much more to Bourdieu's sense of the audience than merely a consideration of judgments of taste, and we can do well to attend to the schematic practical frameworks for understanding that are erected through the media for all kinds of social life. Michèle Lamont adopts "the Bourdieusian view that shared cultural style contributes to class reproduction," while expanding the range of analysis beyond taste in cultural goods.[107] Media audience researchers could take Bourdieu's method for analyzing the frameworks of understanding provided by practice and apply it to media practices, without reducing audience behavior to mere readings of texts. Couldry tells us that Bourdieu's idea of symbolic violence "is…inherent to the media's operations but it can only be unpacked through a theory of the specific rituals and ritualisations that sustain it on a day-to-day basis."[108] A focus on audience habitus would inquire into these ritualizations, asking questions concerning how the audience habitus relates to the symbolic order that is vouchsafed by way of the media. What are the forms that are observed as natural, legitimate, correct by an audience? The logic of classification, of framing, "generates…a political effect to the extent that the social groupings identified are hierarchically differentiated and therefore legitimated."[109] Studying the media audience must involve attempting to understand the differentiating logic at work in messages and in systems of messages, with an appreciation for how audiences relate to the differentiations at work in message systems.

Much of this discussion is relevant to concerns regarding how new media audience behaviors demonstrate that classic models of mass communication will require adjustment. Philip M. Napoli gives us a carefully considered account of how media audiences have changed in recent history. Audience fragmentation is a major development, as we go from "millions of audiences of hundreds instead of hundreds of audiences of millions."[110] As a factor in the ritualized space of the media, this implies that we are experiencing a change in the ritualized space of the media. The sense of connection to a society—and its attendant ritualized boundaries at work—that we once may have gotten from broadcast television or a newspaper has probably changed. This does not imply that it has been eliminated. To put this into Bourdieusian terms, the relatively more differentiated media sphere associated with new media may support a different system of social differentiations that operate in audience member's practical knowledge. In *Distinction* and *The Field of Cultural Production*, Bourdieu put forward an understanding of popular media audiences that painted them as discriminating in their own ways, but as relatively undifferentiated from each other. If this kind of fragmentation of a former 'mass' audience is indeed occurring, we may see either a reason to ignore Bourdieu more than we already have, or (what I suggest) a reason to apply Bourdieu's ideas regarding mutually differentiated systems of classification at work in the field of social interaction that have been adjusted to fit new, fragmented media audiences.

It is important to differentiate this kind of inquiry from a search for centralized myths of legitimacy. The goal is not to recreate a democratic mass audience that may never have truly existed. Couldry pushes us away from "the myth of a valorized social 'centre,'" encouraging us to pursue an understanding of media ritualization that is linked to "a broader analysis of power."[111] So, when faced with the seeming proliferation of differentiations to be made (even by 'dominated' members of society) in the world of the fragmented audience, our response should not be merely to lament the end of the mass audience, nor to applaud the arrival of a seemingly wide-open field of choices. Instead, our job is a murky middle path: that of trying to trace the practical knowledge that emerges from this field of media products, to understand how this has adjusted the ritualized media practices in which audience members engage, and to relate these things to power in a way that preserves the Bourdieusian idea of symbolic violence. To lose sight of the symbolic violence in any idea of a centralized norm[112] is to become part of the symbolic violence at work.

Conclusion: Audience Theory and Methodology

Research concerning media audiences has undergone no small number of adjustments in the last few decades. Sonia Livingstone has argued that the study of the audience needs "a theory which offers an agenda which…not only directs audience research but also ensures that the outcome of such research will serve to connect audience research with production/texts/context."[113] With remarkable clarity, Livingstone points to many of the criticisms that have been leveled at reception studies, and concludes that "the audience becomes…a shorthand way of pointing to ways in which people stand in relationship to each other, rather than a thing of which people may or may not be a member and whose peculiar ways must be discovered."[114] Livingstone sets high expectations for what a theory of the audience should account for. She clearly sees studies that simply conclude that there is, say, 'resistance' to be found in one audience member's read of a particular work of popular culture to be a cop-out.

I argue that Bourdieu's ideas present us with one way to live up to Livingstone's over-riding concern for connections and relations between positions. First, Bourdieu's understanding of the audience is one that comes with a built-in appreciation for the audience member's connections to: other audience members, history, the production of culture, and the text under consideration. Nothing is done in isolation. Certainly much audience research is formulated with that assumption in mind. But it is difficult to find a source for audience theory more focused on these connections than Bourdieu. The habitus/field/capital approach emphasizes the connections at work between all of the things that Livingstone sees as important to audience theory. Beyond this, Bourdieu's idea that 'everything is relational' is a perfect fit for Livingstone's interest in accounting for how 'people stand in relationship to each other.' Livingstone urges us to conceive of audiences "relationally as an analytic concept relevant to, and providing links across, relations among people and media at all levels from the macro economic/cultural to the individual/psychological."[115] As a theorist and researcher whose ideas were developed in an effort to allow us simultaneously to consider the macro and micro, Bourdieu's perspective can get us a long ways toward what Livingstone describes here: an understanding of the audience that takes heed of audience practices in terms of their connections to production processes, and in terms of their relations to other practices.

Beyond helping us to find a better theory of audiences, Bourdieu's methods for studying media audiences also provide some important lessons for audience study. First of all, and most obviously, Bourdieu applied numerous methods to his domains of study, and all of these methods can be incorporated in the study of media audiences. To put a fine point on this, audience research would do well to get beyond its singular association with ethnography. The idea of the habitus can accommodate all kinds of methods. In *Distinction* and *The Love of Art*, Bourdieu uses surveys and interviews to study cultural consumption. In *Outline of a Theory of Practice*, he employs field research. In *The State Nobility*, he ranges from ethnography to statistical analysis to institutional analysis. Loïc Wacquant points out that Bourdieu's loyalty to no method in particular "does not mean that 'anything goes,' …but rather that…the array of methods used must fit the problem at hand." These methods "must constantly be reflected upon *in actu*, in the very movement whereby they are deployed to resolve particular questions."[116] Bourdieu was skeptical of the kinds of qualitative/quantitative splits that tend to reproduce themselves in academic fields.

With this in mind, the method for studying the audience should be fit to the kinds of questions we are asking about audiences. Instead of rejecting surveys as insufficient for the purposes of getting into the finer details of lived experience, or as overly aligned with positivist approaches to the social sciences, an audience researcher could take a page from Bourdieu's book and use surveys that are carefully gauged to the kinds of issues he investigated. David Morley says that the question is not whether or not the method is correct in some way. The question is "always whether *this* particular form of abstraction or 'reduction' is worth the price."[117] To give up on abstraction entirely in the world of audience studies would be to give up on studying patterns at all, including the patterns of perception that audience members apply.

With all of this in mind, the research methods for audience research should be fit to the kinds of questions we ask. Livingstone helpfully points us toward *relational* questions. In doing so, she harmonizes with Bourdieu. In terms of audience methodology, *all* types of methods should be encouraged, but the applications of these methods should be evaluated in terms of how well they draw our attention to the relationality of the audience experience, how it aligns with some other elements of social practice, and how it is set aside from other elements. To chart the Bourdieusian field of audience-ship is to try to come to grips with how media consumption operates as a practice to locate the individual audience member in the social topology. For the researcher, few things would be more contrary to this than simply to focus on interpretation, gratification, or resistance. Until the field of possibles is understood, little can be said.

CHAPTER FOUR

Symbolic Power and Authority: The Power/ Communication Nexus

A politician deems that the finance system is in crisis. A climatologist tells us that global climate change will exact an incalculable human toll. Your auto mechanic tells you that an expensive component of your car's ignition system will need to be replaced. In every case something that is dimly perceived or not perceived at all is made out to be a specific kind of problem, and an audience is given reasons to believe in this explanation. Authority—the issue of how we authorize communicators to create reality—can be found at work in each of these scenarios.

An evergreen intellectual concern in communication relates to how reality is defined in specific ways, and how we come to accept these definitions. For these visions to become effective, societies develop symbolic regimes to sort out legitimacy. Max Weber was famously attentive to this issue, and defined much of it around the term 'authority' as it relates to the state. "If the state is to exist," he claims, "the dominated must obey the authority claimed by the powers that be."[1] For Weber, "the basis of every authority, and correspondingly of every kind of willingness to obey, is a belief, a belief by virtue of which persons exercising authority are lent prestige."[2] The authority at work requires "basic *legitimations* of domination."[3] Without these legitimations that take the form of authority, the system simply does not work.

In the wake of Weber, a focus on legitimations of domination ought to take full measure of the role played by the media in the assertion of authority. James W.

Carey opined that the "rise of the national media represents a centripetal force in social organization." The national media "enhance the control of space…by laying down direct lines of access between national centres and dispersed audiences, and by producing a remarkable *potential* for the centralization of power and authority."[4] Smaller media channels have offered an opposite, "centrifugal," tendency, whereby subsections of a national population come to develop their own regimes of authority.[5] The important thing for the present discussion is this insinuation of the media of communication into the system of authority that Weber identified as so important to organizing society.

Combining the concerns of Weber and Carey, we can develop a sense that authority matters tremendously to how societies are organized, and that the media play a central (if not necessarily centralizing) role in the establishment of authority in a society. Here is where Bourdieu comes in. His perspective on symbolic power gives us a sociological approach to communication that shows a careful concern for the context in which messages are distributed and received. Bourdieu's ideas regarding symbolic power and authority are helpful to think with because they: (a) are broadly applicable to a wide range of communicative situations, from face-to-face conversation to television to blog, (b) are always tied to the field of social practice, and thus invite us to get beyond the content of messages, and (c) help us to think about the role of power in communication. Authority is a notoriously evanescent process, and the cluttered history of mass and digital media does little to make things simpler for the would-be researcher of authority. Bourdieu helps to draw our attention to the interaction between the meanings at work in authority (message) and structures at work in the establishment and corrosion of authority.

Rhetoricians have given us some tools for understanding authority at work in public discourse. John M. Murphy's analysis of George W. Bush's speeches after September 11, 2001, provides an exemplar of rhetorical analysis, with a careful focus on how Bush's "'American' strategies" became part of his construction of his own authority.[6] Murphy's focus—like many other rhetoricians—remains centered squarely on the messages in the speeches themselves. Bourdieu found this kind of analysis of authority to be overly idealist in emphasis; his own focus on praxis would demand an understanding of how authority is grounded in the social. Less discourse-centered directions in rhetoric, like rhetorical materialism[7]—with its potential for grounding rhetorical utterances in social relations—could have tremendous overlap with Bourdieu's vision of authority.

The field of communication has often turned to other fields of inquiry in an effort to develop a theoretical armature. Bourdieu's ideas deserve a place this grand tradition of borrowing/theft because they help us to get beyond the grand theory that is so often used to understand authority. Regimes of legitimation are sometimes very small things. There oft-miniature status does not make them any less important. Bourdieu calls our attention to the interactions between the grand legitimating systems and the oft-unnoticed detail that ensures this legitimation. It is this move to the fine meshes of authority that makes Bourdieu so helpful in looking at how authority is wrought. At its best, and if carefully managed, a Bourdieusian approach to authority can be used to analyze authority in terms of: the identity of the would-be authoritative personage, the audience for authority, the messages at work, and the medium (and media outlet) that is involved. Instead of isolating these factors from each other, Bourdieu gave us the tools for seeing the role played by all of them.

Before we pursue this, it is a good idea to orient the idea of symbolic power, which was the term Bourdieu used most frequently to refer to authority and legitimacy. John B. Thompson identifies symbolic power alongside "economic power,… political power,…[and] coercive power."[8] Symbolic power "stems from the activity of producing, transmitting and receiving meaningful symbolic forms."[9] If Weber's 'legitimations of domination' are to be made effective, it is through communication that such legitimations will operate.

When we think about authority, it is not unusual for us to imagine a situation in which a communicator is ordering someone to do something, as we find in a total institution like the military. This is an obvious and helpful starting place for a discussion of authority. More commonly, however, when we speak of authority, we are often not describing a situation in which the holder and subject of the authority in question are dealing directly with each other. Nor do we always find a command-oriented structure at work. Much of the time, authority in the media takes on a more indirect and diffuse aspect.

The situation of authority at work in the media is reminiscent of Alvin Gouldner's descriptions of modernity and 'the report.' In his description of ideology as it relates to the 'communication revolution,' Gouldner outlined the waning of traditionalism and the waxing of the modern as a situation in which commands have given way to reports. He observed that, "as the new industrialism succeeds,"[10] we move away from command-based means of working out authority, and wind up with ideologies, which are "belief-systems distinguished by the centrality of their concern for What Is and by their world-referencing 'reports,'" working from "publicly scrutable evidence and reasoning."[11] Gouldner put this emergence of ideology in a media context, emphasizing how, with "the growth of the mass media, social interaction [became] less requisite for cultural communality. People might now share information and orientations, facts and values, without mutual access and interaction."[12] Gouldner then turned quickly to a discussion of control via the mass media, and he emphasizes the centralization of opinion, noting that, with the emergence of the mass media, "rational persuasion is then less necessary, and manipulation from a central source can substitute for voluntary persuasion."[13] In sum: largely as a result of changes in communication, we get a dramatic increase in the number of reports about the world, each concerned more directly with 'What Is' than with commands. Ideology is thus set to play out largely through authority, through the concern for securing belief in a range of reports amongst the glut of messages/reports we face.

This move away from authority as a thing possessed, or as a feature of hierarchical bureaucratic arrangements, is an important part of the focus on authority as it plays out in communication. Bruce Lincoln identifies authority as something that "remains distinct from persuasion and coercion alike while being related to them in some very specific and suggestive ways."[14] In language that should spur the imagination of the communication researcher, Lincoln tells us that the "exercise of authority" occurs largely through communication, via "the whole theatrical array of gestures, demeanors, costumes, props, and stage devices through which one may impress or bamboozle an audience."[15] Authority is conveyed through language, but also through other communicative modes and media. It is not so much possessed as expressed, not so much oriented around commands as around reports and the conveyance of content.

Bourdieu offered us numerous solid starting points for an understanding of authority as just this kind of social process; his perspective on symbolic power allows us to consider authority in terms of audiences, producers/speakers, and messages all simultaneously at work. Bourdieu asked us to consider legitimation as a social process whereby social magic is summoned through communication to reproduce—and to contest—the system of power at work. I will begin this story with Bourdieu's ideas regarding language, which can be taken as fundamental to our broader concerns.

Language and Social Structure

Bourdieu outlined a sweeping understanding of language, one that maintains his focus on field, capital, and habitus. The best starting point for an understanding of Bourdieu's take on symbolic power—because it gets us in touch with atomic components of his perspective on authority—is his critique of linguistics and semiotics. Bourdieu insisted that: language is not an independent thing in and of itself, uses of language stem from the social terrain that structures those uses, and language is not a universally accessed range of meanings, available to all people for all purposes at all times.

Bourdieu's understanding of language was directly concerned with social structure. "A structural sociology of language," Bourdieu claimed, "must take as its object *the relationship between the structured systems of sociologically pertinent linguistic differences and the equally structured systems of social differences.*"[16] By bracketing out the social, linguistics has become "a purely internal and formal analysis with the charm of a game devoid of consequences."[17] Using language that seems almost intended for communication scholars, Bourdieu contended that even relatively simple linguistic exchanges involve "a complex and ramifying web of historical power relations between the speaker, endowed with a specific social authority, and an audience, which recognizes this authority to varying degrees, as well as between the groups to which they respectively belong."[18] Utterances are not pulled out of a magical fluency box where all words are equally available to the speaker and listener, but come from a particular distribution of speaker and listener competences as they intersect with the formation of the field of possible utterances, itself largely shaped by power relations.

In this way, Bourdieu treated communication as a practice to take its place alongside other forms of practice; he posited that a full understanding of language could not occur "without placing linguistic practices within the full universe of compossible practices: eating and drinking habits, cultural consumptions, taste in matters of arts, sports, dress, furniture, politics, etc."[19] In keeping with this, language "is a technique of the body, and linguistic (and especially phonological) competency is a dimension of the bodily hexis in which the whole relation to the social world expresses itself."[20] Following Pierre Guiraud,[21] Bourdieu described the "articulatory style" of a speaker as "part and parcel of a lifestyle that has become embodied, *fait corps*, and stands in linked relation with the usages of the body and of time that properly define this lifestyle."[22]

This approach to language, with its invocations of Maurice Merleau-Ponty and Ludwig Wittgenstein, should be reminiscent of Bourdieu's broader concerns relating to the habitus. Reminding us that the habitus is "a set of *dispositions* which incline agents to act and react in certain ways," John B. Thompson clarifies this connection. These dispositions are "acquired through a gradual process of *inculcation* in which early childhood experiences are particularly important." They "literally mould the body and become second nature. The dispositions produced thereby are also *structured* in the sense that they unavoidably reflect the social conditions within which they were acquired."[23] Thompson tells us that Bourdieu's vision of "linguistic exchanges" is portrayed "in such a way that every linguistic interaction, however personal and insignificant it may seem, bears the traces of the social structure that it both expresses and helps to reproduce."[24] We get a sense for how social structures are reproduced in everyday conversation, as the different positions in the social structure are given life by the agents from these positions, mutually constituting each other, holding each other up (as it were).

The importance of language, when contrasted with other forms of practice, is that it is so directly involved in the reproduction of social structure, through its capacity to endow individuals and groups with legitimacy. So, after considering language practices in terms of their similarities to other practice, Bourdieu argued that "the social sciences must take as their object of study the social operations of *naming* and the rites of institution through which they are accomplished." Beyond this, the social sciences must focus on the part that the "struggle over classifications, a dimension of all class struggles, makes to the constitution of classes— classes defined in terms of age, sex or social position, but also clans, tribes, ethnic groups or nations."[25] It is in the act of naming—the socially recognized, legitimate practice of naming—that Bourdieu found much of interest for those studying symbolic power and authority.

We find in language a reiteration a fortiori of Bourdieu's insistence on focusing simultaneously on both the subjective and the objective, through an understanding of the interplay of habitus and field. Social structures can be found in language, and the agents who speak reiterate that social structure. This represents the starting point for Bourdieu's understanding of symbolic power.

The Social Magic of Authority

The broad concern with linguistic practice connects to the topic of authority through a concern for what Bourdieu refered to as 'legitimate language.' In Bourdieu's hands, legitimate language becomes perhaps something similar to the legitimate culture that we associate with the Bourdieu of *Distinction*. We are in the realm of 'capital' here. As with other forms of legitimate culture, "access to legitimate language is quite unequal, and the theoretically universal competence liberally granted to all by linguists is in reality monopolized by some."[26] The unequal distribution of access to legitimate language makes it so that "[c]ertain categories of locutors are deprived of the capacity to speak in certain situations," a situation that sometimes goes fully acknowledged, as by "the farmer who explained that he never thought of running for mayor of his small township by saying: 'But I don't know how to speak!'"[27]

This sense that language operates in part to exclude, to draw lines around communities, led Bourdieu to refer to language as a "*code*, in the sense of a cipher enabling equivalences to be established between sounds and meanings, but also in the sense of a system of norms regulating linguistic practices."[28] The unequal distribution of the 'legitimate language' becomes part of the makeup of the field of social relations so that a style of speaking or writing "exists only in relation to agents endowed with schemes of perception and appreciation that enable them to constitute it as a set of systematic differences, apprehended syncretically."[29]

To focus only on the words is to "forget that *authority comes to language from the outside*, as Benveniste…reminds us in his analysis of the *skeptron* handed, according to Homer, to the orator about to deliver a speech."[30] For Bourdieu, the metaphor of the skeptron called attention to the externality of authority to language as well as the unequal distribution of the power that comes with authority. Some speakers have the skeptron, some do not. If they say the same thing, it would be foolish to expect them to have the same effect on the world around them. Beyond this, the skeptron metaphor leads us to examine the processes underlying this unequal distribution of authorized language.

This skeptron-like power that comes to words from the outside relies extensively on collusion between the communicator and the audience. What Bourdieu called symbolic power[31] is a power that relies very much on the audience. Symbolic power is "defined in and by a definite relation that creates belief in the legitimacy of the words and of the person who utters them, and it operates only inasmuch as those who undergo it recognizes those who wield it."[32] This situation reminded Bourdieu of Marcel Mauss's understanding of magic. As with Maussian magic, the researcher's goal should be to "reconstruct the totality of the social space in which the dispositions and beliefs that make the efficacy of the magic of language possible are engendered."[33] Having wrested the location of authority out of the words themselves, Bourdieu located it in the audience, via the workings of the social field.

Bourdieu's take on symbolic power can be thought of as a way to apply his relational thinking to the study of language. The familiar Austin-ian performative of naming is made possible not by the words, but by the institutions supplying the situation, and an audience who observes the institution's legitimacy. For Bourdieu, the "magical efficacy of these *acts of institution* is inseparable from the existence of an institution defining the conditions (regarding the agent, the time or place, etc.) which have to be fulfilled for the magic of words to operate."[34] The "conditions of felicity" that Austin described "are social conditions,"[35] related to habitus, field, and capital. What was a relatively stable phenomenon for Austin becomes, for Bourdieu, an issue involving power, authority, contestation, and legitimacy. The issue of felicity, in Bourdieu's scheme, takes on a broad ritual significance across almost all social interaction.[36]

The relationship between language and power becomes the point that Bourdieu pursued most doggedly in his writings on language. Symbolic power, exercised largely but not exclusively through language, takes its place along other modalities of power. Symbolic power is secured as capital, exercised in a field, and manifested through habitus. The distance Bourdieu established between himself and Austin—the basic idea that performatives derive their effectiveness from their social context, and must be studied in that way—becomes a jumping-off point for a broader understanding of authority. The "operations of social magic," as Bourdieu referred to Austinian performatives, are "comprised by *acts of authority*," and depend on "the combination of a systematic set of interdependent conditions which constitute social rituals."[37]

That these communicative rituals of naming, classification, and legitimacy are not seen as arbitrary makes them implicit in the reproduction of power. Because the mechanism by which symbolic power operates "[conceals] the link between the qualifications obtained by individuals and the cultural capital inherited by virtue of their social background, this mechanism provides a practical justification of the established order," which allows "those who benefit most from the system to convince themselves of their own intrinsic worthiness, while preventing those who benefit least from grasping the basis of their own deprivation."[38]

Not all communicators are created equal. The "weight of different agents" in a communication context "depends on their symbolic capital, i.e. on the *recognition*, institutionalized or not, that they receive from a group."[39] For Bourdieu, this recognition is what is arranged beforehand, and resides in the audience. Symbolic power is a power to constitute a world, to make effective one's own way of seeing things. It is the "power of constituting the given through utterances,…an almost magical power which enables one to obtain the equivalent of what is obtained through force (whether physical or economic), by virtue of the specific effect of mobilization."[40] The 'magic' at work is the power to construe a world.

The communicator-audience relationship figures prominently here. Because symbolic power "can be exercised only if it is *recognized*," Bourdieu tied it to "a given relation between those who exercise power and those who submit to it, i.e. in the very structure of the field in which belief is produced and reproduced."[41] The "power of words and slogans" derives from "the belief in the legitimacy of words and of those who utter them."[42] Thus does symbolic power exist only in certain circumstances, and always in a manner that derives from the power relations at work in a social system. It is granted to communicators "in the manner of something taken for granted, only under certain conditions,"[43] and it is these conditions that do the heavy lifting for symbolic power. These conditions, "which define legitimate usage," include the following: "it must be uttered by the person legitimately licensed to do so,…it must be uttered in a legitimate situation,…[and] it must be enunciated according to the legitimate forms (syntactic, phonetic, etc.)."[44] When these conditions are met, symbolic power "is a power which the person submitting to [it] *grants* to the person who exercises it, a credit with which he credits him, a *fides*, an *auctoritas*, with which he entrusts him by placing his trust in him. It is a power which exists because the person who submits to it believes that it exists."[45]

Symbolic power is deployed in a manner that points toward the social being of the communicator. This is what Bourdieu meant by saying that the "power of words is nothing other than the *delegated power* of the spokesperson, and his speech…is no more than a testimony, and one among others, of the *guarantee of delegation* which is vested in him."[46] With each utterance partaking of this delegated power, we get a re-performance—a reiteration—of the "subsequent perceptions of linguistic products."[47] As with much other cultural production for Bourdieu, the production of a certain kind of authoritative utterance generates an audience that is attuned to the symbolism at work in the utterance. The system reproduces itself until the field of social relations that underpins the system experiences change.

Working with this idea of words and communication in terms of 'delegated power,' there is plenty for the communication researcher to do. This framework, with its consideration of words and style in terms of capital, at the very least gives us a yardstick by which to measure the exercise of authority in all its contexts. If we do not chart the social space in which the authoritative message is offered, we have only a weak sense of what is going on. A fuller understanding of authority is achieved by developing a sense of: the institutions at work, the other positions staked out by competing authorities, the kinds of fluency required of the audience, and the role played by the audience's enlistment in belief in the authority. In short: research concerning authority must not stop with the messages themselves.

In addition to being an essential starting point, Bourdieu's discussion of language can be linked to issues in the study of media. After all, much as linguists (by Bourdieu's lights) have presumed that language is equally available to all, we frequently find a parallel assumption at work in the realm of the media. Scholars of internet-based and mobile media often describe these new media in terms of how they operate for all, presuming that these are modes of communication equally available to all people. This is a familiar myth pertaining to media, and to 'new' media (and not just today's new media) in particular.[48]

Access to legitimate language is only the beginning of the job to be done. Access to media, and to specific outlets at work in the media, can be treated much as Bourdieu treated access to language. This comes as old news to those who study the digital divide, in its many theoretical incarnations.[49] The idea that access to older forms of mass communication is not evenly distributed through a society comes as no shock at all, and carries with it important implications regarding legitimacy and the media. There remains much work to be done to extend Bourdieu's ideas regarding legitimate language into other media domains.

Another concern here relates to public trust in the media. Intensifying scholarly concern can be found concerning the issue of how much the public trusts the media, and how much the public trust in other institutions—especially the government—can be related to how these institutions are depicted in the media. There is a staggering amount of research linking media consumption to levels of public trust in the government. Few works in the field of communication are more influential to this discussion than Joseph A. Cappella and Kathleen Hall Jamieson's *Spiral of Cynicism*, with its careful dissection of survey and experimental data, and its broad-strokes linkage of media consumption with cynicism, a dependent variable that they link to trust.[50] Patricia Moy and Dietram A. Scheufele author a classic study in the genre. Using survey data, they find that "different types of media [have] different effects on political and social trust."[51] Thomas J. Johnson and Barbara K. Kaye have extended this concern into new media. Their survey data indicated that Weblog users "judged blogs as significantly more credible than other media."[52] All of this only pushes us into the penumbra of the thing that Bourdieu might place at the heart of this: the crucial (if difficult to access) issue of how ostensibly decreasing public trust in the media relates to media influence. Bourdieu suggested that it is our belief—our trust—in the speaker/media that makes it possible for the 'authority effect' to occur. This issue demands more direct consideration.

Symbolic Power and Specialization

Symbolic power is particularly noticeable in the case of specialized discourses, as when scientists communicate with each other and with a broader audience. Bourdieu described a "theory effect" at work in science and other specialized discourses, where, "by expressing in a coherent and empirically valid discourse what was previously ignored…[scientific discourse] transforms the representation of the social world as well as…the social world itself" by "[rendering] possible practices that conform to this transformed representation."[53] The theory effect here is the specialized power to certify certain things as existing, be they the Higgs boson, global climate change, class struggle, or the rules of supply-side economics. To support this vision of the theory effect, Bourdieu approvingly cited Gunnar Myrdal's argument that terms from the field of economics "are always simultaneously descriptive and prescriptive."[54] Specialized discourses as one finds in science do not merely point to things in the world. They also assign roles to the producers of the discourse and the audience, and in a manner similar to that envisioned by framing theory, they set the terms by which reality itself can be judged.

Things get even more interesting when specialized discourses seep out past the always-porous boundaries of the specialist communities from which they originate. This is something that many sociological perspectives on knowledge and science tend to shrug off. The tremendous overlap in the tendencies of professionalization and the extension of the media in the 20th century have made it so that this kind of 'overflow' is far from uncommon. When the expert faces a non-expert audience, we find that specialized discourse resonates with this audience through the play of homologies, much like any other culture. Bourdieu observed that "when esoteric discourses are diffused outside the restricted field," they "undergo a kind of automatic universalization, ceasing to be merely the utterances of dominant or dominated agents within a specific field and becoming statements valid for all dominant or all dominated individuals."[55] Much of the nuance of intrafield rivalries is lost, but symbolic power in some form remains, as the lay audience for messages emanating from a specialist field can attend to the 'style' of a discourse for a sign of the discourse's status as authoritative.

When we speak of consuming culture in functional terms, we are only a short conceptual distance from Bourdieu's idea of 'capital.' He defines linguistic exchange as "a relation of communication between a sender and a receiver, based on enciphering and deciphering, and therefore on the implementation of a code or a generative competence."[56] The play of expertise in a public venue thus becomes an exchange where a code is created to offer authority, and the audience uses its skills to decipher it. The linguistic exchange, Bourdieu claimed, "is also an economic exchange which is established within a particular symbolic relation of power between a producer, endowed with a certain linguistic capital, and a consumer (or a market), and which is capable of procuring a certain material or symbolic profit."[57] This rather blunt application of an economic logic to communication may have its shortcomings, but it does lend itself well to the study of symbolic power and authority. Understood this way, messages can be thought of as something other than "signs to be understood and deciphered,"[58] as the Claude Shannon & Warren Weaver model would have it. Beyond this, messages function as "*signs of wealth*, intended to be evaluated and appreciated, and *signs of authority*, intended to be believed and obeyed."[59] The language of authority is formulated strategically to compel belief through displays that attest to the authority of the communicator.

Authority as Strategy

As we have seen, Bourdieu's ideas regarding authority and symbolic power grow out of a critique of linguistics and semiotics. The basic idea is that not all words and utterances are made the same, and not all speakers (or listeners) are granted identical competences. The language games we play are social, and thus power works its way into language. This power can be understood in terms of field, habitus, and capital. It makes a strong argument, and it orients our thought about communication, but it could be made more directly applicable.

One promising avenue for research concerning authority and communication involves the use of Bourdieu's idea of strategy. It is in terms of strategy that Bourdieu describes how authority comes to us in particular forms, as in the "always semi-conscious strategies" that make up the "game in which the conquest of cultural legitimacy and of the concomitant power of legitimate symbolic violence is at stake."[60] The term 'semi-conscious' is crucial here, for this model of strategic communication presumes that utterances are neither the outcome of totally conscious and rational calculation nor the result of deeply felt unconscious rules. The strategy, in Bourdieu's terms, "is the product of the practical sense as the feel for the game, for a particular, historically determined game."[61] It is this feel for the game that explains how communication could be strategic. One can envision strategic bids for authority via communication as deriving neither from chaos (no rules) nor from predetermined rules.

But simply to posit a 'feel for the game' is to say something rather vague about why communication takes the shape that it does. A slightly more detailed understanding can be achieved if it is further stipulated, as Bourdieu would have it, that the game is played on a field. As with other fields described in this book, "the individuals who participate in these struggles will have differing aims—some will seek to preserve the status quo, others to change it—and differing chances of winning or losing, depending on where they are located in the structured space of positions."[62] From these interlocking different positions come the strategies that individuals will use.

Michel Foucault's focus on "discursive regimes"[63] offers another way to regard the job of prying open the work of authority that we find being carried out in strategies. Foucault considers the "field of strategic possibilities"[64] that is reminiscent of the Bourdieusian use of the terms 'field' and 'strategy,' though Foucault did not go beyond the discourse by attempting to explain it through comparison with the institutional and social framework from which it springs, a position that Bourdieu has criticized.[65]

Communication scholars have also addressed the idea of authoritative strategies. Barbie Zelizer analyzes cultural authority at work in how journalists communicate to the public. She casts cultural authority as a kind of "effect on the communicators,"[66] as the journalists she looks at offer narratives that both establish their authority for an audience while also reminding each other what journalism is. David Eason traces the authority at work in journalism through a tale of its unraveling, the Janet Cooke scandal.[67] Through this story, Eason shows how the evolution of journalism in the 20th century involved "establishing, repairing and transforming the authoritative base for accounts of 'the way it is.'"[68] Rather more broadly, the focus on strategies at work in communication can be found throughout much research conducted in the subfield of political communication. Whether or not Bourdieu is explicitly invoked in this research, there is still a familiar concern for the interests at work in message construction. The study of authoritative strategies is thus not completely new to the field of communication.

Authoritative strategies come from specific actors, and are aimed at specific audiences. Bourdieu asserted that

> all verbal expressions…are marked by their conditions of reception and owe some of their properties…to the fact that…their authors…try to maximize the symbolic profit they can obtain from practices which are, inseparably, oriented towards communication and exposed to evaluation.[69]

The strategic practice of trying to 'maximize profit' (in many ways parallel to Goffman's description of 'face' as a kind of commodity in conversation) can be traced to the workings of the field of production. To find the reason why authority looks like it does means to come to an understanding about the structures that shape how the stakes of the game are defined.

The communicator's anticipation of symbolic profits occurs on a semi-conscious level, by which Bourdieu meant that communicators do this "most often unwittingly, and without seeking to do so."[70] It comes naturally, as it were, and derives its power from the misrecognition of this process as natural. It is the fact that all of this is taken more or less for granted that makes it a relatively seamless ritual act. In a well-executed act of authority, the audience is anticipated but not necessarily reflected upon.

The strategies we associate with authority can be thought of in terms of how they are restricted. Bourdieu dedicated great attention to "censorship" and to "self-censorship," using these terms to refer to "a general feature of markets or fields which requires that, if one wishes to produce discourse successfully within a particular field, one must observe the forms and formalities of that field."[71] The field does not adjust (much) to the individual; the individual, through internalized anticipation of the structure of the field (i.e., the working of the habitus), develops a sense of how to filter expression through the imposition of form. Bourdieu describes this as "euphemism," and asserts that "[d]iscourses are always to some extent euphemisms inspired by the concern to 'speak well,' to 'speak properly.'"[72] The goal (again: internalized, semi-conscious, strategic) is to create messages that "respond to the demands of a certain market," and in pursuit of this, the communicator engages in "compromise formations resulting from a transaction between the expressive interest (what is to be said) and the censorship inherent in particular relations of linguistic production."[73] In this sense, self-censorship becomes the negative space of symbolic power, a dark matter shaping what can be said if authority is to be maintained. This "*dialectical* relation which is established between the expressive interest and censorship" underlies all symbolic production, and I think it plays a major role in communicating authority.[74]

The observation of censorship is what leads an audience to take the message seriously, to consider the message in the glow of legitimacy. Bourdieu stipulated that "[c]ensorship…determines the form of reception," in that to produce a euphemized, formalized unit of discourse is to "produce a product which demands to be received with due formality, that is, with due respect for the forms it has adopted or, as we see in literature, *for its nature as form*."[75] He placed great emphasis on the audience's perception of the artifact. Here, the "imposition of form" gives to the audience an "illusion of the autonomy of the system,"[76] a sense that this utterance is something that is underwritten by legitimacy.

This last point regarding the imposition of form as it relates to legitimacy can certainly be applied to all kinds of media contexts. The imposition of classic journalistic form—inverted-pyramid style, a careful use of quotations, even the font and presentational styles of print—is an excellent example of how the censorship involved in the imposition of form leads an audience to take a message as legitimate. Parallel modes of implied legitimacy can be found attached to all kinds of authoritative-seeming cultural phenomena. Documentary films have a long tradition of pared-down modes of presentation that are very much like the imposition of form that Bourdieu described. When scientists write for lay audiences, their use of scientific terms becomes a way to lead their audience to attend to the observance of form that lends authoritative warrant. To understand the assertions of legitimacy that underlie broad swaths of our culture, an attention to this kind of imposition of form strikes me as necessary.

The idea of looking at authority as a strategy seems vague at first, and certainly Bourdieu was often content to allow it to remain rather general, given his interest in showing how authority plays by many of the same rules as all other social practice. On top of this pervasive vagueness, such strategies—semi-conscious, sometimes silent, functional-because-unremarked—are difficult to notice. As in any other game, the stakes derive much of their power from the fact that they need not be explicitly acknowledged to be effective. Indeed, their power derives from their subtle insinuation into social life and their being misrecognized as natural distinctions. Bourdieu located authority in the relation between the words that are spoken and the space in the social topology that these words point to. The language itself communicates where the speaker is coming from, and the use of specific types of language constitutes a claim to the authority that comes from that authoritative space. Bourdieu's idea of the strategy compels us to attend to how legitimacy depends on silence, and to get beyond that silence. The attempt to describe the meaning of silence is of course difficult terrain. It requires a mapping of the social space at work in the communication of authority, and a sense of the dialectic at work between censorship and expression.

Bourdieu's idea that a would-be authority experiences difficulty communicating with a heterogeneous audience provides an important jumping off point for the study of the media. After all, the mass media—here I am thinking in particular of Carey's 'centripetal' media (see above)—are characterized by their large, heterogeneous audiences. Certainly Bourdieu had face-to-face interaction in mind when he described this problem. When carried over to the mass media, the issue of audience heterogeneity becomes not so much a problem as a fascinating study in what authority should look like. The strategic consideration of 'relative positions of sender and receiver,' I argue, still happens in the cases of authorities communicating via the mass media. The situation leads the communicator to adopt strategies that are even more formal (which is not to say formalized), more informed by the censorship side of the censorship-expression dialectic. The job of the communication researcher would be to find examples and develop a sense of how these censorships come to be, and how they are programmed into authoritative appeals. Digital media more in line with Carey's 'centifugal' media may provide opportunities for a differently shaped censorship-expression relationship, so that authorities who communicate via blogs may come to be valued by more homogeneous audiences and thus be less susceptible to censorship pressures. This may lend itself to different strategies for asserting authority, an issue I have addressed in the context of political bloggers in the early 2000s.[77] However, the issue is complicated by the fact that these centripetal and centrifugal media coexist and overlap with each other. Certainly, authoritative strategies must be adjusted to the medium that is used, and the overlapping worlds of different media no doubt create a tangle of censorship and expressive forces at play. Bourdieu offered little in the way of consideration of the role played by different media; there is every reason for communication researchers to address this gap.

The Break and the Double-Break in the Media

Let us return to Gouldner's assertion that it is 'reports' endowed with legitimacy—and not commands—that hold sway in contemporary society. Alongside massive changes in the media of communication, the expansion of professions dedicated to supplying these reports has made it so that there is no shortage of the kinds of reports Gouldner identified. It is a very common thing to encounter messages in the media that come from communicators claiming to be some kind of authority or another.

Communicators who stake claim to authority via messages in the media inhabit a world of conflicting pressures, many of which they do not necessarily acknowledge in any explicit way. First, they find themselves in a situation where it is clearly in their best interest to refer to whatever it is that separates them from the audience. Clearly, this is something that is best accomplished tacitly, or at least implicitly. That is, they need to find a way to say something to the effect of: 'I know this and you do not. I am a member of a certain elite group, and this group is particularly well-suited to whatever it is I am saying. Those who do not share my position (including you, the audience) could benefit from understanding what an authoritative figure such I have to offer.' This kind of statement is rarely made explicit, because it cues the very things that need to be kept in the background for the social magic to work. I refer to this move as a 'break,' an establishment of difference from an audience, a cleavage from the popular.

Beyond showing some kind of distance from a lay audience, the authority also often writes the audience into their authority by showing that the authority and the audience are really part of the same entity, or at least by showing that the two parties share the same interests, and that the authority is truly acting as a proxy for the audience. In this sense, it is also in the interest of the authority to efface some of the differences between themselves and the audience. Both the erection of the symbolic divide (the break) and the effacement of that same divide (establishing commonality) can occur at the same time. It can be thought of as what Bourdieu called a 'double-break,' as when first establishing a difference from an audience through appeals to one's own authority *while also establishing* a difference from other authorities through assertions of commonalities with an audience. It is this extra move to establish commonality that becomes an important component of the double-break.

This ambivalence at the root of authoritative appeals, the need simultaneously to claim and efface one's identification with an authoritative group, indicates a concern for the public, one that is very much in keeping with the language of censorship and concern for the audience that Bourdieu laid out. It gets to the heart of what Bourdieu described as 'symbolic violence,' wherein symbolic power is accepted by the audience, who become enlisted in the process of submitting to an authority. Symbolic violence is a "domination exerted in the name of a symbolic principle known and recognized both by the dominant and by the dominated."[78] If the audience is to be enlisted into this exertion of symbolic violence via the media, the 'break' between the authority and the audience often must be concealed. Bourdieu shed some light on this issue when he described how "the 'people'…is first of all one of the things at stake in the struggle between intellectuals," and how "the stances adopted towards the 'people' or the 'popular' depend in their form and content on specific interests linked first and foremost to belonging to a cultural field of production and, secondly, to the position occupied within this field."[79]

I would add that this concern for the people, which is always a major concern in intellectual conflicts, is of particular importance when those who stake claim to authority address a relatively large and heterogeneous audience.[80] Because they are addressing those who lack the expertise they have, and because this impels them to highlight their differences from their audience, the need to show some kind of solidarity via appeals to 'the people' becomes all the more urgent.

Bourdieu described the "double-break" as this move to incorporate "the people" into a public stance.[81] When an authority aligns with the people, there is simultaneously a break with the people—the 'break' I established at the beginning of this section—and, additionally, a break with the authoritative, through a contrast with other authorities' ostensible lack of contact with the people. Bourdieu remarked that "the denunciation of professional routine," as one often finds in the work of authorities appealing to a public, can be taken as "official proof of one's charismatic qualifications."[82] By deploying a suspicion that experts and authorities are, by their nature, out of touch with certain essential questions of value by dint of their identification with a legitimating institution, the professional aura can be cast as a stigma, marking a failure to address truly important questions, or to represent the people's interests.

The idea of the break—the difference between authority and audience—lends itself to analysis of all the bits of cultural capital that are deployed strategically to highlight the communicator's difference from the audience. Here the situation is metaphorically similar to the place of the holder of the skeptron. What is it that tacitly addresses the concern that this person should be the *correct* person to say these things, to compel our silence regarding issues of ritual appropriateness of the speaker? Bourdieu held that language does much of this work. The words communicators use function precisely because they classify those who use them as appropriate (or not). Beyond this, following Bruce Lincoln, there is the raft of other issues to be considered, each of which could be aligned strategically with the goals of the would-be authority: the medium that is employed, the media outlet that is used, the placement within the media outlet (Next to classified ads? Or on the front page? At 3 am on public access? From a Twitter account with only ten followers?), the voice of the communicator, the bodily hexis of the communicator, and more. Field theory demands not just a consideration of these strategies, but a consideration of how they relate to each other, where they overlap, and where they conflict. The field of strategies available would not be evenly distributed in any field of authority.

The double-break is of particular relevance to the mass media, largely because media with large audiences will influence the would-be authority to pursue strategies of concealment of any break with the audience. On a structural level, many media lend themselves to double-break appeals. This was quite certainly the case with the bloggers of the early 2000s I have studied, where repeatedly the bloggers returned to the idea that they were ordinary people, unlike the journalists and media celebrities whose authority they contrasted with their own home-grown approach.[83] It was no less the case with the psychoanalysts who wrote for the popular media in the 1940s and 1950s, who positioned themselves as authoritative in large part because they opposed the then-dominant psychiatric approaches, thus lending their own authority the glow of heterodoxy.[84] In both cases, the double-break was employed as a way to bootstrap authority against a field of other commentators accepted as authorities. As with the appeal of the single-break, the double-break can be best understood using the field perspective, understanding the other competing appeals at work, and putting them into conversation with each other. The result of this kind of field-based analysis would be to understand not just that different authoritative strategies exist and can be cataloged, but to develop a careful understanding of how social structures relate to authoritative bids. And that is no mean feat.

Media and Authority

Consideration of strategies, including breaks and double-breaks, helps to focus our attention on how messages are constructed in an effort to assert legitimacy. Scientists want to seem 'science-y'; journalists want to come off as 'journalist-y'[85]; poets want to seem poetic. An even more media-centered approach to Bourdieu's ideas would pay particular attention to how authority and legitimacy relate to something more than linguistic strategies. Authority in the media is a topic that lends itself to a rather dramatic extension of Bourdieu's ideas. In short: much as language can function to mark a discourse as legitimate (or fail to do so), media processes can do much the same thing.

One way to extend Bourdieu's ideas to the study of the media involves lingering on the idea of the 'break,' as described above. Authority stems in many cases from the subtle assertion of some kind of difference between communicator and audience, some sense that the communicator is the right person to address the situation at hand. The idea of the authoritative break can be seen at work in the kinds of separation between communicator and audience in mass communication.

Marshall McLuhan's ideas relating to the printed word are relevant here. McLuhan describes at length how print rearranged social roles. In *The Gutenberg Galaxy*, one of his main points is that typography created a divide between the author and the audience. In a discussion of Machiavelli's ideas as they related to the medium of print, McLuhan surmises that the "effect and meaning of the printed word" was to "[separate] writer and reader, producer and consumer, ruler and ruled, into sharply defined categories."[86] McLuhan explains this through reference to oral communication. With print, there emerges a division of labor, with the new roles of publisher, editor, author/reporter/writer, and audience member. Through the workings of gatekeeping, the audience member occupies a position quite remote from that of the communicator/author. With print, authors became relatively far-off individuals, separated from the audience by space, time, and social position. The same kind of separation of communicator and audience member can be found at work in broadcast media as well; television and radio are classically seen as exemplars of properly 'mediated' communication, with a relatively high degree of separation between the producer of a message and the audience member.

It is not difficult to put this language into something like Bourdieu's ideas regarding authority. First, the separation at work in all of these media between message producers and audience members structures the experience of these media so that there is a break at work between those who create the messages and those who receive them. There is much reason to believe that this simple break has a meaning to authority that Bourdieu did not take fully into account. Beyond this, what is implied by this separation at work in media from print through broadcast is that, in a manner parallel with Bourdieu's discussion of the distribution of access to legitimate language, there is an unequal distribution of access to these media. This unequal distribution underwrites the idea that to be included in programming in these media is to have some kind of symbolic authority.

To theorize the kind of authority that falls to those who come to us via tv, radio, and print is to cue one of the most enduring ideas in media research. Paul F. Lazarsfeld and Robert K. Merton famously proposed the idea that the media confer status on those who are included in their programming. The "mass media," explained Lazarsfeld and Merton, "bestow prestige and enhance the authority of individuals and groups by *legitimizing their status*." Inclusion in mass media programming "testifies that one has arrived, that one is important enough to have been singled out from the large anonymous masses, that one's behavior and opinions are significant enough to require public notice."[87] In the language of Bourdieu, inclusion in the mass media is a kind of symbolic capital, a rare commodity associated with its own ritual observance of importance. Importance is not the same thing as legitimacy, but this idea has tremendous overlap with my broader point regarding media and authority.

Susan Herbst updates and adjusts Lazarsfeld and Merton, arguing that "[a]uthority has a much bigger punch than status conferral, and is decidedly political."[88] She suggests that we adopt the concept of "media-derived authority" to understand the "legitimation one receives through mediated channels."[89] Herbst gets right to what many sociologists miss about communication: its capacity to blur distinctions. As Herbst notes, "the media are not a bounded institution, and this is what makes their influence so profound: They are, for better or worse, the very fabric of the public sphere itself."[90] She outlines four dimensions of this media-derived authority, described here with reference to "individual, organization, or institution X":

A. Volume: X receives high volume of coverage relative to others;
B. Tone: X receives, on balance, decidedly deferential attention of journalists and media gatekeepers, relative to others (e.g., has longer sound bites, or has his or her language/issue frames accepted or valorized);
C. Public Opinion Signal: There are implicit or explicit assumptions that X either represents or can move public opinion;
D. Reasoned Elaboration: X is portrayed as having the capacity to provide logic and persuasive evidence, should that be necessary.[91]

Herbst attempts to deal with how the issue of authority spills out of field-based models, or institution-centered understandings. Each provides a way to consider symbolic power as something that relates relatively directly to the media, in a manner that is relatively independent from other ways for symbolic power to be generated. The media are a "meta-institution,"[92] as Herbst has it.

In his gloss of Bourdieu's arguments in *On Television*, Rodney Benson outlines something very similar to this with his discussion of how "media power is ultimately the power to 'consecrate,' that is, name an event, person, or idea as worthy of consideration."[93] As with Bourdieu's oft-mentioned economic of symbolic goods, it is "[o]nly a handful" that "are picked up by the entire press and attract widespread public attention."[94] Because television has "greater credibility and far larger audiences than the old popular press," it can "bring powerful and 'legitimate' commercial pressure into the heart of the journalistic field and thus pull the entire media field away from the intellectual pole toward the commercial pole."[95]

It becomes apparent in these attempts to apply Bourdieu's ideas regarding symbolic power to the situation of the media that Bourdieu's field theory seems often to point outside of itself. After all, field theory was developed to explain the inter-relationships within fields, and to some extent between fields (though, as we have seen Bourdieu himself seems much more familiar with the former than the latter). This concern for the working of fields can be a poor match for the situation of the media, where messages are less likely to be constrained by circulation within one field. Though produced within a field of journalistic production, a national news broadcast is consumed by millions who are not within that field, and the symbolic power Bourdieu described at work in journalism was something that derived power precisely from its tendency to define reality well beyond the confines of the field of production from which it oriented.

Nick Couldry seizes on this way that field theory seems to stumble on the issue of the media, where media producers are not the boss of the audience, where it is the report and not the command that carries the day. Couldry calls our attention to the mismatch between the hegemony-style arguments that Bourdieu offers in his discussions of symbolic power, and shows how these do not map onto field-based accounts, "because many or most of those over whom hegemony is assumed to be exercised are not members of the fields in question."[96] Couldry concludes that if field-based accounts of media "are to sustain the bold claims [Bourdieu made] about the media's broader 'symbolic power,'" they are "irrevocably pushed towards a type of explanation that spills out beyond the field model."[97] Put differently, "the concept of symbolic systems…implies an explanatory framework that *cuts across* field theory," because "a 'symbolic system' is a structure of misrecognition that works precisely because of its pervasiveness across social space, on account of its totalizing force."[98]

To connect the field-based and extra-field concerns of symbolic power, Couldry takes a cue from Bourdieu's own treatment of the state, and its "preeminence over the definitions, for example, of legal and educational status."[99] This makes the "'field of power' of which the state is the central reference-point…not therefore…a 'field' in Bourdieu's normal sense." Instead, "it is better understood as a general space where the state exercises influence (very much like a general symbolic power) over the *interrelations* between all specific fields (in the usual sense), indeed, perhaps acts upon social space in general."[100] These inter-relations indicate that the state wields a kind of meta-capital that cuts across different fields.

What is true for the state here may be just as applicable to the media. Couldry argues the media have great potential for offering meta-capital to all kinds of other fields. After all, "[a]ll actors in specific fields are likely also to be actors in general social space and general consumers of media messages."[101] The meta-capital associated with the media can act "by influencing what counts as capital in each field," or "through the media's legitimation of influential representations of, and categories for understanding, the social world that, *because of their generality*, are available to be taken up in the specific conflicts in *any* particular field."[102]

With good reason, Couldry focuses most intently on the first of these two functions of media meta-capital, whereby the media "[alter] what counts as symbolic capital in particular fields through [their] increasing monopoly over the sites of social prestige."[103] Imagine a hypothetical case where "media-based symbolic capital developed in one field can under certain conditions be directly exchanged for symbolic capital in another field."[104] Couldry suggests the example of a "well-known television gardener [who] has quickly become a successful popular novelist,"[105] but other examples of parlaying success in one field into another via media exposure can be imagined. Media exposure itself becomes a kind of symbolic capital that can be converted—at different rates, of course—across different fields.

A broader implication of this idea, and one that Couldry notices, "is that in contemporary, highly centralized societies certain institutions have a specific ability to influence all fields at once."[106] Seen this way, we have the strong link between field theory and Bourdieu's other work on symbolic power, for we see that "what is at stake at the level of meta-capital is precisely the type of definitional power across the whole of social space that the latter concepts [those pertaining to symbolic power] capture."[107]

At the heart of all of this is a basic idea that media appearances create a divide between the communicator and the audience. Certainly Lazarsfeld and Merton called our attention to the symbolic importance that is assigned to being included in an element of mass media programming. To have one's name in the paper, to be on television or radio, is to take one's place in a kind of exclusive company. In and of itself, mere inclusion does not constitute symbolic power or authority; Herbst is quite clear on that. But the most fundamental elements of this are reminiscent of Bourdieu's ideas concerning language. As with legitimate language, being included in mass media programming is not equally distributed, and it is associated with legitimacy. Beyond this, different media, and different media outlets, are associated with different kinds of legitimacy. For this reason, I suggest that a model of incorporating Bourdieu's ideas regarding symbolic power take these differences into account. The capital at work in Bourdieu's theory of symbolic power is predominantly considered as a kind of linguistic capital. But there are other forms of capital at work. After all, people do not appear in 'the media.' They say certain things, appearing in specific media programs, carried by specific media outlets, via specific media of communication. The logic of Bourdieu's capital plays out on every one of these levels. They are not all separate fields, necessarily, but a field logic of mutual opposition/alignment plays out on each of these dimensions.

As an example, imagine the case of an expert on international politics appearing on a cable news network's evening analysis program. The symbolic power at work has a number of components, including (but not limited to): the words uttered by this expert, the position of the program in the field of other news programming, the position of the network vis-à-vis other networks, and the position of the medium itself. We might be inclined to consider the medium-level of this not to matter, but this strikes me as incorrect. After all, AM radio, broadcast television, and print journalism each occupies a specific range in the matrix of culture. Bourdieu himself attended to differences between more and less legitimate-seeming media in his *Photography: A Middle-Brow Art.* The symbolic power at work in the media can be extended to take account of all these things in light of Bourdieu's field theory.

New media may reshuffle some of this in ways that change the mediated conditions of staking authority. We certainly find no shortage of speculation regarding how online venues will change—or have already changed—this separation of communicator and audience member. New media are often thought to afford a certain degree of disintermediation, the removal of separation between communicator and audience. One of the more widely cited ideas concerning this online blending of the roles of communicator and audience member is Axel Bruns' idea of "produsage." Bruns asserts that, with new media, individuals are becoming "much more actively involved in shaping their own media and network usage."[108] New online tools, with affordances that lead to greater potential for sharing all kinds of intellectual tasks, create a situation where McLuhan's divided world of print no longer obtains.

Bruns' case for a new world of produsage is laid out in terms that link up clearly with McLuhan's ideas. Bruns notes that, in "an industrial model of content production," boundaries concerning participation in media processes were "clear-cut…: only industrial producers and, to a more limited extent, distributors were directly involved in production processes, while audiences were cast simply in the role of consumers."[109] In the new—online—era of produsage, we have a new model for "collective content creation," which involves four meaningful affordances. The first of these is the affordance for "[p]robabilistic, not directed problem-solving,"[110] where individual users coordinate to solve problems without commands from on high. The second affordance is the replacement of "hierarchy" with "equipotentiality."[111] The third affordance is for "[g]ranular, not composite tasks," and the fourth supports "[s]hared, not owned content."[112] Building from some of the same starting points that Bruns used, Mathieu O'Neil has gone so far as to suggest a typology of "regimes on online authority," designed to account for the new appeals to authority found frequently in online communication.[113] A strict application of the democratic myth of the internet would tell us that the internet is a site where authority has a reduced role, and where the kinds of exclusion that Bourdieu described at work in symbolic power would not pertain. The model of media praxis that comes out of these musings on new media is one that emphasizes disinter-mediation, cooperation, and a blurring of the once-stable divide between producer and consumer/audience member. In some important ways, this is the undoing of much of what McLuhan described as the typographical world.

With all of this in mind, what becomes of authority if, as Bruns and others suggest, the divide between author/producer and audience member becomes less meaningful? Without the divide, the 'break,' between producer/author and au-dience member, what becomes of authority? Bruns offers an important line of thought concerning online authority. If produsage does indeed characterize a sig-nificant amount of online communication (and there is much reason to doubt that it does, so far), I suggest that the authority we associate with media commen-tary—how arguments relevant to the public will be asserted—may be adjusted. It is not difficult to envision that the 'break' between author/producer and audience member may break down. This does seem to be what Bruns anticipates when he describes the coming "transformation of an expert/non-expert or professional/amateur dichotomy into a smooth continuum connecting both ends."[114] In such a situation, we might expect to see an adjustment along both ends of the con-tinuum: the former 'expert' part may be more inclined to voice arguments not as separate from the audience, and the former 'audience' part may be more inclined to approach arguments as something they themselves have created. It is important to consider Matthew Hindman's idea of a "Googlearchy" with respect to this sit-uation. Hindman asserts that the Web supports "winners-take-all patterns"[115] in every niche of the Web, in some ways making the Web more like mass communi-cation than we often presume.

Conclusion

Bourdieu's understanding of authority does a better job of giving us something we can analyze than many other models of authority. Unlike many cultural or rhe-torical understandings of authority, Bourdieu's approach was designed to link up with institutions and other social structures. Social structure becomes a necessary component of any analysis of authority. Unlike some grand theoretical versions of authority, Bourdieu's ideas connect to Alvin Gouldner's suggestion that authority is wrought through 'reports' instead of 'commands'. The communication of legiti-macy is woven into the fine threads running through cultures and social structure, and the media have everything to do with this. Taking a cue from theorists of mediatization[116] who investigate the broad social implications of the role played by the media, we can observe how the emergence of mass media and digital media has linked up with important changes in how legitimacy is asserted, received, and observed. It is this ranginess of Bourdieu's concepts that is their strength. Instead of simply isolating one component of the process of asserting authority, Bourdieu would have us look at the field surrounding each dimension of the process. It is, admittedly, more easily theorized than investigated. The value of this approach can be found in its power to fit a process—legitimacy—that slips through the fingers of nomothetic research approaches.

One theme worth picking out for future research relates to the idea of the fragmented audience. As we have seen, Bourdieu's understanding of the media often divides them into the fields of limited and mass production. As with my earlier suggestion that the fragmentation of the media audience means that we should adjust some of Bourdieu's concerns for studying media production, the consideration of symbolic power in a media field that involves fragmented audiences may mean that we find a fragmentation of authority. Instead of an unevenly distributed, centralized regime of legitimate communication, we may find ourselves in a situation of unevenly distributed, *de*centralized regimes of legitimate communication. There is certainly evidence of the audience for journalism becoming more ideologically divided.[117] On a broader level, changes in how media are programmed and consumed can likely be tied to changes in the kinds of symbolic power we observe. Addressing the fragmentation of the television audience in terms of cultural authority, David Morrison observes that, "from the 1960s to the 1990s, watching television became less and less a public act in the sense of accessing a nationally common offering."[118] To chart the meaning of this change in terms of symbolic power requires a careful analysis of symbolic capital at work in these changing media conditions, and though Bourdieu himself did not directly address this situation, his analytical tools can help us to access just how legitimacy in the media may have shifted with the dramatic changes in the public-ness of media that we have seen in the relatively recent past.

I have made passing mention in this chapter of the idea that there is a sense some social institutions have suffered from losing some of their authority in the recent past. Journalism, for instance, is an institution thought to be in crisis as a result of a relatively low level of public trust; this will come as no surprise to communication scholars, who have been monitoring the many journalism crises for a long time. Scientists encounter major obstacles in their attempts to assert their vision of the world. National governments are widely regarded as facing deficits of legitimation, and this situation has not gone unnoticed. Popular U.S. journalist Chris Hayes' recent book documents an "evaporation of trust"[119] in institutions, especially the state. The recent wave of crises has led an exasperated Tony Judt to argue that "we need to learn to *think* the state again,"[120] a statement that seems to sum up some of the frustration many have had with the erosion of legitimacy in a number of spheres.

Even if all of these crises of legitimacy are merely illusory, they point out one seeming weakness of Bourdieu's model of symbolic power. Like a true Durkheimian, Bourdieu began with the question of what makes symbolic power work, and this draws his attention away from the issue of what happens when symbolic power fails. In his later, more polemic work, he was quite direct about the sources of the problems of legitimacy. He argued that intellectuals should "refrain from entering into complicity and collaboration with the forces which threaten to destroy the very bases of their existence and their freedom, in other words the forces of the market."[121] Market forces, he asserted, undermine the symbolic legitimacy of all that could stand in their way. However, this argument did not occupy much space in his writing on symbolic power. Just because he did not dedicate more attention to the question of the failure of these symbolic structures does not mean that we cannot do so using his ideas. Indeed, there is much to be hoped for in applying his ideas of symbolic capital and field-based analyses to the question of the failure of symbolic power. The crisis becomes a research question, one that is every bit as relevant to our own work as communication researchers (with our own legitimacy at stake) as it is to public life.

CHAPTER FIVE

Reflexivity and the History of the Field of Communication

Bourdieu is best known for his writings on education, cultural production, and symbolic power, as well as for his interventions in political discussions in France. In the field of communication, we often focus most intently on his work concerning cultural production and consumption. However, there is a strong case to be made for using his ideas to understand the history of the field itself. The Bourdieu of *Homo Academicus*, *Science of Science and Reflexivity*, and *An Invitation to Reflexive Sociology* finds him applying his familiar ideas of habitus, capital, and field to arenas of scholarly practice. This approach to the sociology of science has much to offer to those who study the history of the field of communication. Bourdieu's contributions to the sociology of science can help us understand: how the field of communication relates to other scholarly disciplines; how the field's multifarious development can be envisioned in ways that get us beyond a strictly linear narrative; how the field's history[1] relates to obstacles to further legitimation of the field; and how communication scholars can develop a collective reflexivity concerning the field and our shared place in academe.

This last issue—reflexivity—pertains to one of the most important contributions the field of communication can derive from Bourdieu's ideas. The goal of reflexivity is to tie our future endeavors to a well-grounded knowledge of the structural and historical elements at work in the configuration of the field. The feedback loop made possible by reflexivity can open up opportunities for new extensions of the field, as well as for a necessary critical perspective on the field itself. To use sociological ideas to structure the history of a field of inquiry is not much of a leap. There is increasing interaction between social theory and history, and the field of historical sociology is quite strong. Though some may object that history need not take up social theory to operate, there is much precedent for this blended approach, and there is much to be gained from employing social theory in our histories of the field. Bourdieu's ideas help to orient our approach to the history of the field, to explain why we would want to study this history, and to frame the issues at the heart of historical analysis. To take just one example, it is valuable to know the institutional power wielded by the Bureau of Applied Social Research at Columbia University in the 1940s if one wishes to understand why the field of communication has found itself linked to specific questions, research methods, and theories of media 'effects.' To understand the layout of the entire field will require still more historical analysis.

In the context of the field of communication, we see the stirrings of the development of a reflexive move, tied quite closely to the work done on history of the field. Karin Wahl-Jorgensen uses Bourdieu's ideas as a yardstick to judge the extent to which these disciplinary histories "represent a space for a reflexive turn in communication studies."[2] She ultimately finds that this reflexivity was not fully established in any of the histories she studied. She is not surprised by this, telling us that, in pursuit of reflexivity, "[w]e need to read competing histories; open up a dialogue about their meaning; and understand, appreciate, and critique their claims."[3] Jefferson Pooley describes the recent emergence of a "new" history of the field of communication in terms that are in some ways similar to Wahl-Jorgensen's. Pooley urges us to pursue the kinds of careful historiographies of other social science fields, and points out that the survival of a more folkloric sense of the field's past is a testament to the fact that "the discipline has needed all the faith it can muster."[4] An in-depth sociological and historical sense of the field of communication, such as would generate a reflexive understanding of the field, will require a willingness to get past founding myths, and to inquire honestly into the questions that connect the history of the field of communication to the world around it. Many of the attempts to chart a history of the field have functioned more as legitimation dreams than as solid history. The problem is not merely that these dreams make for bad history. Even worse, these stories of the field's founding mislead us, blinding us to avenues of potential intellectual engagement, and covering over threats to the field's well-being with their boosterism.

There is an irony in this boosterism. In a struggle to cast a legitimating glow on the field itself, the authors of these histories have undermined the goals of a more lasting legitimacy. If the goal is to create a field of inquiry that enjoys a better reputation, it would be prudent to develop histories of the field that are somewhat more probing, more in line with the 'reflexive turn' that Wahl-Jorgensen describes.

To Exoticize the Domestic: Studying Our Own World

Bourdieu told us that reflexivity would do more than provide a relativizing counterpoint to 'positivist' research. He hoped that reflexivity could be tied directly to research, and could refine how we pursue research. I argue that reflexivity is one of the most important contributions that an active history of the field of communication can provide, and that Bourdieu's understanding of reflexivity can be helpful in getting us to achieve this goal.

This reflexive move would require an attempt to make strange the everyday things that we do in the field. The point of the reflexive study of his own field of sociology, Bourdieu posited, should not be to "domesticate the exotic, but [to] exoticize the domestic, through a break with [one's] initial relation of intimacy with modes of life and thought which remain opaque to him because they are too familiar."[5] Bourdieu dedicated great effort to undoing what he calls the intellectualist fallacy in academic work, whereby practice is made out to be the result of a calculated, individualized, and explicit model being put into effect. His focus was almost always on the semi-conscious or unconscious components of practice. The unconscious component of scholarly work was the target for much of his sociology of sociology. The point in pursuing a reflexive understanding in scholarship is "seeking in the social structures of the academic world…the sources of the categories of professorial understanding,"[6] categories that often go unspoken, and derive much of their power from this silence.

This pursuit may seem relatively inert, given the lack of any ostensibly 'radical' programmatic. However, on second glance one can sense how such an inquiry may in fact point us toward some of the most contentious questions that we can face. Bourdieu addresses the discomfort—if not outright controversy—that occurs when someone has "revealed the rules of the mandarins' game."[7] There is a sense that a taboo has been revealed, an important censorship has been denied. This is reminiscent of Stephen Brush's consideration of whether or not the history of science should be rated X,[8] because writings in the history of science

> do violence to the professional ideal and public image of scientists as rational, open-minded investigators, proceeding methodically, grounded incontrovertibly in the outcome of controlled experiments, and seeking objectively for the truth, let the chips fall where they may.[9]

Bourdieu's suggestion that we understand the unconscious at work in science de-mands explicit consideration of that which has remained functional in large part because it has been submerged, and to upend the less rational, less open-minded, less methodical, less grounded dimensions of scientific work. His alignment of so-ciology with this kind of reflexivity led Bourdieu to speculate that sociology was "a form of thought detested by 'thinkers' because it gives access to knowledge of the determinations which bear on them and therefore on their thought."[10] A true em-phasis on reflexivity plunges the scholar into a controversial world where no one (least of all oneself) is safe from the determinations of field, habitus, and capital.

This kind of focus on the scientific unconscious will show us how the his-torical unconscious of the communication scholar is shaped by the workings of non-intellectual factors. It is rarely a flattering picture of the scholar. Contrast this with the situation in communication, where many of our histories of the field (to the extent that they exist) are "airbrushed and whiggish,"[11] in Jefferson Pooley's stirring invective, and consisting of little else besides "thin hagiography."[12] A better history of the field will require analytic tools that get us beyond this mire. Bour-dieu's ideas give us a solid sense of how we could carry out this work in a manner that avoids the numerous faults of earlier efforts.

It is the through application of a simultaneously historical and sociological ap-proach to a field that this reflexivity can be employed to uncover the unconscious at work in our field. This is the dark matter of scientific knowledge of all kinds: the tangle of motivations, assumptions, half-thoughts, inclinations, and more. Loïc Wacquant calls attention to how, in the Bourdieusian approach, "[w]hat has to be constantly scrutinized and *neutralized, in the very act of construction of the object*, is the collective scientific unconscious embedded in theories, problems, and (espe-cially national) categories of scholarly judgment."[13] Bourdieusian reflexivity differs from other approaches to reflexivity[14] in "three crucial ways":

> First, its primary target is not the individual analyst but the *social and intellectual un-conscious* embedded in analytic tools and operations; second, it must be a *collective enterprise* rather than the burden of the lone academic; and third, it seeks not to assault but to *buttress the epistemological security of sociology*.[15]

The primary focus on the social and intellectual unconscious, thought out largely in terms of Bourdieu's notion of habitus, is a crucial starting point. Bourdieu sug-gested that we consider the "thought collective which shares a body of knowledge and presuppositions about methodology, observation, acceptable hypotheses and the important problems."[16]

Bourdieu saw in reflexivity a project that was perfectly consistent with the goals of a careful science, ultimately in harmony with (and even necessary to) the goals of scientific sociology. He called reflexivity a *"requirement and form of socio-logical work*, that is, as an epistemological program in action for social science."[17] Instead of relativizing science, reflexivity represents an "effort whereby social science, taking itself for its object, uses its own weapons to understand and check itself" as a means to "[increase] the chances of attaining truth by increasing the cross-controls and providing the principles of a technical critique, which makes it possible to keep closer watch over the factors capable of biasing research."[18] This was Bourdieu's case for a more autonomous science, a science modeled in some ways on other autonomous fields he studied, wherein autonomy developed from the separation of the field from the temporal interests surrounding the field, to the extent that a kind of refinement could be effected.

The call for reflexivity as a collective enterprise intended to buttress epistemological security carries with it an important warning for those conducting histories of the field of communication. The reflexivity at play is meaningless if it is not shared with a broader community. The call of reflexivity should invite an entire field into its analyses, so as to allow for a field-wide reflexivity. Otherwise, histories of the field could become little more than opportunities to build effigies much as, for some time, they functioned largely as efforts to build totems. Properly conceived and executed, the reflexivity that Wahl-Jorgensen found lacking in communication will require tremendous effort, but the potential for grounding the field in enlightened self-knowledge makes it most inviting.

I outline several major avenues of consideration for applying Bourdieusian sociology of science to the history of the field of communication. Bourdieu's ideas can help us: to develop a sense of the field's difficult reputation, to consider the field in light of possible sources of autonomy, to better understand conflicts and divides in the field, to build on this understanding of conflict to develop a decentralized sense of the field's history, and to focus our energies on the individuals who make up the field—the embodied examples of the field's modes of perception and action.

On the Reputation and Autonomy of the Field

One reason that Bourdieu's vision can help us to address the history and sociology of the field of communication is that he focused so intently on issues that have already become central to the debates concerning our field's history. In particular, Bourdieu's theoretical armature can lead us to consider how the field's less-than-healthy academic reputation has been the outcome of particular social forces from inside and outside the field itself. The Bourdieusian focus on symbolic capital and autonomy—both of which play major roles in Bourdieu's science of science—makes Bourdieu a good fit for the issues facing historians of the field who wish to address the reputation of the field.

It is not difficult to find a concern for the field's reputation in considerations of the field's history. Many cite incoherence as a factor in the field's reputation. Addressing this incoherence, Jeremy Tunstall observes that "[t]he fact that a single individual can teach courses in, say magazine editing and research techniques in social psychology is a tribute to human adaptability, not to a well-conceived academic discipline."[19] In a similar vein, John Durham Peters argues that the fact that communication consists of "leftovers from earlier communication research married to dispossessed fields such as academic journalism, drama or speech"[20] leaves us in the position of a toothless hybrid. Robert McChesney finds that a once-gathering "dynamism" is now "extinguished," as "the field has settled into a second-tier role in U.S. academic life, and there is too little research that is distinguished."[21] Jefferson Pooley describes all of this in similar terms, asserting that "the same conditions that fill our lecture halls also guarantee the discipline's low-status obscurity."[22] Because "communication programs are in the business of vocational instruction first[,] academic analysis of the media is an often-resented, parasitic add-on."[23] In Pooley's vision, the "prestige gap opened up by our murky origins is wide enough that very little of our scholarship is much read outside the field."[24] For Pooley, as for Peters, Tunstall, and McChesney, the problem is that the circumstances of the field's history present obstacles to a more intellectually inclined—or autonomous—development.

Bourdieu's concern for symbolic capital is a good match for the reputational issues in the field of communication. Addressing the situation of the individual scientist, Bourdieu declares that "[s]ymbolic capital flows to symbolic capital," in that the "scientific field gives credit to those who already have it."[25] If this can be extended from the domain of the individual to that of the field, we can start to think of the place of communication in terms of how its limited symbolic capital has played out historically, trapping it in a corollary of this rule, in which a lack of symbolic capital tends to reinforce itself over time. Historical approaches that compare and contrast communication's founding and development with the origins of other fields seem likely to yield insights relevant to communication's relative lack of symbolic capital.

One of the signs of a well-established discipline is its power to command the terms by which it is perceived; communication's status as relative newcomer in the field of the social sciences tends to cost the field some legitimacy. Bourdieu described how one of the "main pillars of the older order" is always "ignorance, or, in other words, faith: vagueness has its social function and, as we see with clubs, or with salons in a previous age, the most unimpeachable criteria are those which are the least definable."[26] It is the newer formations whose constituent members experience the need to justify their own existence, to establish themselves. And, as Bourdieu explained, the fact that the question of legitimacy is even raised is an indication of a legitimacy shortage. The vagueness that tacitly protects more established fields in the U.S. (here I am thinking of the natural sciences, but also of economics, sociology, English, and philosophy) is not available to communication. Other social sciences may not be much more than fifty years older than Communication, but that seems to be enough of a difference to allow their origins to have receded into misty half-memory and the dustier sections of the library basement.

Measuring the symbolic capital of a specific field is no easy thing. In part this is because the would-be measures are themselves loaded; these indices are implicated in specific value formations that derive from interested points of view. As Bourdieu put it, "the problems of power and of the principles defining and hierarchizing power, are problems which are already inherently formulated in *the object itself*."[27] There is no easy way simply to step back and find a measure that takes into account all that goes into a field's symbolic power. The preferable option is to take the loaded-ness of the measures—be they citation measures, indications of the power to raise research funds, representation in trans-academic powers—into account from the outset, and write histories from this removed point of view.

As with his other applications of the field as a mode of analysis, Bourdieu's use of the field in the context of the sociology of science often lacked a fuller sense of interfield relationships. This lacuna is even more obvious given Bourdieu's acknowledgment that forces inside and outside the operation of a field are at work in shaping a field's symbolic power. For instance, Bourdieu noted that a description of "the evolution of the symbolic power relationships within the university field" would require a sense of "the processes which led to the weakening of its autonomy and to the growth of the power of external instances of consecration," as one finds with "cultural journalism."[28] This means that the power for communication to amass symbolic capital is shaped in some way by how forces within and outside academe treat the field. Here the field may find itself doubly damned: first in a competition within academia where competing fields often possess the established grounds for legitimation, second, as we find academia's ability to legitimate itself threatened external instances of consecration, we also find other fields outdoing us on what we say is our own turf, as communication scholars occupy relatively little space in journalism as media commentators.

Given Bourdieu's outline for how to approach this kind of thing, the job of turning this into fodder for a history of the field would involve setting up some way to measure symbolic capital, given that there is no neutral measurement one might take. Instead, the history of the field's prestige must involve conceptualizing the variables that can be related to the field's capital, including: research funds, establishment at prestigious universities, links to academic administration, students enrolled in the field, media coverage of the field, journals associated with the field, cross-field citation patterns, and more. Beyond this, little could be established if the field is not put into the context of other academic disciplines. For this reason, cross-disciplinary histories are particularly helpful for understanding the history of the field. Such histories would allow us to understand the meaning of the field's relative absence from the Ivy League universities, the degree to which the field is associated with vocational training, and how university deans and other administrators understand the place of the field.

Concerns related to symbolic capital and symbolic power merely point indirectly in the direction of institutional sources of the field's place in the world. Bourdieu's understanding of the role of autonomy gets us closer to the issue of how the institutional history of communication relates to its position in academe. As with his focus on the fields of art and literature, Bourdieu's interest in the science of science was shaped profoundly by his belief in the importance of autonomy. Autonomy was certainly something he desired for sociology, as can be detected in his declaration that it is only by asserting its autonomy that sociology "will acquire rigorous instruments and thus gain political relevance and potency."[29] The more autonomous field is one in which the forces at work within the structure of the field are "relatively independent of the forces exerted on the field (pressure). It has, as it were, the 'freedom' it needs to develop its own necessity, its own logic, its own *nomos*."[30] *Nomos* here represents a field of reference, a mode of world-construction. Thus, for a field to be relatively autonomous, it must have the power to construct its own vision of the world, and not to have this vision imposed upon it.

If autonomy is the goal, there are numerous obstacles to this goal at work in the social sciences. One difficulty stems from the need for social sciences to "[break] decisively with common sense," which means that "there are always people who, being scientifically dominated, are spontaneously on the side of the preconstructed,…and thus in trying to bring everybody back to the starting line."[31] The social sciences' shared proximity to common sense concerns (far less evident in a field like neuroscience) makes them vulnerable to operators inside and outside the field who would dissolve the grounds for an autonomously derived *nomos*. Beyond this, the fields in the social sciences are relatively weak because, within them, "the most heteronomous researchers and their 'endoxic' truths, as Aristotle put it, have, by definition, more chance of winning social recognition against autonomous researchers."[32] This would seem to be particularly true for communication, which has staked out so much territory adjoining the world of the common sense. Ronald D. Jacobs and Eleanor Townsley make it quite clear how, in the context of public affairs programming, "humanities and social science compete with pundits and think tankers to define questions of broad social and cultural meaning."[33] The field's chosen domains—from interpersonal communication to popular culture to advertising and beyond—frequently make it so that there is a relatively greater tendency for heteronomous researchers to win recognition.

These obstacles to autonomy seem particularly daunting for a field as wide-reaching as communication, where it is difficult to describe any functioning centralized *nomos* at work. Some of Bourdieu's most dramatic language concerns this sense that the social sciences' flexibility makes them relatively easy on those who would play turncoat and side with 'the enemy.' In the social sciences (and other fields where there is less autonomy), "those who are scientifically most dominated are those most inclined to submit to external demands, whether from the right or from the left."[34] It is the fields that enjoy the least autonomy where one finds temptations to violate the *nomos* of the field in pursuit of money, recognition from outside academe, or applied research that is carried out for for-profit concerns. This submission to external demands that tempts those in less autonomous fields is what Bourdieu called "the law of Zhdanovism," whereby "[c]onsiderable freedom is allowed, within the field itself, to those who contradict the very *nomos* of the field and who are protected against the symbolic sanctions which, in other fields, strike those who fall short of the fundamental principles of the field."[35] In an even more downcast tone, Bourdieu warned that "the logic of competition" in a field where Zhdanovism can find purchase may "combine and conjugate with more or less constrained or willing submission to the interests of firms to let whole areas of research drift little by little in the direction of heteronomy."[36] The benefit of autonomy is that "*recognized scientific authority protects you from the temptation of heteronomy.*"[37] When a field lacks autonomy, it provides little reason to accumulate—or 'invest in'—its own native capital.

What is a historian of the field to make of this? This concern for autonomy and heteronomy impels the historian of the field to focus on the space of disciplines, because a "discipline is defined not only by intrinsic properties, but also by properties it owes to its position in the (hierarchized) space of disciplines."[38] If we are to think relationally when we think with Bourdieu, it is communication's relative place in the field of academic work that should be considered. One primary consideration relates to what Bourdieu identified as "two principles of differentiation/hierarchization among disciplines, the temporal principle and the strictly scientific principle."[39] One thing for historians of the field to consider would be how communication has been connected to the "field of power," and the story of the field of communication should be told with a focus on, amongst other things, how communication has related to "scientific 'blue-ribbon' panels, expert reports, and especially on the large philanthropic foundations and institutes of policy research that play a crucial, albeit largely hidden, role in defining the broader directions of research."[40] The quite open question for historians of the field would simply be: to what extent has the field been characterized as one that aligns with the temporal interests (those aligned with capital and with political power) versus an alignment with the strictly scientific focus on matters that arise from within the body of the field? Beyond this: How have these two impulses found power in institutions in the field? And to what extent can the history of the field be told in terms of these two opposing tendencies? Some important historical work has already teased out some of the subtler meanings of the conflicts between the 'administrative' and 'critical' factions in the early days of communication research, but there is much more to do to provide historical perspective for this ongoing struggle.

It is difficult to imagine a better model for the kind of relational history of the social sciences than the work of Andrew Abbott. Abbott's argument in *Chaos of Disciplines* that "the cultural life of the social sciences evolves through an unfolding series of fractal distinctions"[41] calls attention to the divides at work in the social sciences, with an uncommon attention to the rhetorical and material grounds for these distinctions. This sets a high bar for the history of any field, but there are numerous works that address the history of the study of communication with something closely resembling this concern for the inter-relations of different fields. William J. Buxton has documented many of the interstitial tensions made apparent in the context of John Marshall's yeoman labors in the Humanities Division of the Rockefeller Foundation. Buxton shows how Marshall managed interfield, inter-institutional, and inter-continental dynamics in his careful work to push the Humanities Division toward "cross-fertilized traditions" that could be found in the legacy of a number of cultural and research institutions after World War II.[42] Brett Gary's *The Nervous Liberals* tells much the same story, with a greater emphasis on the political context and a broader purview. Gary's narrative is a model of how we can appreciate Abbott's 'fractal distinctions' at work in much of the formative scholarship that helped create what we recognize as the field of communication, including the Rockefeller Foundation's work, in Harold D. Lasswell's pioneering research on propaganda, and more.[43] Willard D. Rowland focuses on the fact that "the first generation of American communication research science emerged simultaneously with and out of the same administrative research programme that engendered the first attempts to create a formal science of policy studies."[44] His analysis takes into account a wide range of competing and colluding fields, institutions, and individuals, with a keen eye for differing visions of how policy should be studied. Finally, Jefferson Pooley and Elihu Katz give us a "speculative"[45] consideration of the history of the study of communication as it relates to the field of sociology, tracing it as it moved out of sociology and into "legitimacy-hungry journalism schools."[46] Across all of these histories, one finds a concern for how the study (if not always the field) of communication has related to the field of academic disciplines. Not surprisingly, these histories require a sense of something more than just origin myth; they grapple with the challenges to the legitimacy of the field, and how the field's need to bootstrap its own legitimacy has led it to pursue particular strategies for advancement and competition within the broader field of disciplines.

As a relatively new arrival in academe, communication finds itself dealing with patterns of self-establishment that are familiar from other new arrivals. Bourdieu described this 'recent arrival' phenomenon as a situation wherein newer disciplines threaten the "previously dominant disciplines," such as "philology, literary history and even philosophy, whose intellectual foundations are threatened by their new rivals."[47] In this conflict, the older disciplines find that "the social foundations of their academic existence are…under siege" from new arrivals who rail against "the archaic nature of their contents and their pedagogical structures."[48] With this in mind, communication can be thought of as the next new arrival in this wave, making much of its anti-archaism, its relevance, its novelty. Historians of the field could learn much about the relative position of the field by looking at arguments made on behalf of communication as the new arrival, and just as much could be learned from attending to the arguments made by those who hope to keep this new arrival at bay.

Much as the novelty of the field of communication gives us material for important historical work, the growth of the field as measured in terms of undergraduate and graduate enrollment also appears to play an important role in the field's history. Addressing the dramatic growth in the number of college students in the 1960s, Bourdieu noted the important connection between "the *external variables*, such as the size of the growth [in number of students] when it occurred, its intensity and duration," and the "*internal variables*, such as the principles controlling appointment and careers in the different faculties and, within them, in the different disciplines."[49] One effect of this is that growth can create "an accelerated career"[50] for those in the growth area, as the relative student glut reduces some of the factors that stall careers. At least as importantly, as the field moves to respond to the increase in the number of students, it becomes less selective in choosing new professors.[51] In this way the growth of a discipline thus becomes a threat to a field's autonomy. The broader issue here for the historian of the field—that of the relationship between the external and internal variables Bourdieu discussed—is one of demographics, and how changes in patterns in enrollment (on the undergraduate and graduate levels) connect with patterns in hiring and in pedagogical and research emphases. This has a particular urgency in communication, where enrollment numbers have swelled for a long time, and where growth has often been the stated or unstated goal. As the field makes moves to become more truly international, there may be phenomena similar to this arising from how the field establishes itself around the world.[52] Is this the professionalizing move of a field developing autonomy, or an index of the field's being positioned as academic cash cow?

Reading these notes on autonomy, one quickly gathers that the field of communication seems particularly heteronomous if Bourdieu's model for autonomy is to be applied. Certainly, Bourdieu would have found numerous examples of heteronomous impulses and failing autonomy if he were ever to have examined the field, such as: the field's near-constant importation of ideas from other fields, the comfortable relationship with many in the for-profit business world, and the association with vocational training. The familiar story is that communication has always been conceptually ambitious, or 'spread out,' while also being defined institutionally in cobbled-together vocational terms (speech and journalism in particular).

It would be absurd of me to pretend that a discussion of the field's heteronomy in and of itself represents any kind of great leap forward. A certain sign that there is broad agreement regarding this situation is that so much of this discussion overlaps with Wolfgang Donsbach's description of the dilemmas facing the field in his presidential address to the International Communication Association in 2005. Donsbach points to a number of the factors that Bourdieu described as threats to a field's autonomy: the quick growth of the field, the lack of cohesion, the "closeness of its object to everybody's reality."[53] There is at least one irony to be found here: one part of the field that Donsbach does not mention—historical inquiry—is the one best suited for providing an empirical analysis of his own claims in his address. The autonomy/heteronomy of the field should be taken as a problem area, demanding careful historical inquiry, and requiring no more in the way of declinist observations regarding all that has been lost. Bourdieu's ideas provide us with ways to frame the question. Only historical research can begin to give us an answer. To cut historical inquiry out of the field is to deny an essential requirement for the field's intellectual development, as well as for its potential autonomy.

Conflicts and Divides Within the Field

One of the pressing issues facing the field of communication has been the question of what the field really means, what 'communication' refers to. And, of course, there has been a deluge of responses to the eternal proseminar question: 'What is Communication?' Divides are not unusual to academic fields, but the divides in communication have their own history, and understanding these divides sheds considerable light on why the field looks like it does.

When I studied communication as an undergraduate, I worked my way through a Department of Communication Studies that divided communication into three subfields: rhetoric, mass communication, and interpersonal communication. The courses pertaining to these different subfields had negligible overlap in terms of terminology, methodology, theoretical approach, or empirical domain. This kind of division of the field was not unusual then, and, depending on whom you ask, these divisions in the field signify either a vigorous field boldly cultivating a thousand gardens, or a fractured mess of a would-be academic specialty watered down by other pretenders.

These divisions make the field an excellent empirical object of inquiry for Bourdieu's ideas regarding the history and sociology of science. He observed that "contacts between sciences, like contacts between civilizations, are occasions when implicit dispositions have to be made explicit," so that "interdisciplinary groups that form around a new object… would be a particularly favourable area for observing and objectivating these practical schemes."[54] Communication could be understood as a very large interdisciplinary group that has formed around an object, and this makes the field a fascinating example, a test case in what happens when multiple disciplinary orientations from the social sciences (sociology, anthropology, psychology, economics) come into contact with disciplinary orientations from the humanities (English/modern languages, rhetoric, art, philosophy), and both rub elbows with a tradition of vocational/professional training.

As Craig Calhoun has recently observed, the field of communication is a particularly 'edgy' field, with contacts all over the academic and non-academic map. Calhoun notes that "communication researchers study lots of intellectual problems and empirical topics, at lots of different scales and in lots of different places,"[55] which is "heterogeneous not just in the mix of fields it embraces, but in the organizational and curricular models it has produced for itself."[56] With such a tremendous metaphorical ratio of surface area to volume, communication finds itself touching on all kinds of other fields' self-understandings, and it brings together scholars who have so little in common that one thing that defines the field is the tremendous work that must be performed simply to explain what part of 'communication' one is in. This has become even more obvious with the rise of so-called 'new media,' a development that may very well have amplified the field's 'edginess.'

Division, or what might be called the social construction of division,[57] plays a major role in Bourdieu's sociology, and, as with the divides between academic fields, Bourdieu's ideas find ready application to the divides within communication, as well as to how these divisions in the field of communication relate to each other, compete with each other, and collaborate with each other. The strategic moves made by different factions in an academic field "will depend on the structure of the field,…but [the field] will always be organized around the principal opposition between the dominant…and the dominated, the challengers."[58]

Within this scheme of dominant versus challengers, the dominant have the power "to impose the representation of science most favourable to their interests," to establish "the 'correct', legitimate way to play and the rules of the game and therefore of participation in the game."[59] The dominant players in an academic field "enjoy decisive advantages in the competition," in part because "they constitute an obligatory reference point for their competitors."[60] The dominant enjoy the position of having their own ideas, theories, and methods being taken as given. Conflicts between dominant and dominated are inevitable, and the "polemical exchanges" that take place between these positions show us how each position relates to the others.[61] The history of communication research would do well to consider more fully the kinds of polemical exchanges that have occurred in the history of the field, if only to understand where the lines get drawn, and from what kind of symbolic reserves different positions in the field derive their own self-understanding.

One of the things that makes Bourdieu's sociology of science a particularly good match for a sociological and historical consideration of the field of communication is his emphasis on mutually conflicting impulses within any field at a given point in time. This puts him at odds with what he calls the "'communitarian' vision" in the sociology of science, which "fails to grasp the very foundation of the scientific world as a universe of competition for the 'monopoly of the legitimate handling' of scientific goods," by which Bourdieu means the definition of "the correct method, the correct findings, the correct definition of the ends, objects and methods of science."[62]

Bourdieu does not so much reject the Durkheimianism of much sociology of science so much as he projects how it would work in terms of a number of competing functional regimes, each operating in simultaneous conflict and collusion with others. He asserts that the "notion of the field…destroys all kinds of common oppositions, starting with the one between consensus and conflict."[63] This field-oriented vision "sweeps away the naively idealist view of the scientific world as a community of solidarity" while also being "opposed to the no less partial view of scientific life as a 'war of all against all'."[64] Thusly emplotted, the field no longer resembles one in which simple consensus or conflict can be understood to be at work. What Bourdieu's field theory presents is a way to understand the intertwining of different capital formations, each of them vying for power, using strategies that follow from their position in the field, while also giving us a sense of how to understand the field's position relative to other fields.

The history of the field has often taken the form of attempts to write legitimacy into the field, frequently in part through playing down any such internecine conflict. More recent histories of the field have gotten past this unfortunate preoccupation for legitimacy, often through an exploration of other points of view. Bourdieu's ideas regarding divisions within fields call for the application of a dialectical imagination to how the dominant and the dominated come into contact with each other, each spurring the other on to new things. A history of 'polemical exchanges' and 'classificatory epithets' could do much to detail precisely how the field of communication has come to be what it is.

Alongside this opposition between dominant and dominated, Bourdieu emphasized the importance to all academic fields of "the opposition between the agents and institutions which are orientated mostly towards research and scholarly goals…and those which are orientated more towards the reproduction of the cultural order and the body of reproducers."[65] In communication, the divide here could easily be encoded in terms of research-based applications in teaching and academic work and those approaches to the field that take vocational training—including journalism, public relations, advertising, and marketing—to be their goal. The tension between journalism educators and social scientists is nothing new to communication. Jake Highton metonymically described a similar tension in 1967 as one between "green eye-shades [those teaching journalism] vs. Chi squares [the social scientists],"[66] and the same tension can be found today, as the field's long-standing association with vocational/professional education conflicts with the field's development of research and scholarship as the proper emphasis.

Bourdieu outlined a similar axis of division in a field with his discussion of the "two principles of domination in the scientific field, temporal and intellectual," which basically involve the domination coming from the forces interior to the field, representing the ostensibly 'pure' (autonomous) impulses of researchers, versus those of the 'outside,' temporal powers (state and market), whose impulses push fields toward a different kind of outward-looking anticipation of profits.[67] Here, the question of division concerns the degree to which communication scholarship can be affected in some way by forces outside the field. Here I am reminded of Willard Rowland's study of *The Politics of TV Violence*,[68] which explains how media effects researchers attempting to develop greater legitimacy for the field of communication played a rather convenient role for the U.S. government and the media industry. The "service of" the interests of legitimacy for the field of communication—a low-status field more willing to accommodate the temporal powers—"militated against any comprehensive, intellectually grounded discussion of the role and meaning of mass communications in society and culture."[69] It is a classic story about the temporal domination of a field. Todd Gitlin's classic consideration of the "dominant paradigm"[70] of media sociology asserts that Paul F. Lazarsfeld's links to funding agencies at the Bureau of Applied Social Research guided the course of communication research toward compromise with the temporal powers. The result, in Lazarsfeld's words, was "a kind of joint enterprise between industries and universities."[71] When considered in terms of divisions within the field, the temporal/intellectual distinction calls our attention to the oppositions between research and teaching done on the field's own terms and the potential sources of heteronomy, including: 'sponsored' research (research funded by organizations with their own interests in the findings), the need to vet research interests to match national and international governments' funding interests, and college and university administrators' interests in pushing communication teaching away from the intellectual pole.

Still another division that Bourdieu offered as grist for historians of the sciences concerns the oppositions between "older professors, and those best provided with strictly academic titles of consecration," and "younger professors, who are defined above all negatively, by their lack of institutional signs of prestige and by the possession of inferior forms of academic power."[72] These agents are distinguished by their different uses of time. It is this opposition that leads fields to nurture innovation and conflict. The dialectic at work here pits the side of tradition, with its investment in the way things already are, against the side of "modernism," which points to the existence of an ostensibly hide-bound tradition as a rationale for "limited innovations" which are "bound to serve to found a new academic routine."[73]

Agents in different positions relate differently to the field, as the possession of different levels and types of capital reproduce a tension between the established and the new. For Bourdieu, academic fields are not easily sorted into categories where we find "on the one side 'progress' and 'progressives' and on the other 'reaction' and 'conservatives.'"[74] Instead, tendencies toward orthodoxy and heterodoxy are intertwined, and one should attend to "the solidarities and complicities which are affirmed even in antagonism."[75] Applied to the history of the field of communication, one is prompted to consider the numerous schools of thought, each of which struggles (and, in less obvious ways, collaborates) with others to establish itself in the field as legitimate or dominant. A proper history would show the grounds for these struggles, charting the space in which they happened, maintaining a sense not only of the disagreements between each subfield and school of thought, but also of the alliances and the varying capital opportunities available to agents within each movement. An excellent model for this can be found in Craig Calhoun and Jonathan VanAntwerpen's historical treatment of the reaction against so-called 'mainstream sociology,' a classificatory epithet[76] developed by younger "insurgent sociologists" to "[project] the politicized categories of their present onto the past, retelling the history of postwar sociology in the process."[77] The extant history of the field provides rather less consideration of the kinds of insurgencies that have been fought, and many of these considerations come from major players, with obvious stakes in the game. The history of the field could do much to distance itself from originating impulses of the field and consider the give and take between the old and the new that we find with, for instance: the emergence of cultural studies as a challenge to orthodoxy, the scholars who first led the field into the consideration of the internet and other 'new' media, the incorporation of game studies into the field, and the responses to all of these phenomena.

An equally relevant distinction in capital acquisition occurs between different methods of creating and presenting academic work. Bourdieu described the different kinds of capital deployed by those who work at research centers, who "can no longer surround themselves with the charismatic aura which attached to the traditional writer or professor, small producers exploiting their own independent cultural capital."[78] The "'reports' and 'accounts'" that come from the research performed at research centers are written differently, "bound to sacrifice all to a display of the amount of work accomplished…rather than to an interpretation or a systematization of the results," making them "just as different from a book or a scientific article as are the most traditional doctoral theses, which are also marked by the social need to have their labour displayed and appreciated."[79] For the field of communication, which has banked considerable symbolic coin in the world of research institutes, it is worth considering what kinds of methods of academic presentation have sustained the field. What kind of 'charismatic aura' has defined the work in the field? To what degree has the field's U.S. origins in research centers (including: the Bureau of Applied Social Research, the Office of Radio Research, the Institutes for Communication Research) affected the field's sense of itself? More contemporary examples, such as the Pew Foundation's Internet and American Life Project and the Annenberg Public Policy Center, offer important new pockets for communication research, and important stories in the history of the field of communication. The promise of the field's alignment with research institutes (with their reports, their focus on particular methodological alignments, their large collaborative projects) is that such associations will bring to communication some of the home-base legitimacy found in other fields. The opposition opened up by this—between more 'charismatic' theorizing and scholarship vs. the institute-based approach—no doubt underlies many of the intellectual, methodological and other disputes in the field.

Beyond the Kuhnian Model

One vision of the history of change in the field of communication has involved a narrative that mimics Thomas Kuhn's familiar story of scientific revolutions, wherein a dominant paradigm develops, encounters problems, faces explicit challenges, and is in time replaced by another dominant paradigm.[80] Thus the field can be and has been interpreted in terms of the dominant schools of thought that have moved through the field. Bourdieu's ideas give us something that I think fits the field better than Kuhn's take.

Bourdieu's problem with Kuhnian histories of science was that they adhere to a vision of a scientific world "where there are no struggles—or at least, no struggles over what is at stake in the struggles."[81] Though Kuhn "has drawn attention to the discontinuities [and] revolutions" in science, his description of "the scientific world from a quasi-Durkheimian perspective, as a community dominated by a central norm" means that he lacks "a coherent model for explaining change."[82] In the Kuhnian scheme, it is as if a spontaneous adjustment in the general will occurs, resulting in a near-universal shift in how 'regular' science is carried out.

For Bourdieu, meaningful changes come almost entirely from outside of the field. As David Swartz points out, "[c]hange comes about when traditional strategies are deployed in relation to novel phenomena."[83] What kind of novel phenomena? Swartz identifies the following as the kinds of things that lead to meaningful change:

> Intrusion of external events into fields, increase in sheer number of field participants, uneven development and conjuncture of crises among different fields, growth in types of capital, and social struggles that expose field *doxa* necessitating new forms of symbolic domination and new reproduction strategies by agents.[84]

Rodney Benson addresses this most pithily by saying, in sum, that the field model posits "more churn than change."[85] More grandly, Benson argues that "it takes a shock to the entire system to produce substantial change." He explains that

> [f]inancial crises, electoral political realignments, scandals, or environmental cataclysms may provide the heretofore lacking symbolic and material resources necessary for the rising generation to force out the old guard and create fundamentally new rules of the game.[86]

The shift in a field resulting from this kind of external 'shock' Benson describes arranges things so that old strategies no longer have the same magic, the oppositions once thought to be stable become forgotten, the habitus at work in an individual no longer applies to the new arrangement. It may be yet another indication of the field of communication's place in the academy that it can be considered to be particularly vulnerable to these kinds of external shocks.

When scientific fields are subjected to these kinds of changes, new opportunities arise for challenges to the orthodoxy. Kuhn left things decidedly murky when it comes to explaining much about how these revolutions in science get worked out. From a Bourdieusian perspective, the revolutionary in a field is not just anyone; it is someone whose interests are structured to lead them to pursue a revolutionary strategy, impelled in large part by that agent's place in the field. More specifically, it is "necessarily someone who has capital" who can act as a revolutionary, or someone who has "a great mastery of the accumulated collective resources, and who therefore necessarily conserves what he supersedes."[87] Beyond this, the focus on numerous competing subfields and agents leads us to look beyond the apparent agreement at work when normal science is being conducted, to gain a sense of the roiling controversies within any field at any time, because struggles (and struggles over the grounds of struggle itself) are carried out constantly. This seems like a particularly good fit for communication, where numerous and widely divergent subfields do not remind one of the kind of more consensus-based community of scholars Kuhn implicitly described. In short, communication is much closer to the kind of *bellum omnium contra omnes* that Bourdieu expected us to find, and the revolutions/changes that occur come not out of anywhere (or nowhere); they come from those who inhabit positions of accumulation of cultural capital in subfields in the dominated position in the field.

For Bourdieu, change in a field related to the strategies available to different agents within that field. Because Bourdieu described strategies themselves largely in terms of reproduction of pre-existing features of fields, one may wonder how change in a field can ever happen. With the model of the field close at hand, Bourdieu remarked that "changes within a field are often determined by redefinitions of the frontiers between fields, linked (as cause or effect) to the sudden arrival of new entrants endowed with new resources."[88] With a field as given to adjustments in boundaries as communication, this insight is of profound importance to anyone attempting to tell the history of the field. It invites reference to the constantly changing interfield dynamics at work that have made communication's borders so porous.

Another reason for change in a field, of course, relates not to new ideas pursued, but to older ideas that are left behind. Maria Löblich and Andreas Matthias Scheu describe the relative failure of critical theory in German communication studies, connecting this failure to inter-related intellectual, biographical, and institutional sources, all traced onto Bourdieu's field approach. Ultimately, they find that critical communication studies has been thrown to the margins in German communication studies as a result of "the 'critical scholars' themselves, the established power structures within the discipline, and a lack of autonomy from the political field combined with the [field of communication's] need for legitimatization."[89] Far from being locked into a hermetic determinism, Bourdieusian sociology of science can be used to conceptualize the development of new ideas in the field, as well as the demise or marginalization of other ideas.[90]

This focus on the ongoing struggles in fields is of striking relevance to the field of communication, where new entrants endowed with new resources are a regular component of the texture of the field. A most obvious example for the field today concerns so-called 'new media' and their linkage to new domains, researchers, departments, theories, and methods associated with the field. Looking back on the history of the field, one finds similar changes with other changes in media, and from other redefinitions of the frontiers between fields: sociology's disassociation from the study of media, the long and complicated relationship between social psychology and the study of communication and the media, the development of communication's own versions of cultural studies in the 1970s, George Gerbner's attempt to merge critical and social scientific perspectives in his cultural indicators project, and more. In all of these examples, what we find are multi-party conflicts whose outcome never really gets settled, with a playing field whose contours are being reshaped at all times. This complicated mess is the stuff of Bourdieu's sociology of science.

Biographies and the History of the Field

One promising avenue for research on the history of the field that Bourdieu's ideas help us to open up concerns scholarship that focuses on the role of the individual. Though Bourdieu's ideas are by no means individualistic, he did place great emphasis on the individual in his discussion of how the sociology of science could be executed. He saw the goal of the sociology of science as "assist[ing] the [individual] scientists in the work of making explicit the practical schemes that underlay their decisive choices—the choice of this or that discipline, laboratory or journal."[91] The overall goal of reflexivity was to feed back into the scientific pursuit, which was (and on this Bourdieu was nothing if not consistent) treated very much as all other pursuits.

The focus on how individuals go about their scholarship took on a Wittgensteinian aspect in Bourdieu's work, as he noted that "[o]ne does not act in accordance with a method, any more than one follows a rule, by a psychological act of conscious adherence." Instead it is "by letting oneself be carried along by a sense of—a feel for—the scientific game that is acquired through prolonged experience of the scientific game, with its regularities as much as its rules."[92] The individual scholar gets to a point where the feel for the game takes over, through experience with the more or less explicitly formulated rules for research, the instruments of measurement, and "by indices embedded in the very functioning of the field."[93] Through this emphasis on how individual scientists come to internalize the workings of the field, Bourdieu concluded that a "scientist is a scientific field made flesh, an agent whose cognitive structures are homologous with the structure of the field and, as a consequence, constantly adjusted to the expectations inscribed in the field."[94] This means that the job of the historian of the field should be at least in part oriented toward understanding individuals as starting points for historical inquiry. The point would not be to tell the story of a person so much as to tell the story of a field by using the individual as prism, refracting the field from one position, and thus offering some kind of access to an entire field of functioning along a set of historically connected points.

Continuing with this, Bourdieu described how the "rules and regularities" at work in individual scientists' proclivities are granted their power "only because they are perceived by scientists endowed with the habitus that makes them capable of perceiving and appreciating them, and both disposed and able to implement them."[95] In sum: "the rules and regularities determine the agents only because the agents determine themselves by a practical act of cognition and recognition which confers their determining power on them."[96] Individuals are not to be considered as "simple particles," nor as "rational subjects working to fulfill their preferences as far as circumstances permit." Instead they are to be conceptualized as

> socialized agents…endowed with transindividual dispositions, and [who] therefore tend to generate practices which are objectively orchestrated and more or less adapted to objective requirements, that is irreducible either to the structural forces of the field or to individual dispositions.[97]

One approach to the history of the field of communication (and this would no doubt hold true for other fields as well) could do well to start with histories of individual scholars, in an effort to track these 'transindividual' modes of perception that Bourdieu described at work as systematic methods for perception.

This being Bourdieu, there is still a leading role for institutions to play. Histories of individuals could be considered not only in terms of modes of perception, but also in terms of the concerns that Bourdieu applies in *Homo Academicus*, where he examined all kinds of background institutional information that played a role in positioning the individual in a field. Examples of variables Bourdieu addressed included, broadly: "educational determinants[,]…the capital of academic power[,]…capital of scientific power[,]…capital of scientific prestige[,]…capital of intellectual renown[,]…capital of political or economic power… [, and] 'political' dispositions in the widest sense."[98] His goal in much of *Homo Academicus* is to show the connection between connections to institutions and worldviews as maintained by individual players in the game. He considers the "educational system" as something that operated "as pleasure principle and reality principle," capable of stimulating "the *libido sciendi*, and the *libido dominandi* which this conceals, and which…assigns [scholars] limits, causing the agents to internalize frontiers between what it is legitimate to obtain,…and what it is legitimate to hope for, to desire, to like."[99] The individual as starting point can give us a sense of how these frontiers of thought are constructed, practiced, lived.

A renewed interest in focusing on individuals in the history of the social sciences can be traced to Andrew Abbott's call to focus on individuals in historical inquiry. Abbott's language bears more than a passing similarity to Bourdieu's ideas regarding the issue. Abbott asserts that "individuals are central to history because it is they who are the prime reservoir of historical connection from past to present." It is this that makes for what Abbott calls the "historicality of individuals."[100] Taking inspiration from Abbott, Peter Simonson has suggested (in language even more suggestive of Bourdieu than Abbott's) that we understand how individuals play the role of "thread ends," who are "metaphorically at the end of a thread that is woven into the broader social, cultural, institutional, and geographical fabrics of their historical moments," and because of this, "any given individual can serve as a point of entry into that fabric."[101] Individuals have much to offer to the history of the social sciences, and to the history of the field of communication.

Taken together, Bourdieu, Abbott, and Simonson offer an extensive sense of what focusing on individuals can do for history more generally, and in particular, what they can offer to the history of the social sciences, including communication. None suggests that the focus on individuals in history should get us started on a 'great man' approach to history. Instead, individuals are seen historiographically in terms of: how they understand a field, how certain questions come to matter, how debates become ingrained in practice, how problems come to be defined, how motivations to join fields operate, and more. Individuals come to matter in this approach not because great ones are seen as being the driving force of history, but because it is through individuals that history happens. If a scientist is the scientific field made flesh, it is worth examining the individual scientist.

One need not look far to find an individual-based history of the field of communication. One of the most widely read books concerning the history of the field is based on biographical study: Everett M. Rogers' *A History of Communication Study:*

A Biographical Approach. Rogers' work in this book, however, is not the kind of history Bourdieu envisioned. *A History of Communication Study* takes a titular "biographical approach," but its emphasis is patently whiggish, and its biographical approach functions rather poorly if historical work is to be judged according to the degree to which it allows us to understand the constraints at work through individuals.

Other work on the history of the field offers a much closer approximation of the Bourdieusian ideal for examining the individual in context. Simonson's own focus on the individual was developed as a prologue for his excellent consideration of the role William McPhee played in the history of media research. The approach is not explicitly Bourdieusian, but it has much that Bourdieu hoped the focus on the individual could do for the history of science. In particular, Simonson focuses on the interaction between McPhee's own background (which led to him being described as "a hick" at Columbia[102]) and the workings of the field of sociology and media research in the 1950s. Not only does this biographical work approximate the focus on agent-field interactions that Bourdieu outlines, but it also treats its subject as a "thread end," in a sense unlocking the workings of the field through reference to the individual. On top of this, by taking McPhee as his subject, Simonson demonstrates (as Bourdieu implies) that it is not only the celebrated 'great men' in a field who can further our knowledge of the field; there is much understanding to be gleaned from less consecrated individuals.

Biographical historical work in the history of communication research is not uncommon. Much of it does take major, central figures in the field. John H. Summers' work on C. Wright Mills is an important example of work on the history of the field of communication that gets to the level of transindividual dispositions and issues in strategic use of capital as they related to the Bureau of Applied Social Research in the 1940s and 1950s.[103] David E. Morrison's studies of Paul Lazarsfeld do much the same thing.[104] As I point to these two exemplars of dirty-fingernails history on individuals in the field, however, I also highlight an unfortunate pattern that has emerged in histories that focus on individuals: the tendency to focus almost exclusively on a small number of figures who are seen as central to the field, and who have already been written about before.[105] This is a kind of Matthew effect echo. Bourdieu—and Abbott, and Simonson—call for individual-focused histories that get us past the 'great man.' Despite having no shortage of subjects for this kind of history in the field, much of this work simply has yet to be done. Promising work seems likely to come from new oral history projects associated with the Project on the History of Communication Research, and with Michael Meyen (who has already conducted oral history interviews with all living International Communication Association Fellows[106]). As with much else related to the history of the field, this should be only the beginning.

Conclusion

I should note some critical gaps in Bourdieu's approach to the sociology of science. Perhaps the most important problem is that Bourdieu's focus on fields helps us very much to conceptualize what occurs within fields, and even helps us to understand how external shocks (in Rodney Benson's language) shift the working of fields. Though there is much benefit to this, it must be admitted that the concept of the field cannot explain *all* that happens. Bourdieu never intended for the idea of the field to do that kind of impossible heavy lifting. The field of communication provides an example of how things that did not happen within the field (or, properly speaking, 'in' any other academic field) shaped the emergence of the field. The development of the internet is an even better example of a phenomenon that certainly did not happen inside the field, and the effects on the field are only beginning to be felt. The point here is simple: though it is good to think in terms of the within- and across-field dynamics that Bourdieu lays out, these are not the complete picture of things. The history of the field cannot be told only in terms of things that happened as a result of field dynamics, no matter how tempting it might be to find in the field a readymade explanatory tool.

Another problem with applying Bourdieu's sociology of science to the history of the field—or to any other history—derives from the risk that any sociological ideas pose to good history. The history of the sciences ought not to be judged solely in terms of how easily we can cram the relevant historical details into any social scientific model, even one as flexible and context-sensitive as those proposed by Bourdieu. History becomes no less important, and perhaps even more interesting, when it fails to fit into sociological schemes. This reminder is particularly relevant to those who do what is now called 'communication history,' an approach that John Nerone has claimed still finds itself very much attracted to "grand narrative," and theoretical insight.[107] Bourdieu's ideas give us ways to ask good questions for the history of the field, initial avenues of inquiry that assist us in putting pieces together, assembling narratives, developing a sense of the mutually constitutive nature of social existence as it occurs in the history of the field. They do not provide a yardstick in and of themselves for 'good history.'

A third problem I wish to call attention to is Bourdieu's own limits with respect to what happens when, as Sergio Sismondo describes it, "science meets non-science."[108] This is perhaps just a different version of the critique of Bourdieu's internalist tendencies described above, but there is a different slant here. The problem is that Bourdieu's understanding of capital leads him to presume that the holders of the relevant capital (say, environmental scientists talking about climate change) are to be understood on their own terms, and (even more dramatically) *will* be accepted as experts on their own terms. Sismondo points out that while the "standard model of expertise [which Bourdieu accepts] assumes that science trumps all other knowledge traditions,"[109] there seems to be much more play at work in this, and recent examples of scientists (in the U.S., and around the world) being challenged by other authorities provide ample cause to doubt the potential of science to hold all the trumps Bourdieu seemed to think it held.

But the benefits of a Bourdieu-inflected history of the field of communication would be substantial. First, Bourdieu's emphasis on 'the field' as a frame for analysis lends itself well to the study of academic fields. With this vision of the field in place, the historian is invited to consider a wide variety of empirical themes, including: border maintenance, intra- and interfield conflicts, margins, and centers. When combined with the idea of capital, the whole thing becomes much less consensus-oriented and the issue of variable levels of power comes fully into play. It is the combination of field and capital that allows Bourdieu's sociology of science to benefit from the insight that 'everything is relational,' while still retaining the critical bite that allows him to point out that just because everything is relational does not mean that all are equal. The accumulation of capital can take many forms, and the values attributed to capital can vary dramatically. Capital becomes Bourdieu's way to make certain that considerations of power are never left far behind.

In addition to this twinned concern for field/capital, Bourdieu's concern for autonomy and heteronomy seems a promising avenue for histories of the field. Without uncritically imbibing all that Bourdieu has to say about the proper role of autonomy in an academic field, the question of autonomy/heteronomy does push us toward fruitful areas of inquiry. In particular, it leads us to ask questions about how the field relates to other fields, and to the field of power. The question of critical vs. administrative research (a construct in and of itself, of course) has never been far from the minds of many of us in the field, and the basic question Robert Lynd asked of sociology—*Knowledge for What?*—could be posed to communication just as well. The autonomy/heteronomy divide ties directly to concerns for reflexivity that I have proposed as a central goal of histories of the field. How do our institutional alliances function to shape the questions we ask? What are the ultimate goals of our pedagogical and research programs? If the field is not in control of itself, who is our master?

Last, Bourdieu's focus on individuals and on habitus give historians of the field of communication a valuable, if at times frustrating and puzzling, starting point for what good 'dirty-fingernails' history could look like. Individuals in the field are seen here as functioning as storing the history they experience. To understand the history of a field with a respect for the habitus means in large part to try to remember that historical subjects do not operate from a written to-do list. Much as the pragmatists would have it, the individuals operate historically by having internalized (on the level of the disposition) the ways things work. The job of the historian is to attempt—through use of interviews, archival records, images, anything—to dig deep enough to gain access to the world-construction that happens on the bodily level, the things that go without saying, the obvious and evanescent, the practices that recreate the system at work. This is no mean feat, but if this level of detail can be tied to a broader field-based analysis, we would learn much that is important about our own chosen field of inquiry.

CHAPTER SIX

Conclusion: Communication as Practical, Relational, Historical, and Reflexive

At the end of the *Tractatus Logico-Philosophicus*—which is to say, at the conclusion of a challenging treatise regarding logical propositions and their connections to the universe—Wittgenstein wrote that his "propositions serve as elucidations" in that "anyone who understands me eventually recognizes them as nonsensical, when he has used them—as steps—to climb up beyond them." The reader "must, so to speak, throw away the ladder after he has climbed up it."[1] It is one of the great punch lines in philosophy, and it helps to illuminate one of the most important elements of Bourdieu's thought. Bourdieu was a great admirer of Wittgenstein, and shared with Wittgenstein a skepticism regarding the supposed human adherence to rules of logic or to idealist schemata. Though Bourdieu's ideas evolved considerably during his career, this anti-idealism can be found at work in all that he wrote.

It is this anti-idealism at work in Bourdieu that makes it difficult to sum up his thoughts, or to outline a program of research that ought to develop from these thoughts. There is a danger that his ideas will be taken up mechanically, and applied as if they were a set of pre-packaged independent and dependent variable relationships to be mapped onto innumerable fields of inquiry. I have attempted to bring Bourdieu's ideas more fully into conversation with some of the arenas of theoretical consideration that matter to those of us who study the media: media production, media audiences, symbolic power and authority, the history of the field. However, this should not be the end of the story. Bourdieu's ideas are too all-encompassing simply to be parceled into pre-existing problem areas in the field of communication. I thus conclude with a review of some of the major elements of Bourdieu's thought that ought to continue to challenge those who consider the field of communication. We can get the most value out of Bourdieu's thought by considering at length his ideas related to: embodiment, the relational element of practice, an appreciation of the historical dimension of practice, and reflexivity.

Habitus and Practical Reason

It is Bourdieu's afore-mentioned anti-idealism that led him to admire Marx's afore-mentioned admonition that we not mistake "the things of logic for the logic of things."[2] When applied to the study of communication, Bourdieu's focus on what he called the logic of practice draws our attention to processes we often regard as secondary to what it is that we study. Whereas communication researchers often focus on meanings, ideologies, and texts, Bourdieu spoke of the elementary things that we do in order to make these grander hermeneutic enterprises possible: practices and perceptions. Bourdieu developed the concept of habitus in an attempt to emphasize the embodiment of practice. The idea was that we do not go about our lives simply consulting the meanings we hold dear, and then living up to them. Instead, Bourdieu argued that our behavior in the world—including all sorts of seemingly 'pure' behaviors, such as attending art openings, writing philosophy,[3] or appreciating avant-garde cinema—is more accurately and helpfully understood as a kind of practice that involves certain bodily dispositions. It is at the bodily—habitus—level that we perceive and experience the world. This is similar to Anthony Giddens' discussion of "practical consciousness,"[4] and sets Bourdieu apart from many of the approaches to communication we come to think of as 'culturist' in any sense.

When applied to issues of communication, as I have done in the preceding chapters, the idea of habitus leads us to inquire into the practical aspects of different questions of communication. It is by no means revolutionary to think of the production of mediated culture as a practice, but there is much to be gained by considering what practices are actually at work in media production, from journalists, to comic book artists, to movie producers, and more. In all of these contexts, a concern for habitus leads us to ask about the kinds of taken-for-granted activities that constitute the everyday labor of these media producers. This in turn leads to questions regarding how these practices lead to certain perceptions of: what exists, what is important, what is preferred, and more. In the context of media audiences, habitus leads us to take the seemingly purely intellectual process of interpretation as a practical process of orientation, while also pointing us toward questions regarding how audience members regard some content as entertaining, appropriate, or relevant. In the context of authority, habitus pushes us to understand the strategies of asserting authority that come to seem natural to speakers and to listeners. For inquiry into the history of the field of communication, habitus pushes us to consider the bodily/practical elements of communication scholarship in the past, to consider how the work that communication scholars have done has shaped their perceptions of where the field has come from, where it should go, what constitutes 'good' research, how to evaluate evidence, and more.

In all of these ways, habitus is at the very least a reminder that, though we may sometimes pretend otherwise, communication is a process that always involves the body, and more broadly, always involves materiality. The emphasis on practice that comes out of the term 'habitus' bears comparison with pragmatism, political economy, and materialist communication history. As with habitus, these approaches to the study of communication get us beyond inquiring only into the work of the interactions of signifiers. It seems unlikely that this common ground will produce much in the way of a powerful common cause, but at the very least it does seem that habitus has much to tell us about a question that Nick Couldry poses as the basic issue we all face: "*what are people doing that is related to media?*"[5] I believe that habitus gets us in touch with this essential question. Perhaps surprisingly for a term to come from such a prolix and prolific intellectual as Bourdieu, habitus allows us to strip away a lot of the less essential issues that surround and complicate this question. Bourdieu shows us how to go right to the issues that matter, if only by first showing us—à la Wittgenstein—what ladder we need to kick out from under us after we get up to where we need to be.

The Relational

The idea of habitus has roots in phenomenological thought, and Bourdieu was perfectly clear about this in his citations. It is when the idea of habitus is married to the concept of the field that the idea takes on a social meaning. The idea of the field makes habitus a social phenomenon, and not just an aspect of individual experience. When Bourdieu asserted that 'everything is relational,' he meant that everything we do is done in relation to some set of possibilities that is associated with each position within a field. When we engage in any practice, we are engaging with a particular relation to the field of possibilities of practices that exist. The existence of these fields precedes us; we cannot stand outside of the fields. Much as structuralists like Ferdinand de Saussure considered meaning in terms of the differences—the distinctions—that are established in words before we speak them, Bourdieu considered the same kinds of systems of difference at work in practices. The idea of the field extends this concern for difference in a way that presumes that not everyone has the same perspective on these differences.

To treat habitus hand in hand with the field is to envision a society that is made meaningful by its differences. From each locale in a given field, a certain practical sense of the world is engendered by habitus, bearing with it a particular (if flexible) sense of what seems natural, what is correct, how to behave, how to speak, and what to do. The idea of the field links subjective experience—how we understand the world, how we see it—to objective social structure—the social position we occupy in the world. The relation between habitus and field involves both "conditioning," wherein the "field structures the habitus, which is the product of the embodiment of the immanent necessity of a field," and "[h]abitus contributes to constituting the field as a meaningful world, a world endowed with sense and value, in which it is worth investing one's energy."[6] From each point in the field, a particular feel for the game will resonate. Of course, the distribution of capital within these fields is not equal. We do not all have access to the same resources. The capital at work in fields—economic, social, cultural, symbolic—is not distributed equally, and the values and strategies that emerge from interactions within and between fields reflect (and often reproduce) these inequalities.

The idea of the field puts forth a relational (not to be confused with relativist) understanding of meaning and practice. The field of communication has much to gain from appropriating this kind of relational understanding of how society functions. At the very least, the idea that 'everything is relational' cues us to ask comparative questions about the communication issues we face. The meaning is found neither in the text, nor in the corporation that produces it, but in the relation that any given subject has to that which surrounds it. This would lead us toward a particular brand of something-more-than-comparative studies: of media corporations, of approaches to journalism, of motion picture content and genres, of audience responses, and of course much more. The idea that fields have dominant and dominated components no doubt can shape much of these kinds of analyses, and it gives us an appreciation for power at work in all of the contexts we survey. The idea of the field pushes us away from looking at any communication phenomenon without consulting the structures that lend social specificity to what we are studying. Rodney Benson describes how "[m]edia field researchers…argue that the first step toward change is to bring to consciousness the invisible structures of belief and practice that lead actors to unwittingly reproduce the system, even as they struggle within it."[7] This is a justifiably ambitious program for the field-based study of the media.

The Historical Dimension of All Communication

One of the broadest points to make regarding what the field of communication can learn from Bourdieu concerns the importance he assigned to history. In the field of communication, history has remained on the margins. The divisions in the field—media effects versus cultural studies, quantitative versus qualitative, critical versus administrative—rarely seem to involve history much at all. To a great extent, history has been left to itself, occasionally aligning with one faction or another, but rarely being taken up as a cause from within the field. This may be changing. John Nerone tells us that communication history has started to "come to awareness of itself,"[8] and we who agree with Nerone have much to point to as evidence of this burgeoning self-awareness.[9]

Bourdieu's ideas have much to offer to communication history as it begins to emerge as an increasingly self-sustaining part of the field. It may seem strange to look to a sociologist in search of ideas for history, but Bourdieu's work was quite thoroughly imbued with a concern for the diachronic. One of the most important criticisms of Bourdieu was that he was a determinist,[10] and one of the most important responses he had to this argument was his emphasis on diachronic change, on history. George Steinmetz has argued that "[e]ach of Bourdieu's main theoretical concepts (habitus, cultural and symbolic capital, and field) is inherently historical,"[11] and he makes a strong case.

It is easy to detect the centrality of history to Bourdieu's work. We find Bourdieu praising attention to historical detail as an important component of social inquiry in his recurring use of the term 'accumulation.' The basic fact that capital can be accumulated over time by social actors, that it can vary in its fungibility at different times, that actors' strategies relate differently to different time frames, that the fields of interaction wherein different forms of capital compete are subject to their own historical variance, can all be taken as reasons why history must be accounted for in our visions of the social world. Bourdieu considered social agents to be "the product of history, of the history of the whole social field and of the accumulated experience of a path within the specific subfield."[12]

When asked about the difference between a field (as a mode of explanation) and an apparatus, Bourdieu responded that "an essential difference" was

> struggles, and thus historicity! I am very much against the notion of apparatus, which for me is the Trojan horse of 'pessimistic functionalism': an apparatus is an infernal machine, programmed to accomplish certain purposes no matter what, when, or where.[13]

To devise a theory that admits nothing of history is to give up on the all-important role of context, to create an abstraction machine that may help to 'explain' something merely by substituting the logic of the researcher for that of the social actor. Bourdieu emphasized the role played by history in his use of the idea of the field, explaining that, though "a synchronic analysis" of a field's structure was necessary, "we cannot grasp this structure without a historical, that is, genetic, analysis of its constitution and of the tensions that exist between positions in it, as well as between this field and other fields, and especially in the field of power."[14] History is no sideshow here.

One of the most sweeping statements Bourdieu made on behalf of historical inquiry came from his consideration of how scientists operate. "Each scientific act, like every practice," he explained, "is the product of the encounter between two histories, a history embodied, incorporated in the form of dispositions, and a history objectified in the very structure of the field and in technical objects (instruments), writings, etc."[15] These two histories—embodied in the habitus and objectified in the field—loom large in all that Bourdieu did. The historical inquiry that Bourdieu considered necessary to the social sciences—and that grew quite naturally from his concepts of habitus, field, and capital—represented an effort to effect a fidelity to the social world we represent. Much as habitus grew out of Bourdieu's discomfort with treating praxis in an abstract manner, history represented to Bourdieu a way to be consistent in this resistance against abstraction.

When we apply this to the field of communication, we get a sense of how history can do something much more than just play bridesmaid to studies of popular culture or to political economy, two subfields that have taken up history as a component of what they do, but rarely embraced historical inquiry as vigorously as I think Bourdieu would have preferred. What Bourdieu proposed for social inquiry is a sense of history that is both sweeping in scope and attentive to detail. If we have not examined the accumulated histories of the things we study in communication, we have done a poor job of understanding the human agents in our studies or the backgrounds in which they operate. History is at work all the time in communication, whether or not we are accustomed to using history to understand it. From interpersonal contexts to large-scale popular culture phenomena, from political campaigns to SNS fandom discussions, history shapes agents and fields. Few social theorists offer to communication history a better philosophy—or modus operandi—than Pierre Bourdieu.

Reflexivity and the Field of Communication

Bourdieu's concern for history was linked closely to his more noticeable arguments on behalf of reflexivity. It is the historical consideration of our own concepts and practices that allows reflexivity to become possible. He criticized historians who "forget that [their] *concepts* and the reality they capture are themselves the product of historical construction,"[16] and offered much the same critique of scholars in other fields who mistake their own concepts for the reality they attempt to identify and analyze.

When Bourdieu argued on behalf of greater reflexivity, he was drawing on a tradition of reflexivity in the social sciences, which itself stems from what Fernando Bermejo has called "the observer-related nature of knowledge,"[17] an idea that has also found adherents in anthropology, economics, philosophy, and many more fields. In sociology, Alvin Gouldner's ideas in *The Coming Crisis of Western Sociology*[18] represent an important precursor of what Bourdieu would say on the subject.[19] Instead of merely representing an opportunity for what may become navel-gazing and introspection, Bourdieu saw reflexivity as a necessary component of the process of research. Bourdieu's vision of reflexivity demanded that social scientists consider what the stakes of our research are, why we have come to the understandings that we have, what kinds of alignments underlay our own actions, and what power dynamics are at work in the constitution of our own knowledge. Bourdieu proposed reflexivity not as a way to reduce scientific knowledge "to its historical conditions," but instead "to enable those who do science to better understand the social mechanisms which orient scientific practice,"[20] in order to make science (of all kinds) stronger. In this sense, Bourdieu was the consummate radical empiricist.

When considered from the point of view of the field of communication—a field that has at least begun to assimilate and apply the idea of the 'observer-related nature of knowledge'—the concern for reflexivity prompts us to inquire into the history and structure of the field of communication. Reflexivity could give the field a critical sense of its own project. Though it is easy to imagine the idea of reflexivity being used as a cudgel by one faction hoping to take down a (presumably 'dominant') faction, a more useful approach would be to give the field a deeper sense of its own historical shifts, giving *all* factions within the field a sense of where their tools for understanding have come from, and how they have developed. Beyond this, a reflexive understanding of the field can give us a sense of the sources of and threats to the field's autonomy, its power to develop its own questions, methods, and theories. In a field like communication, with its unusual place in academe, there is much to be hoped for in the kinds of reflexive accountings that, in Karin Wahl-Jorgensen's words, consider "our stakes as producers of knowledge."[21] The growing bibliography concerning the history of communication study offers promise, but there is much more to be done; the work has barely been started.

Though some might imagine reflexivity as code for navel-gazing, Bourdieu positioned reflexivity as a way to engage the world. As a scholar who played a significant role in the politics of his time—to the point where he would be remembered as "France's foremost public intellectual after the passing of Foucault"[22]—Bourdieu channeled his reflexive efforts in such a way as to connect with the world outside academe. Instead of simply using plugging himself into media appearances in a manner that would have made him yield to the heteronomous, market-based logics of media reportage,[23] Bourdieu wrote for the public in a way that preserved his own skepticism regarding how the issues were framed before he arrived on the scene. If any scholars should understand the potential pitfalls that could occur when reaching out to a public via the media, one would hope that media scholars would be in the vanguard.

Characteristically, Bourdieu did not think that the ideal of the lone intellectual addressing a mass audience was likely to sustain a meaningful engagement between good science and the public. He called reflexivity "the absolute prerequisite to any political action by intellectuals,"[24] and hoped to create "new forms of communication between researchers and activists."[25] "Cultural producers," including knowledge-workers like communication scholars, must "agree to work collectively for the defence of their own interests," to counteract "technocrats," and to "defend the economic and social conditions of the autonomy of these socially privileged universes in which the material and intellectual instruments of what we call Reason are produced and reproduced."[26] Bourdieu was skeptical of any and all laissez-faire arrangements, and in this, he was the ultimate believer in structure. If the defense of 'what we call Reason' were to succeed, there should be little doubt about the fact that we will need structures in order to defend it. Bourdieu lamented that the "autonomy that science had gradually won against the religious, political or even economic powers, and, partially at least, against the state bureaucracies... has been greatly weakened."[27] The only way to begin to defend science—and, in particular, social science—would be to create structures that could defend this autonomy anew, and to do so in a global context.

The result of this intense reflexive focus would be, he hoped, quite the opposite of an inwardly focused field. Instead, reflexivity could lead to a more meaningful engagement with the public. He hoped to create a collective intellectual structure that would "invent new forms of communication between researchers and activists, which means a new division of labor between them."[28] He suggested that scholars "create...a structure for collective research, interdisciplinary and international, bringing together social scientists, activists, [and] representatives of activists."[29] Scholars in this context would be able to help "non-professionals to equip themselves with specific weapons of resistance, so as to combat the effects of authority and the grip of television, which plays an absolutely crucial role."[30]

The field of communication has changed quickly in the last several decades. It has grown tremendously, it has become more intellectually diverse, and it shows signs of meaningful internationalization. This has come at a time of major shifts in higher education. In the U.S., many treasured sources of intellectual autonomy in the academy have been threatened by: adjustments in faculty labor arrangements as found in the increasing reliance on part-time teaching, budget pressures on higher education that pit many universities against other publically funded entities, the development of for-profit educational organizations that adjust the operations of the field of higher education, and political involvement in university policies. In short, it is difficult to imagine a more pressing issue for the field of communication than its own place—and its future—in this environment. Are we creating the kinds of scholars who are required to formulate a scholarly response to these pressures? Or are we becoming a field that is engineered to offer a convenient, tuition- and grant-generating solution to short-term political, labor, and budgetary problems, only to let down the public? If the field cannot hold these forces in abeyance, there is little hope for our future value to the public. Bourdieu gave to communication and media studies a compelling vision of how collective self-understanding in a field can be put in the service of the profession *and* the public. It would be a shame to ignore him.

Notes

Chapter One: Pierre Bourdieu's Legacy and the Study of Communication

1. Jenkins, *Pierre Bourdieu*, 12.
2. Sallaz and Zavisca, "Bourdieu in American Sociology," 26.
3. Ibid., 27.
4. Lizardo, "The Three Phases of Bourdieu's U.S. Reception," 242.
5. See Benson and Neveu, *Bourdieu and the Journalistic Field*.
6. See, in particular, Hesmondhalgh, "Bourdieu, the Media and Cultural Production."
7. See Thompson, *The Media and Modernity*.
8. See Couldry, *Media Rituals*, and Couldry, *Media, Society, World*.
9. Craig, "Communication Theory as a Field," 119.
10. See, in particular, Swartz, *Culture and Power*.
11. Amongst other things, such a promise would neglect to account for the habitus of communication researchers.
12. Grenfell, *Pierre Bourdieu: Agent Provocateur*, 26.
13. Bourdieu, *Outline of a Theory of Practice*, 73.
14. This is the most frequently cited similarity between the idea of habitus and Anthony Giddens' structuration theory. *See* Giddens, *The Constitution of Society*.
15. Bourdieu, *Outline of a Theory of Practice*, 78.
16. Ibid.
17. Bourdieu, *The Logic of Practice*, 53.

18. Bourdieu and Wacquant, *An Invitation to Reflexive Sociology*, 126.
19. Swartz, *Culture and Power*, 290.
20. Grossberg, "Cultural Studies vs. Political Economy," 72.
21. Presumably, this will supply those of us in communication not with peace, but with new squabbles. Much as Bourdieu's work has provoked controversy in sociology, let us hope it has the power to do the same in communication.
22. Bourdieu, *The Logic of Practice*, 67.
23. Ibid.
24. This is not to imply that communication (or any other field of academic study) can stand completely outside of these routinized, evanescent, and embodied processes. Indeed, Bourdieu's call for scholarly reflexivity was a recognition of these same dimensions of social processes in our own attempts to describe social processes.
25. Johnson, in Bourdieu, *The Field of Cultural Production*, 6.
26. Ibid.
27. Bourdieu and Wacquant, *Invitation to Reflexive Sociology*, 97.
28. Ibid.
29. Ibid.
30. Ibid.
31. Thompson, *The Media and Modernity*, 12.
32. Ibid.
33. Bourdieu and Wacquant, *Invitation to Reflexive Sociology*, 96.
34. Ibid., 104.
35. Ibid.
36. Ibid., 105.
37. Ibid.
38. Ibid., 110.
39. Ibid.
40. Swartz, *Culture and Power*, 119.
41. Ibid.
42. Benson and Neveu, "Introduction" in *Bourdieu and the Journalistic Field*, 11.
43. Bourdieu, *Field of Cultural Production*, 162.
44. Bourdieu, "The Forms of Capital," 46.
45. Ibid.
46. Bourdieu, *Language and Symbolic Power*, 230.
47. Bourdieu, "The Forms of Capital," 47.
48. Ibid.
49. Ibid., 51.
50. Ibid., 52.
51. Ibid.
52. Bourdieu, *Language and Symbolic Power*, 43.
53. Ibid., 72.
54. Bourdieu, *In Other Words*, 45. It is worth pointing out that the same passage finds Bourdieu describing how he developed the "notion of the field" both *against* Weber and *with* Weber," and suggesting the utility of thinking "with Durkheim against Durkheim."

55. Bourdieu, "The Forms of Capital," 47.
56. Ibid., 54.
57. Ibid.
58. Bourdieu and Wacquant, *Invitation to Reflexive Sociology*, 30. The Burke quotation comes from Burke, *On Symbols and Society*, 282.
59. Mills, *The Sociological Imagination*, 50.

Chapter Two: The Field of Media Production

1. See Hallin and Mancini, *Comparing Media Systems*, esp. Chap. 4.
2. Hesmondhalgh, "Bourdieu, the Media and Cultural Production," 211.
3. Ibid., 212.
4. Ibid., 215.
5. Ibid., 217.
6. Ibid.
7. Ibid., 220.
8. Ibid.
9. Garnham, "Bourdieu, the Cultural Arbitrary and Television," 189.
10. Hesmondhalgh, "Bourdieu, the Media and Cultural Production," 220. Garnham, "Bourdieu, the Cultural Arbitrary and Television," 189.
11. Marx & Engels, *The German Ideology*, 47.
12. Krais, "Gender and Symbolic Violence," 169.
13. Mosco, "Revisiting the Political Economy of Communication," 95.
14. Ibid., 96.
15. Ibid., 97.
16. Ibid., 103.
17. Bourdieu, *Outline of a Theory of Practice*, 183.
18. For more on this, see Craig Calhoun's "Habitus, Field, and Capital," 68.
19. Bourdieu and Wacquant, *An Invitation to Reflexive Sociology*, 124–126.
20. Bourdieu, *Language and Symbolic Power*, 66.
21. The author thanks Lee Artz for this way of putting it.
22. Miège, "Capitalism and Communication," 88.
23. Streeter, "Romanticism in Business Culture."
24. Smythe, "Communications: Blindspot of Western Marxism."
25. Darras, "Media Consecration of the Political Order," 166.
26. Ibid.
27. Bourdieu, *Outline of a Theory of Practice*.
28. Thomas, *Doing Critical Ethnography*.
29. Pendakur, "Political Economy and Ethnography."
30. Jenkins, *Convergence Culture*, 234.
31. Silverstone, "What's New About New Media," 10.
32. Bourdieu, *The Field of Cultural Production*, 30.

33. Ibid., 45.
34. Couldry, "Media Meta-Capital," 659.
35. Swartz, *Culture and Power*, 128.
36. Bourdieu, *Language and Symbolic Power*, 38.
37. Bourdieu, *On Television*, 37.
38. Benson, "News Media as a 'Journalistic Field,'" 198.
39. Benson, *Shaping Immigration News*, 129.
40. See Fourcade, *Economists and Societies*.
41. Alexander, "The Mass News Media."
42. Hallin, "Field Theory, Differentiation Theory," 226.
43. Ibid., 227.
44. Ibid.
45. Ibid., 231.
46. Ibid., 233.
47. Ibid., 235.
48. See Schudson, "Autonomy from What?"
49. Hallin, "Field Theory, Differentiation Theory," 240.
50. Ibid., 236.
51. Ibid.
52. Swartz, *Culture and Power*, 120.
53. Ibid., 123.
54. Benson, "Field Theory in Comparative Context," 463.
55. Ibid., 479.
56. Ibid., 481.
57. Ibid.
58. Swartz, *Culture and Power*, 125.
59. Ibid., 124.
60. Ibid., 131.
61. Cross-media platforms demonstrate that individual media are not perfectly stable differentiators of fields. However, the continuing power of fields seems to be demonstrated in how stubbornly media producers continue to cling to within-media competition. We still speak of a motion picture industry, a music industry, and so forth. This is evidence of a field-ness that is linked to individual medium.
62. See Bourdieu, *On Television*, especially 48–59.
63. See Bennett et al., *Culture, Class, Distinction*, especially chapter 8.
64. Owen and Wildman, *Video Economics*, 54.
65. Bourdieu, *The Field of Cultural Production*, 33.
66. See Turow, *Breaking Up America*, 1997.
67. Janet Stager and Sabine Hake, *Convergence Media History*, ix.
68. Hesmondhalgh, "Bourdieu, the Media and Cultural Production," 221.
69. Bourdieu, *The Field of Cultural Production*, 115.
70. Ibid.
71. Bourdieu, *The Rules of Art*, 217.
72. Ibid.

73. Ibid.
74. Bourdieu, *The Field of Cultural Production*, 39.
75. Ibid., 168.
76. Ibid., 169.
77. It is worth pointing out that Bourdieu himself developed much more versatile uses of the term autonomy, especially in his later writings on journalism.
78. Bourdieu, *On Television*, 62.
79. Bourdieu, *The Rules of Art*, 299.
80. Bourdieu, *The Field of Cultural Production*, 115.
81. Bourdieu, *The Rules of Art*, 216.
82. Ibid., 220–221.
83. Ibid., 218.
84. Ibid., 345.
85. Ibid.
86. Lippmann, *Public Opinion*, 238.
87. Jansen, *Walter Lippmann*, 117.
88. Habermas, *The Structural Transformation of the Public Sphere*.
89. Bourdieu, *The Rules of Art*, 344.
90. Hesmondhalgh, "Bourdieu, the Media and Cultural Production," 222.
91. Menzel, "Quasi-Mass Communication," 407.
92. Ibid., 406–407.
93. See, for instance, Bourdieu, *Distinction*, 442.
94. Atton, *Alternative Media*, 25. Atton rejects most of Bourdieu's field model for application to independent media, in large part because he finds it lacks a sufficient account for the potential for the emergence of radicalism.
95. Duncombe, *Notes from Underground*, 56.
96. Benson, "Commercialism and Critique," 122.
97. O'Neil, *Cyberchiefs*, 2.
98. Benkler and Nissenbaum, "Commons-based Peer Production and Virtue," 394.
99. McLuhan, *Understanding Media*, ix.
100. Peters, "And Lead Us Not," 23.
101. Acland, "Introduction," xix–xx.
102. Bourdieu, *Distinction*, 5. Acland cites this in his introduction for *Residual Media*, xv.
103. Bourdieu, "The Forms of Capital," 54.
104. Ibid., 43.
105. Hesmondhalgh, "Bourdieu, the Media and Cultural Production," 220.
106. Ibid., 222.
107. There is much reason to believe that this strategy is not so new. US television programming in the 1950s often displayed a concern for countering concerns that it was low culture. Comic books in the 1950s were often produced in part to counter claims that comic books were merely trash culture.
108. Bourdieu, *The Field of Cultural Production*, 50.
109. Ibid., 50–51.
110. Ibid., 51.

111. Ibid.
112. Ibid., 121.
113. This is certainly an argument advanced by Robert Darnton, in "Writing News and Telling Stories," and by Barbie Zelizer in "Journalists as Interpretive Communities," and considered in numerous chapters in Rodney Benson and Erik Neveu's *Bourdieu and the Journalistic Field.*
114. Rosenbaum, *Movie Wars*, 93.
115. Hesmondhalgh, "Bourdieu, the Media and Cultural Production," 222.
116. Neuman, *The Future of the Mass Audience*, 13.
117. See Turow, *Niche Envy.*
118. Katz, "And Deliver Us from Segmentation," 22, 33.
119. Benson, "Field Theory in Comparative Context," 483.
120. Ibid., 483–484.
121. Ibid., 484.
122. Ibid., 487.
123. Ibid.
124. Ibid.
125. Ibid., 488.
126. Bourdieu, *The Rules of Art*, 234.
127. Ibid., 253.

Chapter Three: The Media Audience: Fluency, Strategy, and *Le Sens Practique*

1. Christian Vermehren observes that the field of communication's search for strong media effects in the audience leaves media effects theories vulnerable to the Bourdieusian charge that they are merely "constructing prophecies…which serve as symbolic weapons in the same social struggle they hope to explain." See Vermehren, "Bourdieu and Media Studies," 188.
2. Curran, "The New Revisionism," 151. My line of reasoning here follows from Jeff Pooley's "Lost in Traslation."
3. Vermehren, "Bourdieu and Media Studies," 191.
4. Couldry, *Media, Society, World*, 39.
5. See Pooley, "Lost in Translation," for more specific insight regarding the negligence of Bourdieu in the field of communication
6. Neveu, "Bourdieu and the Frankfurt School," 204.
7. Ibid.
8. Ibid., 205.
9. Ibid., 208.
10. Ibid.
11. Ibid., 209.
12. Ibid.
13. Cicourel, "Structural and Processual Epistemologies," 94.

14. Bourdieu, *The Logic of Practice*, 31.
15. Bourdieu, *In Other Words*, 61
16. Bouveresse, "Rules, Dispositions, and the *Habitus*," 51.
17. Bourdieu, *In Other Words*, 61.
18. Ibid.
19. Bourdieu, *The Logic of Practice*, 69
20. Certainly Bourdieu himself was aware of the similarities between his own understanding of praxis and the views of the pragmatists. See Bourdieu and Wacquant, *An Invitation to Reflexive Sociology*, 122.
21. See Radway, *Reading the Romance*.
22. Taylor, "To Follow a Rule," 50.
23. Ibid.
24. LaRose, "The Problem of Media Habits," 194.
25. Ibid., 196.
26. Gross, "Modes of Communication," 62.
27. Ibid., 57.
28. Ibid., 62.
29. Ibid., 65
30. Gross, "How True Is Television's Image?," 29.
31. Ibid., 30.
32. Bourdieu, *Practical Reason*, 55.
33. Bourdieu, *Distinction*, 1.
34. Bourdieu, *Distinction*, 2.
35. Bourdieu and Darbel, *The Love of Art*, 37.
36. Thompson, Editor's Introduction to Bourdieu, *Language and Symbolic Power*, 14.
37. Indeed, it is tempting to suggest that 'symbolic competence' is simply a better term than 'cultural capital.'
38. Bourdieu, *Sociology in Question*, 151.
39. Bourdieu and Darbel, *The Love of Art*, 111.
40. See Kellner and Share, "Toward Critical Media Literacy."
41. Peterson and Kern, "Changing Highbrow Taste," 903–904.
42. Bennett et al., *Culture, Class, Distinction*, 92.
43. Ibid., 112.
44. Ibid., 137.
45. Hall, "Encoding/Decoding," 130.
46. Ibid., 135.
47. Ibid.
48. Ibid., 136–138.
49. Benson, "Field Theory in Comparative Context," 463.
50. du Gay et al., *Doing Cultural Studies*, 3.
51. Entman, *Democracy Without Citizens*, 17–19.
52. McChesney, *The Problem of the Media*, 200–201. It is worth pointing out that Say's Law was not originally proposed as a way to understand communication codes, and that McChesney's usage of the term may cause some economists to experience a hacking cough.
53. Bourdieu and Darbel, *The Love of Art*, 37.

54. Ibid.
55. Ibid., 59
56. Ibid., 68–69.
57. Bourdieu, *The Rules of Art*, 253.
58. Nakamura, "Interrogating the Digital Divide," 71.
59. Ibid., 80.
60. Ibid.
61. Nakamura, *Digitizing Race*, 33.
62. Marvin, *When Old Technologies Were New*, 9.
63. Ibid., 15.
64. Bourdieu, *Distinction*, 6.
65. Bourdieu, *Practical Reason*, 3.
66. Ibid., 4–5
67. Bourdieu, *Distinction*, 232
68. Wiener, *The Human Use of Human Beings*, 70.
69. Bourdieu, *Distinction*, 233.
70. Ibid.
71. Ibid., 234.
72. Bourdieu, "The Production of Belief," 268.
73. McMurran, "Brandon Tartikoff."
74. I am indebted to an anonymous reviewer for this point regarding the relevance of homologies to mass production and its audiences.
75. Bourdieu, *Distinction*, 32.
76. Bourdieu, *Photography*, 17.
77. Benson, "Field Theory in Comparative Context," 485.
78. Peters, *Speaking into the Air*, 62.
79. Turow, *Breaking Up America*, 3
80. Rheingold, *The Virtual Community*, 145.
81. Sundén, 3. Cited in boyd & Ellison, "Social Network Sites."
82. boyd & Ellison, "Social Network Sites."
83. Livingstone, "Taking Risky Opportunities," 408.
84. Papacharissi, "Without You, I'm Nothing."
85. Bourdieu, *Distinction*, 482.
86. Rubin, "Ritualized and Instrumental Television Viewing," 76.
87. Ibid.
88. Swartz, *Culture and Power*, 87.
89. Ibid.
90. Ibid.
91. Carey, *Communication as Culture*, 18.
92. Ibid., 20
93. Ibid., 21
94. Couldry, *Media Rituals*, 4.
95. Ibid.
96. Ibid., 49.

97. Bourdieu, *Pascalian Meditations*, 135.

98. Couldry, *Media Rituals*, 29.

99. Silverstone, *The Message of Television*, 182.

100. Couldry, *Media Rituals*, 26.

101. Silverstone, *The Message of Television*, 182.

102. Bourdieu, *The Logic of Practice*, p. 75

103. Ibid.

104. Time-shifting (the consumption of mediated texts at times other than the moment of their transmission) has the power to disrupt this. Much as narrow-casting may lend itself to a social disunity based on content, time-shifting may sow the seeds of disunity of a temporal form.

105. Dayan and Katz, *Media Events*, 16.

106. Ibid., 16–17.

107. Lamont, *Money, Morals, & Manners*, 181.

108. Couldry, *Media Rituals*, 41.

109. Swartz, *Culture and Power*, 87.

110. Napoli, *Audience Evolution*, 57. Napoli cites notes from the International Advertising Bureau's 2008 Audience Measurement Leadership Forum in New York.

111. Couldry, *Media Rituals*, 35.

112. Here I draw from Grenfell, *Pierre Bourdieu*, 173.

113. Livingstone, "Relationships Between Media and Audiences," 244.

114. Ibid., 251.

115. Ibid.

116. Bourdieu and Wacquant, *An Invitation to Reflexive Sociology*, 30.

117. Morley, *Media, Modernity, and Technology*, 81.

Chapter Four: Symbolic Power and Authority: The Power/Communication Nexus

1. Weber, "Politics as a Vocation," 78.

2. Weber, *Economy and Society*, 263.

3. Weber, "Politics as a Vocation," 78.

4. Carey, "The Communications Revolution," 24.

5. Ibid., 26.

6. Murphy, "'Our Mission and Our Moment,'" 621.

7. *See* Ronald Walter Greene, "Rhetorical Materialism."

8. Thompson, *The Media and Modernity*, 17.

9. Ibid., 16.

10. Gouldner, *The Dialectic of Ideology and Technology*, 33.

11. Ibid., 33.

12. Ibid., 95.

13. Ibid., 96.

14. Lincoln, *Authority*, 4.
15. Lincoln, *Authority*, 5.
16. Bourdieu, *Language and Symbolic Power*, 54.
17. Bourdieu, *Language and Symbolic Power*, 34. The point is, of course, largely consistent with many of the insights to come from sociolinguistics. Space limitations prevent a fuller discussion of this. For more on sociolinguistics, see Labov, *Language in the Inner City* and *Sociolinguistic Patterns*, or Bernstein, *Class, Codes, and Control*.
18. Bourdieu and Wacquant, *An Invitation to Reflexive Sociology*, 142–143.
19. Ibid., 149.
20. Bourdieu and Wacquant, *An Invitation to Reflexive Sociology*, 149.
21. Guiraud, *Le Français Populaire*.
22. Bourdieu and Wacquant, *An Invitation to Reflexive Sociology*, 149.
23. Thompson, Editor's Introduction in Bourdieu, *Language and Symbolic Power*, 12.
24. Ibid., 2.
25. Bourdieu, *Language and Symbolic Power*, 105.
26. Bourdieu and Wacquant, *An Invitation to Reflexive Sociology*, 146.
27. Ibid.
28. Bourdieu, *Language and Symbolic Power*, 45.
29. Ibid., 38–39.
30. Bourdieu and Wacquant, *An Invitation to Reflexive Sociology*, 147.
31. Bourdieu was not always careful to separate his discussion of symbolic power and authority. At the very least, these two terms have substantial overlap in Bourdieu's writings.
32. Bourdieu and Wacquant, *An Invitation to Reflexive Sociology*, 148.
33. Ibid.
34. Bourdieu, *Language and Symbolic Power*, 73.
35. Ibid.
36. Here Bourdieu also implicitly invokes Erving Goffman's "Felicity's Condition."
37. Ibid., 111.
38. In Bourdieu, *Language & Symbolic Power*, 24–25.
39. Bourdieu, *Language and Symbolic Power*, 72.
40. Ibid., 170.
41. Ibid.
42. Ibid.
43. Ibid., 113.
44. Ibid.
45. Ibid., 192.
46. Ibid., 107.
47. Bourdieu, *Language and Symbolic Power*, 82.
48. Alice Crawford does a terrific job skewering this myth of new media. As she has it, because "our linguistic practices themselves carry the markings of our backgrounds, betraying or trading on the training of a certain position," online communication is by no means free from the social processes of credentialing or authorization. Crawford, "The Myth of the Unmarked Net Speaker," 101.
49. See Epstein, "The Analog History of the 'Digital Divide.'"

50. Cappella and Jamieson, *Spiral of Cynicism.*
51. Moy and Scheufele, "Media Effects," 751–752.
52. Johnson and Kaye, "Wag the Blog," 634.
53. Bourdieu, *Language and Symbolic Power*, 133.
54. Ibid., 134.
55. Ibid., 41.
56. Ibid., 66.
57. Ibid.
58. Ibid.
59. Ibid.
60. Ibid., 137.
61. Ibid.
62. In Bourdieu, *Language & Symbolic Power*, 14.
63. Foucault, *Power/Knowledge*, 113.
64. Quoted in Bourdieu, *The Field of Cultural Production*, 33.
65. Bourdieu, *The Field of Cultural Production*, 33.
66. Zelizer, *Covering the Body*, 2.
67. Janet Cooke won a Pulitzer Prize for her *Washington Post* story about a heroin-addicted eight-year-old boy from Washington, D.C. This story was later demonstrated to have been fabricated.
68. Eason, "On Journalistic Authority," 431.
69. Bourdieu, *Language and Symbolic Power*, 77
70. Ibid.
71. In Bourdieu, *Language & Symbolic Power*, 20.
72. Bourdieu, *Language and Symbolic Power*, 79.
73. Ibid.
74. Ibid., 139.
75. Ibid.
76. Ibid., 141–142.
77. Park, "Blogging with Authority."
78. Bourdieu, *Masculine Domination*, 2.
79. Bourdieu, *In Other Words*, 150.
80. Another way of putting this would be to say that when experts communicate with each other, as is the case with material published in professional journals, 'the people' is a less pressing concern. It will be fascinating to see how (or if) this situation changes with the creation of more open-access journals.
81. Bourdieu, *In Other Words*, 152.
82. Bourdieu, *The Field of Cultural Production*, 124.
83. Park, "Blogging with Authority."
84. Park, "The Couch and the Clinic."
85. The ostensible 'crisis' in journalism relates in no small part to the fact that journalists currently find themselves re-appraising how to accomplish this goal, how to develop a kind of monopoly over legitimate journalistic discourse.
86. McLuhan, *The Gutenberg Galaxy*, 209.

87. Lazarsfeld and Merton, "Mass Communication, Popular Taste, and Organized Social Action," 561.
88. Herbst, "Political Authority in a Mediated Age," 489.
89. Ibid.
90. Ibid.
91. Ibid., 490.
92. Ibid., 499.
93. Benson, "Field Theory in Comparative Context," 469.
94. Ibid.
95. Ibid., 470.
96. Couldry, "Media Meta-Capital," 663.
97. Ibid.
98. Ibid., 665.
99. Ibid., 666.
100. Ibid.
101. Ibid., 668.
102. Ibid.
103. Ibid.
104. Ibid., 669.
105. Ibid.
106. Ibid.
107. Ibid.
108. Bruns, *Blogs, Wikipedia, Second Life, and Beyond*, 15.
109. Ibid., 17.
110. Ibid., 19.
111. Ibid.
112. Ibid., 20.
113. O'Neil, *Cyberchiefs*, 80.
114. Bruns, *Blogs, Wikipedia, Second Life, and Beyond*, 215.
115. Hindman, *The Myth of Digital Democracy*, 57.
116. See Lundby, *Mediatization*.
117. See Iyengar & Hahn, "Red Media, Blue Media."
118. Morrison, "Cultural and Moral Authority," 126.
119. Hayes, *Twilight of the Elites*, 11.
120. Judt, *Ill Fares the Land*, 199.
121. Bourdieu, *Acts of Resistance*, 76.

Chapter Five: Reflexivity and the History of the Field of Communication

1. My focus here will be placed on the field of communication in the U.S., for the sake of convenience. Some of my claims can be extended to histories of the field in other nations, but I lack sufficient space here to begin to address all of these histories.

2. Wahl-Jorgensen, "Rebellion and Ritual," 87.
3. Ibid., 112.
4. Pooley, "The New History," 60.
5. Bourdieu, *Homo Academicus*, xi.
6. Ibid., xii.
7. Ibid., 5.
8. Brush, "Should the History." I am indebted to Jeff Pooley for introducing me to this comparison.
9. Brush, "Should the History," 183.
10. Bourdieu, *Pascalian Meditations*, 131.
11. Pooley and Park, "Introduction," 1.
12. Ibid., 4.
13. Bourdieu and Wacquant, *An Invitation to Reflexive Sociology*, 40.
14. Wacquant refers in particular to Alvin W. Gouldner's version of reflexivity as expressed in Gouldner's *The Coming Crisis in Western Sociology*.
15. Bourdieu and Wacquant, *An Invitation to Reflexive Sociology*, 36.
16. Bourdieu, *Science of Science and Reflexivity*, 65.
17. Bourdieu and Wacquant, *An Invitation to Reflexive Sociology*, 38.
18. Bourdieu, *Science of Science and Reflexivity*, 89.
19. Tunstall, "The Trouble with U.S.," 93.
20. Peters, "Institutional Sources," 543.
21. McChesney, *Communication Revolution*, 6.
22. Pooley, "Another Plea," 1442.
23. Ibid.
24. Ibid., 1453.
25. Bourdieu, *Science of Science and Reflexivity*, 56.
26. Bourdieu, *Homo Academicus*, 151.
27. Ibid., 9.
28. Ibid., 119.
29. Bourdieu and Wacquant, *An Invitation to Reflexive Sociology*, 187.
30. Bourdieu, *Science of Science and Reflexivity*, 47.
31. Bourdieu and Wacquant, *An Invitation to Reflexive Sociology*, 184.
32. Bourdieu, *Science of Science and Reflexivity*, 88.
33. Jacobs and Townsley, *The Space of Opinion*, 98.
34. Bourdieu, *Science of Science and Reflexivity*, 87.
35. Ibid., 88.
36. Ibid., viii.
37. Bourdieu and Wacquant, *An Invitation to Reflexive Sociology*, 183–184.
38. Bourdieu, *Science of Science and Reflexivity*, 66.
39. Ibid.
40. Bourdieu and Wacquant, *An Invitation to Reflexive Sociology*, 77.
41. Abbott, *Chaos of Disciplines*, 157.
42. Buxton, "John Marshall and the Humanities in Europe," 152.
43. Gary, *The Nervous Liberals*.
44. Rowland, "American Telecommunications Policy Research," 165.

45. Pooley and Katz, "Further Notes on Why American Sociology," 767.
46. Ibid., 776.
47. Bourdieu, *Homo Academicus*, xxiv.
48. Ibid., xxiv.
49. Ibid., 129.
50. Ibid.
51. Ibid., 137.
52. Also: there is reason to suspect that this is not only a recent issue for the field, inside or outside of the Anglo-American world.
53. Donsbach, "The Identity of Communication Research," 445.
54. Bourdieu, *Science of Science and Reflexivity*, 41–42.
55. Calhoun, "Communication as Social Science," 1480.
56. Ibid., 1481.
57. Obviously, Bourdieu's *Distinction* addresses this, and there is no small amount of sociological work dedicated to symbolic divides and differences. See *Cultivating Differences*, Michèle Lamont and Marcel Fournier, eds.
58. Bourdieu, *Science of Science and Reflexivity*, 35.
59. Ibid.
60. Ibid.
61. Bourdieu, *Homo Academicus*, 14.
62. Bourdieu, *Science of Science and Reflexivity*, 45.
63. Ibid., 46.
64. Ibid.
65. Bourdieu, *Homo Academicus*, 74.
66. Highton, "Green Eye-Shades Vs. Chi Squares."
67. Bourdieu, *Science of Science and Reflexivity*, 46.
68. Rowland, *The Politics of TV Violence*.
69. Ibid.
70. Gitlin, "Media Sociology."
71. Lazarsfeld, "An Episode," 315, quoted in Gitlin, "Media Sociology."
72. Bourdieu, *Homo Academicus*, 79.
73. Ibid., 113.
74. Ibid.
75. Ibid.
76. The term 'classificatory epithet,' used by Calhoun and VanAntwerpen, comes from Bourdieu, *Homo Academicus*, 14.
77. Calhoun and VanAntwerpen, "Orthodoxy, Heterodoxy, and Hierarchy," 410.
78. Bourdieu, *Homo Academicus*, 125.
79. Ibid.
80. Kuhn, *The Structure of Scientific Revolutions*.
81. Bourdieu, *Science of Science and Reflexivity*, 11.
82. Ibid., 15.
83. Swartz, *Culture & Power*, 213.
84. Ibid., 217.

85. Benson, "On the Explanatory and Political Uses," 5.
86. Ibid., 5–6.
87. Ibid., 17.
88. Ibid., 35–36.
89. Löblich and Scheu, "Writing the History of Communication Studies," 15.
90. In keeping with Bourdieu's dialectical approach, the discarded ideas themselves become eligible for homologous linkages with marginalized positions in the field, and thus become potential avenues for rediscovery, for new bids to challenge the central.
91. Bourdieu, *Science of Science and Reflexivity*, 44.
92. Ibid., 40–41.
93. Ibid., 41.
94. Ibid.
95. Ibid.
96. Ibid.
97. Bourdieu, *Homo Academicus*, 150.
98. Ibid., 40.
99. Ibid., 143–144.
100. Abbott, "The Historicality of Individuals," 3.
101. Simonson, "Writing Figures into the Field," 294.
102. Ibid., 300.
103. See Summers, "Perpetual Revelations."
104. See Morrison, "Opportunity Structures."
105. See Pooley and Park, "Communication Research."
106. See Meyen, "The Founding Parents of Communication."
107. Nerone, "The Future of Communication History," 255.
108. Sismondo, "Bourdieu's Rationalist Science of Science," 94.
109. Ibid.

Chapter Six: Conclusion: Communication as Practical, Relational, Historical, and Reflexive

1. Wittgenstein, *Tractatus Logico-Philosophicus*, 89.
2. Bourdieu, *In Other Words*, 61.
3. The best example of Bourdieu's demonstration of the 'impurity' of philosophy is his *The Political Ontology of Martin Heidegger*.
4. Giddens, *The Constitution of Society*, xxiii.
5. Couldry, *Media, Society, World*, 35.
6. Bourdieu and Wacquant, *An Invitation to Reflexive Sociology*, 127.
7. Benson, "Field Theory in Comparative Context," 477.
8. Nerone, "The Future of Communication History," 260.
9. For example, recent years have witnessed the founding of history sections in the International Communication Association (ICA), the European Communication Research and Education

Association (ECREA), and the International Association for Media and Communication Research (IAMCR).

10. See, in particular, Jenkins, "Pierre Bourdieu and the Reproduction of Determinism" for an excellent version of this critique.
11. Steinmetz, "Bourdieu, Historicity, and Historical Sociology," 51.
12. Bourdieu and Wacquant, *Invitation to Reflexive Sociology*, 136.
13. Ibid., 102.
14. Ibid., 90.
15. Bourdieu, *Science of Science and Reflexivity*, 35.
16. Bourdieu and Wacquant, *Invitation to Reflexive Sociology*, 94.
17. Bermejo, "Introduction," in *On Communicating*, 3.
18. Gouldner, *The Coming Crisis of Western Sociology*.
19. Bourdieu distanced himself explicitly from Gouldner's approach to reflexivity. See Bourdieu and Wacquant, *An Invitation to Reflexive Sociology*, 72.
20. Bourdieu, *Science of Science and Reflexivity*, viii.
21. Wahl-Jorgensen, "Rebellion and Ritual," 87.
22. Calhoun and Wacquant, "'Everything Is Social'," 3.
23. Bourdieu, *On Television*, 77.
24. Bourdieu, *Firing Back*, 19.
25. Bourdieu, *Acts of Resistance*, 57.
26. Bourdieu, *The Rules of Art*, 348.
27. Bourdieu, *Science of Science and Reflexivity*, vii.
28. Bourdieu, *On Television*, 57.
29. Ibid., 56.
30. Ibid., 57.

References

Abbott, Andrew. *Chaos of Disciplines*. Chicago: University of Chicago Press, 2001.
———. "The Historicality of Individuals." *Social Science History* 29, no. 1 (2005): 1–13. doi:10.1215/01455532-29-1-1.
Acland, Charles R. "Introduction." In *Residual Media*, edited by Charles R. Acland, xiii–xxvii. Minneapolis: University of Minnesota Press, 2007.
Alexander, Jeffrey. "The Mass News Media in Systemic, Historical and Comparative Perspective." In *Mass Media and Social Change*, edited by Elihu Katz and Tamás Szecskö, 17–52. Beverly Hills, CA: Sage, 1981.
Atton, Chris. *Alternative Media*. London: Sage, 2002.
Benkler, Yochai and Helen Nissenbaum, "Commons-based Peer Production and Virtue." *The Journal of Political Philosophy* 14, no. 4 (2006): 394–419. doi: 10.1111/j.1467-9760.2006.00235.x
Bennett, Tony and Mike Savage, Elizabeth Silva, Alan Warde, Modesto Gayo-Cal, and David Wright. *Culture, Class, Distinction*. London: Routledge, 2009.
Benson, Rodney. "Commercialism and Critique." In *Contesting Media Power: Alternative Media in a Networked World*, edited by Nick Couldry and James Curran, 111–127. Lanham, MD: Rowman & Littlefield, 2003.
———. "Field Theory in Comparative Context: A New Paradigm for Media Studies." *Theory and Society* 28, no. 3 (1999): 463–498.
———. "News Media as a 'Journalistic Field': What Bourdieu Adds to New Institutionalism, and Vice Versa," *Political Communication* 23, no. 2 (2006): 187–202. doi: 10.1080/10584600600629802.

———. "On the Explanatory and Political Uses of Journalism History." *American Journalism* 30, no. 1 (2013): 4–14.

———. *Shaping Immigration News: A French-American Comparison*. New York: Cambridge University Press, 2013.

Benson, Rodney and Erik Neveu, eds. *Bourdieu and the Journalistic Field*. Cambridge, UK: Polity Press, 2005.

Bermejo, Fernando. "Introduction." In *On Communicating: Otherness, Meaning, and Information*, by Klaus Krippendorff, edited by Fernando Bermejo, 1–8. New York: Routledge, 2009.

Bernstein, Basil B. *Class, Codes and Control. Volume I: Theoretical Studies Towards a Sociology of Language*. London: Routledge, 1971.

Bourdieu, Pierre. *Acts of Resistance: Against the Tyranny of the Market*. Translated by Richard Nice. New York: The New Press, 1998.

———. *Distinction: A Social Critique of the Judgement of Taste*. Translated by Richard Nice. Cambridge, MA: Harvard University Press, 1984.

———. *The Field of Cultural Production: Essays on Art and Literature*. Edited and Introduced by Randal Johnson. New York: Columbia University Press, 1993.

———. *Firing Back: Against the Tyranny of the Market 2*. Translated by Loïc Wacquant. New York: The New Press, 2003.

———. "The Forms of Capital." Translated by Richard Nice. In *Education: Culture, Economy, and Society*, edited by A. H. Halsey, Hugh Lauder, Phillip Brown, and Amy Stuart Wells, 46–58. Oxford, UK: Oxford University Press, 1997.

———. *Homo Academicus*. Translated by Peter Collier. Stanford, CA: Stanford University Press, 1988.

———. *In Other Words: Essays Towards a Reflexive Sociology*. Translated by Matthew Adamson. Stanford, CA: Stanford University Press, 1990.

———. *Language and Symbolic Power*. Translated by Gina Raymond and Matthew Adamson. Edited and Introduced by John B. Thompson. Cambridge, MA: Harvard University Press, 1991.

———. *The Logic of Practice*. Translated by Richard Nice. Stanford, CA: Stanford University Press, 1990.

———. *Masculine Domination*. Translated by Richard Nice. Stanford, CA: Stanford University Press, 2001.

———. *On Television*. Translated by Priscilla Parkhurst Ferguson. New York: The New Press, 1998.

———. *Outline of a Theory of Practice*. Translated by Richard Nice. Cambridge, UK: Cambridge University Press, 1977.

———. *Pascalian Meditations*. Translated by Richard Nice. Stanford, CA: Stanford University Press, 2000.

———. *Photography: A Middle-Brow Art*. Translated by Shaun Whiteside. Stanford, CA: Stanford University Press, 1990.

———. *The Political Ontology of Martin Heidegger*. Translated by Peter Collier. Stanford, CA: Stanford University Press, 1991.

———. *Practical Reason: On the Theory of Action*. Stanford, CA: Stanford University Press, 1998.

————. "The Production of Belief: Contribution to an Economy of Symbolic Goods." *Media, Culture and Society* 2, no. 3: 261–293. doi: 10.1177/016344378000200305

————. *The Rules of Art: Genesis and Structure of the Literary Field.* Translated by Susan Emanuel. Stanford, CA: Stanford University Press, 1995.

————. *Science of Science and Reflexivity.* Translated by Richard Nice. Chicago: University of Chicago Press, 2004.

————. *Sociology in Question.* Translated by Richard Nice. London: SAGE, 1993.

Bourdieu, Pierre and Alain Darbel. *The Love of Art: European Art Museums and Their Public.* Translated by Caroline Beattie and Nick Merriman. Stanford, CA: Stanford University Press, 1990.

Bourdieu, Pierre and Loïc J. D. Wacquant. *An Invitation to Reflexive Sociology.* Chicago: University of Chicago Press, 1992.

Bouveresse, Jacques. "Rules, Dispositions, and the *Habitus.*" In *Bourdieu: A Critical Reader,* edited by Richard Shusterman, 45–63. Oxford: Blackwell, 1999.

boyd, danah and Nicole Ellison. "Social Network Sites: Definition, History, and Scholarship." *Journal of Computer-Mediated Communication* 13, no. 1 (2008): 210–230. doi: 10.1111/j.1083-6101.2007.00393.x

Bruns, Axel. *Blogs, Wikipedia, Second Life, and Beyond: From Production to Produsage.* New York: Peter Lang, 2008.

Brush, Stephen G. "Should the History of Science be Rated X?," *Science* 183, no. 4130 (1974): 1164–1172. doi: 10.2307/1737848.

Burke, Kenneth. *On Symbols and Society.* Chicago: University of Chicago Press, 1989.

Buxton, William J. "John Marshall and the Humanities in Europe: Shifting Patterns of Rockefeller Foundation Support." *Minerva* 41, no. 2 (2003): 133–153.

Calhoun, Craig. "Habitus, Field, and Capital: The Question of Historical Specificity." In *Bourdieu: Critical Perspectives,* edited by Craig Calhoun, Edward LiPuma, and Moishe Postone, 61–88. Chicago: University of Chicago Press, 1993.

————. "Communication as Social Science." *International Journal of Communication* 5 (2011): 1479–1496.

Calhoun, Craig and Jonathan VanAntwerpen. "Orthodoxy, Heterodoxy, and Hierarchy: 'Mainstream' Sociology and Its Challengers." In *Sociology in America: A History,* edited by Craig Calhoun, 367–410. Chicago: University of Chicago Press, 2007.

Calhoun, Craig and Loïc Wacquant. "'Everything Is Social': In Memoriam, Pierre Bourdieu (1930–2002)." *Footnotes* 30, no. 2 (2002). http://www.asanet.org/footnotes/feb02/fn5.html

Cappella, Joseph A. and Kathleen Hall Jamieson. *Spiral of Cynicism: The Press and the Public Good.* New York: Oxford University Press, 1997.

Carey, James W. *Communication as Culture: Essays on Media and Society.* New York: Routledge, 1992.

————. "The Communications Revolution and the Professional Communicator." *Sociological Review Monograph,* no. 13: 23–38.

Cicourel, Aaron V. "Aspects of Structural and Processual Theories of Knowledge." In *Bourdieu: Critical Perspectives,* edited by Craig Calhoun, Edward LiPuma, and Moishe Postone, 89–115. Chicago: University of Chicago Press, 1993.

Couldry, Nick. "Media Meta-capital: Extending the Range of Bourdieu's Field Theory." *Theory and Society* 32, no. 5–6 (2003): 653–677. doi: 10.1023/B:RYSO.0000004915.37826.5d.

———. *Media Rituals: A Critical Approach.* London: Routledge, 2003.

———. *Media, Society, World: Social Theory and Digital Media Practice.* London: Polity, 2012.

Craig, Robert T. "Communication Theory as a Field." *Communication Theory* 9, no. 2 (1999): 199–161. 10.1111/j.1468-2885.1999.tb00355.x.

Crawford, Alice. "The Myth of the Unmarked Net Speaker." In *Critical Perspectives on the Internet*, edited by Greg Elmer, 89-104. Lanham, MD: Rowman & Littlefield, 2002.

Curran, James. "The New Revisionism in Mass Communication Research: A Reappraisal." *European Journal of Communication* 5, no. 2 (1990): 135–164. doi: 10.1177/0267323190005002002.

Darnton, Robert. "Writing News and Telling Stories." *Daedalus* 104, no. 2 (1975): 175–194.

Darras, Eric. "Media Consecration of the Political Order." In *Bourdieu and the Journalistic Field*, edited by Rodney Benson and Erik Neveu, 156–173. London: Polity.

Dayan, Daniel and Elihu Katz. *Media Events: The Live Broadcasting of History.* Cambridge, MA: Harvard University Press, 1992.

Donsbach, Wolfgang. "The Identity of Communication Research." *Journal of Communication* 56, no. 3 (2006): 437–448. doi: 10.1111/j.1460-2466.2006.00294.x.

du Gay, Paul, Stuart Hall, Linda Janes, Hugh Mackay, and Keith Negus. *Doing Cultural Studies: The Story of the Sony Walkman.* London: SAGE, 1997.

Duncombe, Stephen. *Notes from Underground: Zines and the Politics of Alternative Culture.* London: Verso, 1997.

Eason, David L. "On Journalistic Authority: The Janet Cooke Scandal." *Critical Studies in Mass Communication* 3, no. 4 (1986): 429–447. doi: 10.1080/15295038609366674.

Entman, Robert M. *Democracy Without Citizens: Media and the Decay of American Politics.* New York: Oxford University Press, 1989.

Epstein, Dmitry. "The Analog History of the 'Digital Divide.'" In *The Long History of New Media*, edited by David W. Park, Nicholas W. Jankowski, and Steve Jones, 127–144. New York: Peter Lang, 2011.

Foucault, Michel. *Power/Knowledge: Selected Interviews and Other Writings, 1972–1977.* Edited by Colin Gordon. Translated by Colin Gordon, Leo Marshall, John Mepham, and Kate Soper. New York: Pantheon.

Fourcade, Marion. *Economists and Societies: Discipline and Profession in the United States, Britain, and France, 1890s to 1990s.* Princeton, NJ: Princeton University Press, 2009.

Garnham, Nicholas. "Bourdieu, the Cultural Arbitrary, and Television." In *Bourdieu: Critical Perspectives*, edited by Craig Calhoun, Edward LiPuma, and Moishe Postone, 178–192. Chicago: University of Chicago Press, 1993.

Gary, Brett. *The Nervous Liberals: Propaganda Anxieties from World War I to the Cold War.* New York: Columbia University Press, 1999.

Giddens, Anthony. *The Constitution of Society: Outline of the Theory of Structuration.* Berkeley, CA: University of California Press, 1984.

Gitlin, Todd. "Media Sociology: The Dominant Paradigm." *Theory and Society* 6, no. 2 (1978): 205–253.

Goffman, Erving. "Felicity's Condition." *American Journal of Sociology* 89, no. 1 (1983): 1–53.

Gouldner, Alvin W. *The Coming Crisis of Western Sociology*. New York: Basic Books, 1970.

Gouldner, Alvin W. *The Dialectic of Ideology and Technology: The Origins, Grammar, and Future of Ideology*. New York: Seabury Press, 1976.

Greene, Ronald Walter. "Rhetorical Materialism: The Rhetorical Subject and the General Intellect." In *Rhetoric, Materiality, and Politics*, edited by Barbara A. Biesecker and John Louis Lucaites, 43–65. New York: Peter Lang, 2009.

Grenfell, Michael. *Pierre Bourdieu: Agent Provocateur*. New York: Continuum, 2004.

Gross, Larry. "How True is Television's Image?" In *Getting the Message Across*, no editor listed, 23–52. Paris: UNESCO Press, 1975.

Grossberg, Lawrence. "Cultural Studies vs. Political Economy: Is Anybody Else Bored With This Debate?" *Critical Studies in Mass Communication* 12, no. 1 (1995): 72–81. doi: 10.1080/15295039509366920.

Guiraud, Pierre. *Le Français Populaire*. Paris: Presses Universitaires de France, 1965.

Habermas, *The Structural Transformation of the Public Sphere: An Inquiry into a Category of Bourgeois Society*. Translated by Thomas Burger with the assistance of Frederick Lawrence. Cambridge, MA: MIT Press, 1989.

Hall, Stuart. "Encoding/Decoding." In *Culture, Media Language: Working Papers in Cultural Studies, 1972–79*, edited by Stuart Hall, Dorothy Hobson, Andrew Lowe, and Paul Willis, 128–138. London: Routledge, 1992.

Hallin, Daniel C. "Field Theory, Differentiation Theory, and Comparative Media Research." In *Bourdieu and the Journalistic Field*, edited by Rodney Benson and Erik Neveu, 224–243. London: Polity, 2005.

Hallin, Daniel C. and Paolo Mancini, *Comparing Media Systems: Three Models of Media and Politics*. Cambridge, UK: Cambridge University Press, 2004.

Hayes, Christopher. *Twilight of the Elites: America After Meritocracy*. New York: Crown, 2012.

Herbst, Susan. "Political Authority in a Mediated Age." *Theory and Society* 32, no. 4 (2003): 481–503.

Hesmondhalgh, "Bourdieu, the Media and Cultural Production." *Media, Culture & Society* 28, no. 2 (2006): 211–231. doi: 10.1177/0163443706061682.

Highton, Jake. "Green Eye-Shades Vs. Chi Squares." *Quill*, February 1967: 10–13.

Hindman, Matthew. *The Myth of Digital Democracy*. Princeton, NJ: Princeton University Press, 2009.

Iyengar, Shanto and Kyu S. Hahn. "Red Media, Blue Media: Evidence of Ideological Selectivity in Media Use." *Journal of Communication* 59, no. 1 (2009): 19–39. doi: 10.1111/j.1460-2466.2008.01402.x.

Jacobs, Ronald N. and Eleanor Townsley, *The Space of Opinion: Media Intellectuals and the Public Sphere*. New York: Oxford University Press, 2011.

Jansen, Sue Curry. *Walter Lippmann: A Critical Introduction to Media and Communication Theory*. New York: Peter Lang, 2012.

Jenkins, Henry. *Convergence Culture: Where Old and New Media Collide*. New York: New York University Press, 2006.

Jenkins, Richard. *Pierre Bourdieu*. New York: Routledge, 1992.

———. "Pierre Bourdieu and the Reproduction of Determinism." *Sociology* 16, no. 2 (1982): 270–281. doi: 10.1177/0038038582016002008.

Johnson, Thomas J. and Barbara K. Kaye. "Wag the Blog: How Reliance on Traditional Media and the Internet Influence Credibility Perceptions of Weblogs Among Blog Users." *Journalism and Mass Communication Quarterly* 81, no. 3 (2004): 622–642. doi: 10.1177/107769900408100310

Judt, Tony. *Ill Fares the Land*. New York: Penguin, 2010.

Katz, Elihu. "And Deliver Us from Segmentation." *Annals of the American Academy of Political and Social Science* 546 (July, 1996): 22–33.

Kellner, Douglas and Jeff Share. "Toward Critical Media Literacy: Core Concepts, Debates, Organizations, and Policy." *Discourse: Studies in the Cultural Politics of Education* 26, no. 3 (2005): 369–386. doi: 10.1080/01596300500200169.

Krais, Beate "Gender and Symbolic Violence: Female Oppression in the Light of Pierre Bourdieu's Theory of social Practice" In *Bourdieu: Critical Perspectives*, edited by Craig Calhoun, Edward LiPuma, and Moishe Postone, 156–177. Chicago: University of Chicago Press, 1993.

Kuhn, Thomas S. *The Structure of Scientific Revolutions*, Second Edition. Chicago: University of Chicago Press, 1970.

Labov, William. *Language in the Inner City: Studies in the Black English Vernacular*. Philadelphia: University of Pennsylvania Press, 1972.

———. *Sociolinguistic Patterns*. Philadelphia: University of Pennsylvania Press, 1972.

Lamont, Michèle. *Money, Morals, and Manners: The Culture of the French and American Upper-Middle Class*. Chicago: University of Chicago Press, 1992.

Lamont, Michèle and Marcel Fournier, eds. *Cultivating Differences: Symbolic Boundaries and the Making of Inequality*. Chicago: University of Chicago Press, 1992.

LaRose, Robert. "The Problem of Media Habits." *Communication Theory* 20, no. 2 (2010): 194–222. doi: 10.1111/j.1468-2885.2010.01360.x.

Lazarsfeld, Paul F. "An Episode in the History of Social Research: A Memoir." In *The Intellectual Migration, Europe and America, 1930–1960*, edited by Donald Fleming and Bernard Bailyn, 270–337. Cambridge, MA: Harvard University Press, 1969.

Lazarsfeld, Paul F. and Robert K. Merton. "Mass Communication, Public Taste, and Organized Social Action." In *The Communication of Ideas*, edited by Lyman Bryson, 95–118. New York: Harper & Brothers, 1948.

Lincoln, Bruce. *Authority: Construction and Corrosion*. Chicago: University of Chicago Press, 1994.

Lippmann, Walter. *Public Opinion*. New York: Free Press, 1997.

Livingstone, Sonia. "Relationships Between *Media and Audiences: Prospects for Audience Reception Studies.*" In *Media, Ritual and Identity: Essays in Honor of Elihu Katz*, edited by Tamar Liebes and James Curran, 237–255. London: Routledge, 1998.

———."Taking Risky Opportunities in Youthful Content Creation: Teenagers' Use of Social Networking Sites for Intimacy Privacy and Self-Expression." *New Media & Society* 10, no. 3 (2008): 393–411. doi: 10.1177/1461444808089415.

Lizardo, Omar. "The Three Phases of Bourdieu's U.S. Reception: Comment on Lamont." *Sociological Forum* 27, no. 1 (2012): 238–244. doi: 10.1111/j.1573-7861.2011.01310.x.

Löblich, Maria and Andreas Scheu, "Writing the History of Communication Studies: A Sociology of Science Approach." *Communication Theory* 21, no. 1 (2011): 1–22. doi: 10.1111/j.1468-2885.2010.01373.x.

Lundby, Knut. *Mediatization: Concept, Changes, Consequences*. New York: Peter Lang, 2009.

Marvin, Carolyn. *When Old Technologies Were New: Thinking About Electric Communication in the Late Nineteenth Century*. New York: Oxford University Press, 1988.

Marx, Karl and Frederick Engels. *The German Ideology*. Edited and introduced by C. J. Arthur. New York: International Publishers, 1947.

McChesney, Robert W. *Communication Revolution: Critical Junctures and the Future of Media*. New York: The New Press, 2007.

———. *The Problem of the Media: U.S. Communication Politics in the Twenty-First Century*. New York: Monthly Review Press, 2004.

McLuhan, Marshall. *Understanding Media: The Extensions of Man*. New York: Mentor/Penguin, 1964.

———. *The Gutenberg Galaxy*. Toronto: University of Toronto Press, 1962.

McMurran, Kristin. "Brandon Tartikoff." *People* 22, no. 20 (November 12, 1984): 103.

Menzel, Herbert. "Quasi-Mass Communication: A Neglected Area." *The Public Opinion Quarterly* 35, no. 3 (1971): 406–409.

Meyen, Michael. "The Founding Parents of Communication: 57 Interviews with ICA Fellows." *International Journal of Communication* 6 (2012): 1451–1459.

Miège, Bernard. "Capitalism and Communication: A New Era of Society or the Accentuation of Long-Term Tendencies?" In *Toward a Political Economy of Culture: Capitalism and Communication in the Twenty-First Century*, edited by Andrew Calabrese and Colin Sparks, 83–94. Lanham, MD: Rowman & Littlefield, 2004.

Mills, C. Wright. *The Sociological Imagination*. Fortieth Anniversary Edition. New York: Oxford University Press, 2000.

Morley, David. *Media, Modernity, and Technology: The Geography of the New*. London: Routledge, 2007.

Morrison, David. "Cultural and Moral Authority: The Presumption of Television." *Annals of the American Academy of Political and Social Science* 625, no. 1 (2009): 116–127. doi: 10.1177/0002716209338351.

———. "Opportunity Structures and the Creation of Knowledge: Paul Lazarsfeld and the Politics of Research." In *The History of Media and Communication Research: Contested Memories*, edited by David W. Park and Jefferson Pooley, 179–203. New York: Peter Lang, 2008.

Mosco, Vincent. "Revisiting the Political Economy of Communication." In *Marxism and Communication Studies: The Point Is to Change It*, edited by Lee Artz, Steve Macek, and Dana L. Cloud, 87–110. New York: Peter Lang Press, 2006.

Moy, Patricia and Scheufele, Dietram A. "Media Effects on Political and Social Trust." *Journalism and Mass Communication Quarterly* 77, no. 4 (2000): 744–759. doi: 10.1177/107769900007700403

Murphy, John M. "'Our Mission and Our Moment': George W. Bush and September 11th." *Rhetoric & Public Affairs* 6, no. 4 (2003): 607–632. doi: 10.1353/rap.2004.0013.

Nakamura, Lisa. *Digitizing Race: Visual Cultures of the Internet*. Minneapolis: University of Minnesota Press, 2008.

———. "Interrogating the Digital Divide: The Political Economy of Race and Commerce in New Media." In *Society Online: The Internet in Context*, edited by Philip N. Howard and Steve Jones, 71–83. Thousand Oaks, CA: SAGE, 2004.

Nerone, John. "The Future of Communication History." *Critical Studies in Media Communication* 23, no. 3 (2006): 254–262.

Neuman, W. Russell. *The Future of the Mass Audience*. Cambridge, UK: Cambridge University Press, 1991.

Neveu, Erik. "Bourdieu, the Frankfurt School, and Cultural Studies: On Some Misunderstandings." In *Bourdieu and the Journalistic Field*, edited by Rodney Benson and Erik Neveu, 195–213. Cambridge, UK: Polity, 2005.

O'Neill, Mathieu. *Cyberchiefs: Autonomy and Authority in Online Tribes*. London: Pluto Press, 2009.

Owen, Bruce M. and Steven S. Wildman. *Video Economics*. Cambridge, MA: Harvard University Press, 1992.

Papacharissi, Zizi. "Without You, I'm Nothing: Performances of the Self on Twitter." *International Journal of Communication*, 6 (2012): 1989–2006.

Park, David W. "Blogging with Authority: Strategic Positioning in Political Blogs." *International Journal of Communication* 3 (2009): 250–273.

———. "The Couch and the Clinic: The Cultural Authority of Popular Psychiatry and Psychoanalysis." *Cultural Studies* 18, no. 1 (2004): 109–133. doi:10.1080/0950238042000181638.

Pendakur, Manjunath. "Political Economy and Ethnography: Transformations in an Indian Village." In *Illuminating the Blindspots: Essays Honoring Dallas W. Smythe*, edited by Janet Wasko, Vincent Mosco, and Manjunath Pendakur, 82–108. Norwood, NJ: Ablex Publishing, 1993.

Peters, Benjamin. "And Lead Us Not into Thinking the New Is New: A Bibliographic Case for New Media History." *New Media & Society* 11, no. 1/2 (2009): 13–30. doi: 10.1177/1461444808099572.

Peters, John Durham. "Institutional Sources of Intellectual Poverty in Communication Research." *Communication Research* 13, no. 4 (1986): 527–559. doi: 10.1177/009365086013004002.

———. *Speaking Into the Air: A History of the Idea of Communication*. Chicago: University of Chicago Press, 1999.

Peterson, Richard A. and Roger M. Kern. "Changing Highbrow Taste: From Snob to Omnivore." *American Sociological Review* 61, no. 5 (1996): 900–907.

Pooley, Jefferson. "Another Plea for the University Tradition: The Institutional Roots of Intellectual Compromise," *International Journal of Communication* 5 (2011): 1442–1457.

———. "Lost in Translation: Pierre Bourdieu in the History of Communication Research." Paper presented at the Annual Meeting of the International Communication Association, New Orleans, LA, May 2004.

———. "The New History of Mass Communication Research." In *The History of Media and Communication Research: Contested Memories*, edited by David W. Park and Jefferson Pooley, 43–69. New York: Peter Lang, 2008.

Pooley, Jefferson and Elihu Katz. "Further Notes on Why Sociology Abandoned Mass Communication Research." *Journal of Communication* 58, no. 4 (2008): 767–786. doi: 10.1111/j.1460-2466.2008.00413.x.

Pooley, Jefferson and David W. Park, "Communication Research." In *The Handbook of Communication Research*, edited by Peter Simonson, Janice Peck, Robert T. Craig, and John P. Jackson, Jr., 76–90. New York: Routledge, 2013.

———. "Introduction." In *The History of Media and Communication Research: Contested Memories*, edited by David W. Park and Jefferson Pooley, 1–15. New York: Peter Lang, 2008.

Radway, Janice A. *Reading the Romance: Women, Patriarchy, and Popular Literature*. Chapel Hill: University of North Carolina Press, 1984.

Rheingold, Howard, *The Virtual Community: Homesteading on the Electronic Frontier*. Reading, MA: Addison-Wesley, 1993.

Rogers, Everett M. *A History of Communication Study: A Biographical Approach*. New York: The Free Press, 1994.

Rosenbaum, Jonathan. *Movie Wars: How Hollywood and the Media Conspire to Limit What Films We Can See*. Chicago: A Capella, 2000.

Rowland, Willard D., Jr. "American Telecommunications Policy Research: Its Contradictory Origins and Influences." *Media, Culture and Society* 8, no. 2 (1986): 159–182.

———. *The Politics of TV Violence: Policy Uses of Communication Research*. Beverly Hills, CA: Sage, 1983.

Rubin, Alan M. "Ritualized and Instrumental Television Viewing." *Journal of Communication* 34, no. 3 (1984): 67–77. doi: 10.1111/j.1460-2466.1984.tb02174.x

Sallaz, Jeffrey J. and Jane Zavisca. "Bourdieu in American Sociology, 1980–2004." *Annual Review of Sociology* 33 (2007): 21–41. doi: 10.1146/annurev.soc.33.040406.131627.

Schudson, "Autonomy from What?" In *Bourdieu and the Journalistic Field*, edited by Rodney Benson and Erik Neveu, 214–223. London: Polity, 2005.

Silverstone, Roger. *The Message of Television: Myth and Narrative in Contemporary Culture*. London: Heinemann Educational, 1981.

———. "What's New About New Media?" *New Media & Society* 1, no. 1 (1999): 10–24.

Simonson, Peter. "Writing Figures into the Field: William McPhee and the Parts Played by People in Our Histories of Media Research." In *The History of Media and Communication Research: Contested Memories*, edited by David W. Park and Jefferson Pooley, 291–320. New York: Peter Lang, 2008.

Sismondo, Sergio. "Bourdieu's Rationalist Science of Science." *Cultural Sociology* 5, no. 1 (2011): 83–97. doi: 10.1177/1749975510389728.

Smythe, Dallas W. "Communications: Blindspot of Western Marxism." *Canadian Journal of Political and Social Theory* 1, no. 3 (1978): 1–27.

Stager, Janet and Sabine Hake, eds. *Convergence Media History*. New York: Routledge, 2009.

Steinmetz, George. "Bourdieu, Historicity, and Historical Sociology." *Cultural Sociology* 5, no. 1 (2011): 45–66. doi: 10.1177/1749975510389912.

Streeter, Thomas. "Romanticism in Business Culture: The Internet, the 1990s, and the Origins of Irrational Exuberance." In *Toward a Political Economy of Culture: Capitalism and Communication in the Twenty-First Century*, edited by Andrew Calabrese and Colin Sparks, 286-306. Lanham, MD: Rowman & Littlefield, 2004.

Summers, John H. "Perpetual Revelations: C. Wright Mills and Paul Lazarsfeld." *Annals of the American Academy of Political and Social Science* 608 (November, 2006): 25–40.

Sundén, Jenny. *Material Virtualities: Approaching Online Textual Embodiment*. New York: Peter Lang, 2003.

Swartz, David. *Culture and Power: The Sociology of Pierre Bourdieu*. Chicago: The University of Chicago Press, 1997.

Taylor, Charles. "To Follow a Rule…" In *Bourdieu: Critical Perspectives*, edited by Craig Calhoun, Edward LiPuma, and Moishe Postone, 45–60. Chicago: University of Chicago Press, 1993.

Thomas, Jim. *Doing Critical Ethnography*. Newbury Park, CA: Sage, 1993.

Thompson, John B. *The Media and Modernity: A Social Theory of the Media*. Stanford, CA: Stanford University Press, 1995.

Tunstall, Jeremy. "The Trouble with U.S. Communication Research." *Journal of Communication* 33, no. 3 (1983): 92–95. doi: 10.1111/j.1460-2466.1983.tb02410.x

Turow, Joseph. *Breaking Up America: Advertisers and the New Media World*. Chicago: University of Chicago Press, 1997.

———. *Niche Envy: Marketing Discrimination in the Digital Age*. Cambridge, MA: MIT Press, 2006.

Vermehren, Christian. "Bourdieu and Media Studies." In *Pierre Bourdieu: Language, Culture and Education*, edited by Michael Grenfell and Michael Kelly, 187–210. Oxford: Peter Lang, 1999.

Wahl-Jorgensen, Karin. "Rebellion and Ritual in Disciplinary Histories of U.S. Mass Communication Study: Looking for 'The Reflexive Turn.'" *Mass Communication and Society* 3, no. 1 (2000): 87–115.

Weber, Max. *Economy and Society: An Outline of Interpretive Sociology*. Edited by Guenther Roth and Claus Wittich. Berkeley, CA: University of California Press, 1978.

———. "Politics as a Vocation." In *From Max Weber: Essays in Sociology*, edited by Hans H. Gerth and C. Wright Mills, 77–128. New York: Oxford University Press, 1946.

Wiener, Norbert. *The Human Use of Human Beings: Cybernetics and Society*. Boston: Da Capo, 1954.

Wittgenstein, Ludwig. *Tractatus Logico-Philosophicus*. Translated by D. F. Pears and B. F. McGuiness. New York: Routledge, 2001.

Zelizer, Barbie. "Journalists as Interpretive Communities." *Critical Studies in Mass Communication* 10, no. 3 (1993): 219–237. doi: 10.1080/15295039309366865.

———. *Covering the Body: The Kennedy Assassination, the Media, and the Shaping of Collective Memory*. Chicago: University of Chicago Press, 1992.

Index

A

Abbott, Andrew, 114, 126, 127
Acland, Charles, 42–43
affordances, 71, 101–102
Alexander, Jeffrey, 28–29
American Film Institute (AFI), 48
American Idol (tv series), 47, 49
AMC (tv network), 46
Annenberg Public Policy Center (APPC), 121
art, 1, 8, 38–39, 41–43, 46–48, 54, 59–60, 63–64, 68–69, 77, 83, 101, 112, 117, 132
Atton, Chris, 40–41, 145n94
audience. *See* media audience
Austin, J. L., 85–86
authority, viii, 1, 3, 10, 14–15, 17, 79–104, 113, 131, 133, 138. *See also* symbolic power
autonomy, 7, 10, 21, 25, 28–31, 36–41, 43, 45, 47, 51, 92, 109–113, 115–116, 124, 129, 137–139

B

Benkler, Yochai, 41
Bennett, Tony, 61
Benson, Rodney, ix, 2, 11, 28, 31–32, 41, 49–51, 62, 69, 98, 122, 128, 134, 146n113
blogs, 8, 42, 70, 71, 80, 88, 93, 96
Bouveresse, Jacques, 56
boyd, danah, 70
Breaking Bad (tv series), 46
Bruns, Axel, 101–102
Brush, Stephen, 107
Bureau of Applied Social Research (BASR) (Columbia University), 106, 120, 121
Burke, Kenneth, 16
Buxton, William J., 114

C

Calhoun, Craig, 117, 120
capital (Bourdieu's basic concept), viii, 3, 9, 12–15, 20, 23, 26, 32, 33–35, 38–39, 42,

43, 44–51, 55, 60, 61, 65, 68, 72, 77, 82, 84, 85–87, 89–90, 95, 99–101, 103, 104, 105, 108, 109, 111–114, 118, 120–123, 126, 128–129, 134, 135–136

Cappella, Joseph A., 88

Carey, James W., 72–73, 79–80, 93

Cassirer, Ernst, 8

Carson, Johnny, 41

Children's Hospital (tv series), 41

Cicourel, Aaron V., 55–56

cinema, 33, 43, 132. *See also* film, motion pictures, movies

circuit of culture, 62–63

classification, 70–72, 75–76, 84, 86, 119–120, 154n76

Comic Book Code, 44

communication competence. *See* symbolic competence

consumption, viii, 5, 8, 20, 26, 55, 58, 63–64, 69–71, 74, 77–78, 83, 88, 105, 149n104

Couldry, Nick, ix, 2, 27, 54, 73–76, 99–100, 133

Craig, Robert T., 2,

critical theory, viii, 123

cultural capital, 13–14, 26, 35, 45–46, 48–49, 60–61, 65, 68, 86, 95, 121, 123, 147n37

cultural production, 8, 11, 19–20, 27–28, 33, 37–38, 40–42, 46, 50, 68, 87, 105 *See also* media production

Curran, James, 53

D

Darras, Eric, 24

Dayan, Daniel, 75

de Saussure, Ferdinand, 35, 68, 133–134

distinction, viii, 8, 21, 35, 41, 46–47, 48, 50, 68–69, 71, 72, 92, 98, 114, 120, 121, 154n57

Donsbach, Wolfgang, 116

double-break, 93–96

doxa, 23–24, 57, 122

du Gay, Paul, 63

Duncombe, Stephen, 41

Durkheim, Émile, 72–73, 104, 118, 122, 142n54

E

Eason, David, 90–91

economic capital, 12, 14–15, 20, 44–45, 49

Ellison, Nicole, 70

embodiment, 3–4, 8, 13, 21–22, 24, 27, 55, 73, 83, 109, 132, 134, 136, 142n24

Engels, Friedrich, 22

Entman, Robert, 63

F

Facebook, 71

Federal Communications Commission (FCC), 30

field (Bourdieu's basic concept), 6–21, 24–51, 54, 55, 57, 62, 63–64, 66, 68–70, 72, 73, 76, 77–78, 80, 82, 83, 84–85, 86, 87, 89, 90, 91, 95–96, 98–100, 101, 103, 106, 108, 110, 111–116, 118, 119–120, 122–130, 133–139

field of power, 10, 27–28, 36–38, 99, 113, 129, 136

film, 48, 66 *See also* cinema, motion pictures, movies

Foucault, Michel, 90, 138

Fourcade, Marion, 28

Fox Television Network, 32

G

Garnham, Nicholas, 20

Gary, Brett, 114

Gerbner, George, 124

Giddens, Anthony, 132, 141n14

Gitlin, Todd, 32, 119–120

Gouldner, Alvin W., 81–82, 93–94, 102, 137, 153n14, 156n19
Grenfell, Michael, 4
Gross, Larry, 59
Grossberg, Lawrence, 6

H

Habermas, Jürgen, 39–40
habitus, 3–7, 9–12, 17, 20–27, 42, 50, 51, 55, 56, 57, 60, 63, 72, 74–77, 82, 83, 84, 85–86, 91, 105, 108, 122, 125, 129, 132–133, 141n11
Hake, Sabine, 36
Hall, Stuart, 32, 62
Hallin, Daniel C., 19, 28–32
Hayes, Christopher, 103
Herbst, Susan, 98, 100
Hesmondhalgh, David, ix, 2, 19–20, 30, 31, 36, 40, 45, 48
heteronomy, 21, 29, 36, 39, 113, 116, 120, 129
Hindman, Matthew, 102
Highton, Jake, 119
historiography, 106, 126
history, 1, 3, 5, 12, 17, 28, 29, 36, 38–39, 42–43, 46, 77, 80, 83, 90, 105–130, 131–133, 135–136
Hoggart, Richard, 54
Home Box Office (HBO) (tv network), 45–46
homologies, 9, 27, 33, 54, 58, 62, 66–69, 125, 148n74, 155n90

I

illusio, 7–8
intellectualism, 56, 57–58, 71, 74, 107
intellectuals, 28, 29, 40, 49, 54, 95, 104, 138
interfield relationships, 10, 27–31, 49–51, 111, 114, 123, 129

internet, 23, 41, 43, 64–65, 70, 87, 101–102, 121, 128
interpersonal communication, 5, 59, 113, 117, 136
intrafield relationships, 27, 31–36, 50, 89, 129

J

Jacobs, Ronald D., 112–113
James, William, 57
Jamieson, Kathleen Hall, 88
Jansen, Sue Curry, 39
Jenkins, Henry, 25–26
Johnson, Randal, 8
Johnson, Thomas J., 88
journalism, 2, 5, 11, 22, 24, 28–32, 34, 38, 41, 46, 47, 49–50, 63, 90–92, 96, 98–99, 101, 103, 110, 111, 115, 116, 119, 134, 145n77, 151n85
Judt, Tony, 103–104

K

Katz, Elihu, 48, 75, 114
Kaye, Barbara K., 88
Kern, Roger, 61
Krais, Beate, 22
Kuhn, Thomas, 122

L

Lamont, Michèle, 75, 154n57
language, viii–ix, 10, 14, 55, 57, 65, 74, 82–90, 93–98, 100, 117
LaRose, Robert, 58
Law & Order (tv series), 8
Lazarsfeld, Paul F., 97–98, 100, 120, 127
Lincoln, Bruce, 82, 95
Lippmann, Walter, 39

Livingstone, Sonia, 70, 76–78
Lizardo, Omar, 2
Löblich, Maria, 123–124
Lynd, Robert, 129

M

Mancini, Paolo, 19, 30
Maron, Marc, 41
Martin, George R. R., 8
Marvin, Carolyn, 65–66
Marx, Karl (and Marxism), 15, 22, 24, 25, 32, 50, 56, 132
Marshall, John, 114
Mauss, Marcel, 85
mass communication, 5, 46, 48, 69, 76, 87, 97, 117, 119
McChesney, Robert W., 63, 110, 147n52
McLuhan, Marshall, 42–43, 97, 101–102
McPhee, William, 127
media audience, ix, 1, 3, 6, 14, 23–25, 26, 33–35, 38, 40–41, 43, 46–49, 53–78, 79–83, 85, 88, 90–103, 131, 132–133, 134, 138, 146n1, 148n74
media literacy, 60–62
media production, ix, 1, 2, 3, 11, 17, 19–51, 57, 63, 67, 69, 103, 131, 132 See also cultural production
mediatization, 102–103
Menzel, Herbert, 40
Merton, Robert K., 97–98, 100
meta-capital, 99–100
Meyen, Michael, 127
middle-brow, 46, 49, 54, 101
Miège, Bernard, 23
Mills, C. Wright, 127
misrecognition, 15, 26, 45. 59, 91–92, 99
mobile media, 69, 87
Morley, David, 78
Morrison, David E., 103, 127
Mosco, Vincent, 22–23

motion pictures, 30, 43, 45, 47, 134, 144n61 See also cinema, film, movies
movies, 11, 34, 36, 48, 132 See also cinema, film, motion pictures
Moy, Patricia, 88
multi-user dungeons (MUDs), 70
music, vii–viii, 26, 30, 32, 43, 47, 61, 144n61
Myrdal, Gunnar, 88

N

Nakamura, Lisa, 64–65
NBC (National Broadcasting Company) (tv network), 68
Nerone, John, 128, 135
Neuman, W. Russell, 48
Neveu, Erik, 2, 11, 54, 146 n113
Nissenbaum, Helen, 41
nomos, 112–113

O

objectivism, 6, 11
O'Neil, Mathieu, 41, 101
Owen, Bruce M., 34

P

Papacharissi, Zizi, 70
Parsons, Talcott, 28
Pendakur, Manjunath, 25
Perry, Katy, 49
Peters, Ben, 42
Peters, John Durham, 110
Peterson, Richard, 61
Pew Foundation, 121
political economy of the media, 21–25, 29–32, 133, 136
Pooley, Jefferson, 106, 108, 110, 114–115, 146n2, 146n5

R

radio, vii, viii, 33, 36, 39, 40, 43, 49, 69, 74, 97, 100, 101
Radway, Janice, 57
reception of communication, 5–6, 33, 47, 54–55, 58–60, 62–64, 68, 71, 91–92. *See also* media audience
reflexivity, 17, 54, 105–109, 124, 129, 132, 136–138, 142n24, 153n14, 156n19
relationality, 5, 7, 8–9, 20, 27, 40, 54, 66, 70, 77–78, 85, 113, 114, 129, 131–134
residual media, 43–44
Rheingold, Howard, 70
Ritual, 17, 48, 55, 71–76, 85–86, 91, 95, 98
Rogers, Everett M., 126–127
Rosenbaum, Jonathan, 48
Rowland, Willard, 114, 119
Rubin, Alan M., 71–72

S

Sallaz, Jeffrey J., 1
Say's Law, 63, 147n52
Scheu, Andreas Matthias, 123–124
Scheufele, Dietram A., 88
sens practique, 26, 57
Shannon, Claude, 89
Showtime (tv network), 45
Silverstone, Roger, 26, 74
Simonson, Peter, 126–127
Sismondo, Sergio, 128–129
Smythe, Dallas, 23–24
social capital, 13–14
sociology of science, ix, 105, 109, 111, 117–118, 124, 128–129
Spider Man (motion picture), 47
Stager, Janet, 36
Steinmetz, George, 135

strategy, viii, 8, 9, 14, 21, 23, 27, 32–34, 45, 51, 55–56, 58, 80, 89–93, 95–96, 115, 118, 122–123, 127, 135, 145n107
structure/agency divide, 3, 4, 6, 11
subculture(s), vii, 59
subjectivism, 6, 11
Summers, John, 127
Sundén, Jenny, 70
Swartz, David, 5, 27, 31–33, 122
symbolic capital, 14–15, 39, 86, 97, 100, 103–104, 109–112, 135
symbolic competence, 14, 59–65, 83, 84, 89–90, 147n37
symbolic power, viii–ix, 1, 2–3, 14, 17, 72, 79–104, 105, 111–112, 131
symbolic violence, 35, 45, 72, 75–76, 90, 94–95

T

Tartikoff, Brandon, 68
Taylor, Charles, 57–58
television, 8, 28, 29, 30, 32, 33–34, 36, 38, 39, 41, 43, 45–47, 48, 49, 61, 68–70, 71, 74, 76, 80, 97, 99–101, 103, 138, 145n107
temporality, 12, 74–75
theoreticism, 16–17
The Wire (tv series), 46
Thomas, Jim, 25
Thompson, E. P., 54
Thompson, John B., 2, 9, 60, 81, 83
Thorn, Jesse, 41
Townsley, Eleanor, 112–113
Tunstall, Jeremy, 110
Turow, Joseph, 35, 69
Twitter, 70, 95

V

VanAntwerpen, Jonathan, 120–121
Vermehren, Christian, 54, 146n1

W

Wacquant, Löic, 8–9, 16, 77–78, 108
Wahl-Jorgensen, Karin, 106–107, 109, 137
Weaver, Warren, 89
Weber, Max, 79-81, 142n54
Wiener, Norbert, 67
Wildman, Steven S., 34
Williams, Raymond, 54

Willis, Paul, 54
Wittgenstein, Ludwig, 56, 83, 124, 131, 133
World of Warcraft (computer game), 8

Z

Zavisca, Jane, 1
Zelizer, Barbie, 90, 146n113

A CRITICAL INTRODUCTION TO **MEDIA** AND **COMMUNICATION** THEORY

David W. Park
Series Editor

The study of the media in the field of communication suffers from no shortage of theoretical perspectives from which to analyze media, messages, media systems, and audiences. One of the field's strengths has been its flexibility as it incorporates social scientific and humanist ideas in pursuit of a better understanding of communication and the media. This flexibility and abundance of ideas threaten to muddle the study of communication as it stakes out an interdisciplinary identity.

This series puts on center stage individuals and ideas whose importance to the study of communication can be reconfigured, reinvented, and refocused. Each of the specially commissioned books in the series shares a concern for the history of theory in the field of communication. Books provide sophisticated discussions of the relevance of particular theorists or theories, with an emphasis on re-inventing the field of communication, whether by incorporating ideas often considered to be 'outside' the field or by providing fresh analyses of ideas that have long been considered vital in the field's past. Though theoretical in focus, the books are at all times concerned with the applicability of theory to empirical research and experience and are designed to be accessible, yet critical, for students—undergraduates and postgraduates—and scholars.

For additional information about this series or for the submission of manuscripts, please contact:

David W. Park
park@lakeforest.edu

To order other books in this series, please contact our Customer Service Department:

(800) 770-LANG (within the U.S.)
(212) 647-7706 (outside the U.S.)
(212) 647-7707 FAX

Or browse online by series:
www.peterlang.com

Lightning Source UK Ltd.
Milton Keynes UK
UKHW021333251122
412842UK00029B/231